SPEAKING OUR MINDS

A GUIDE TO PUBLIC SPEAKING FOR CANADIANS

Sandie Barnard

Centennial College

Prentice-Hall Canada Inc.
Scarborough, Ontario

Prentice-Hall, Inc., Englewood Cliffs, New Jersey
Prentice-Hall International, Inc., London
Prentice-Hall of Australia, Pty., Ltd., Sydney
Prentice-Hall of India Pvt., Ltd., New Delhi
Prentice-Hall of Japan, Inc., Tokyo
Prentice-Hall of Southeast Asia (Pte.) Ltd., Singapore
Editora Prentice-Hall do Brasil Ltda., Rio de Janeiro
Prentice-Hall Hispanoamericana, S.A., Mexico

ISBN 0-13-825894-5

Canadian Cataloguing in Publication Data

Barnard, Sandie, 1946-
    Speaking our minds: a guide to public speaking
    for Canadians

ISBN 0-13-825894-5

1. Public speaking. 2. Oratory.   I. Title.

PN4121.B37 1989   808.5′1   C89-093999-3

Copyeditor: Peter Buck
Production Editor: Jamie Bush
Designer: Jack Steiner Graphic Design
Production Coordinator: Sandra Paige
Typesetting: Jay Tee Graphics

1 2 3 4 5 IG 94 93 92 91 90

Printed and bound in Canada

For Sheila, D, Donna, and Kay
  with thanks,

  and my students
    with admiration for their outrageous and
    unremitting perception, honesty, and
    compassion.

CHAPTER 4   **We Can Work It Out: Small
                Group Communication 102**

CHAPTER 5   **Puttin' On The Ritz:
                The Social Speech 150**

P R E F A C E

During a public speaking workshop in Halifax, I asked the group to outline the essential qualities of a good speaker. They answered that every speaker needs backbone and heart — courage and compassion. This text attempts to meet the requirements of people learning to speak and of those who teach them. It deals equally with design and delivery: the basic organizational skills required to refine an idea or thesis and organize research and proof, and the techniques of speaking to and with an audience.

The title, *Speaking Our Minds*, reminds us that speaking is indeed the result of thought; it is not an automatic response. Before we speak, we need to think, to examine our purpose and organize our ideas. We need to consider how best to reach our audience and bring them to an awareness of our position. We also need to speak from the heart — to be brave enough to speak the truth, to make a stand for the things we believe in, and to trust that our conviction will help us reach our audience.

Do we need a special text for Canadians? That was often the first question I was asked by the people interviewed in this book. Yes we do. Our history, our manners, our boldness, our sense of responsibility, and our humour are special, sometimes extremely so. This text provides Canadian examples, references and anecdotes to make the learning more immediate.

In over 15 years of teaching this subject, I have been continually impressed by the honesty and integrity of my students. Despite their initial terror, they have found the courage to speak. What students need is a clear, step-by-step approach. That's what this text provides. Beginners should start giving speeches early in the semester or workshop so that they may have as many speaking opportunities as possible during the course. To that end, I have made sure that although each chapter builds on the previous one, there is enough information in the first chapter to enable a person to start making short speeches immediately. The result is a complete course, with each new chapter adding techniques and refinements to the bare structure outlined in Chapter 1. Many instructors, of course, like to proceed in their own way, and the text offers flexibility as well. It is possible to use the Table of Contents to design a course suitable to individual needs and methods.

Why are there so many exercises, quizzes and games? The key to being a good speaker is practice. When participants increase their speaking competence through social exchange, debate, and playing games, they gain an understanding of effective speaking as part of their lives, rather than as an exercise in Speaking 101. Confidence is another key to developing good speakers. A supportive group atmosphere is essential for a good class or workshop experience. As anyone who has recently spoken to a group can attest, you feel yourself on the line when you give a speech. Instructors should remember this and work to develop a learning environment that respects each person's abilities and encourages each person's performance.

Recently the sound and the atmosphere of many classrooms has changed. Softer voices, different philosophies, accents and rhythms are present. Each one has a place, and good listening skills and adequate sound systems are more appropriate than repeated whispers to "speak louder."

This book is enriched by interviews with and speeches by eight outstanding Canadians. Their generosity in making time for the interviews and the thoroughness with which they answered my questions made the preparation of this text especially exciting. After all, why should students rely solely on the advice of their instructors? I set out to discover if people whose life's work involves speaking use similar techniques and have the same concerns as we in the classrooms. The forthrightness of the interviews reinforces the lessons of the chapters; they provide practical back-up for the theory. All the interviews were taped and transcribed; they have the rhythm and feeling of talking with the person concerned.

All of the speeches are transcriptions — they too have the flow of spoken English. When I started this book I never anticipated how few speeches by contemporary Canadians we have on record. Their remarks are part of our history, and I hope that others will begin to share the task of taping and preserving them.

Knowing how easy it is to forget simple things, especially under pressure, I have included the checklists. A group of experienced speakers and facilitators provided input. The results are sometimes serious, often humorous, and always helpful.

Speaking Our Minds: A Guide to Public Speaking for Canadians should provide you with a practical working tool. Nothing, however, can replace the efforts of thoughtful teachers and honest, supportive students. I believe that speaking does make a difference in our lives and I commend this book to you.

ACKNOWLEDGEMENTS

This is a thank-you speech I am happy to make; I am truly grateful for the outstanding generosity of many people. Roberta Bondar, June Callwood, Edward L. Greenspan Q.C., Rick Hansen, David Nichol, Jeanne Sauvé, and David Suzuki graciously permitted their interviews and speeches to be used, as did Rose Anne Hart and Thomas Coon. John DeShano, Cynthia Patterson, B.J. Danylchuk, and Gail Heaslip provided firsthand information. Arranging interviews is a challenge and I am thankful for the endless patience and courtesy of Anne Doremus, Shirley Macaulay, Elaine Paterson, Susan Petersen, and Marie Bender, press secretary to Her Excellency, the Governor General.

I am also indebted to the musicians who allowed their work to appear in the text and to my students who provided speeches, ideas, exercises, and inspiration.

Various editors gave me guidance at different stages: Peter Buck, Jamie Bush, Jean MacDonald, Monica Schwalbe, and, of course, Patrick Ferrier. Paul Mason, cartoonist extraordinaire, cracked me up with his interpretations of the text and I am delighted to have worked with him. To the reviewers who provided input in the early days, Alban Goulden of Vancouver Community College, Nancy McKenna of Sheridan College, and Dr. Robert Price of Seneca College, thank you.

My colleagues at Centennial College helped me many times: Jon Redfern and Margaret van Dijk generously shared their inventiveness; Dorothy Kelleher and Colleen Marlin helped with the evaluation material; Ken Bryant, Marilynn Daye and Madeline Sim of College Communications were astute enough to record and preserve keynote speeches. Michael Evans, a Social Service Worker instructor provided much of the background material for the chapter on small group communication, and Lori Martin, a journalism student, taught me by example how to interview.

Marguerite Rogers and other members of the Ontario Council of the Girl Guides of Canada gave me endless support, and Professor Richard Coe of Simon Fraser University kindly contributed the material on jargon and bafflegab. Sheila McLeod, reference librarian at the Whitchurch-Stouffville library, ordered in every single book I ever needed.

I would especially like to thank Jack David and David Kent who advised and encouraged me throughout the long process of writing my first textbook. Their passion for teaching, writing, and publishing has been exciting to share. Liz Armstrong interrupted my writing to take me across the country on a series of speaking workshops that taught me how courageous workers can be when they decide to take a stand. And Shelia Goulet, my best and most loyal audience, contributed the material on logic and showed an unflagging interest in every word.

My development as a speaker owes much to my mother, Marie Boddam, who listened to each of my grade eight speeches hundreds of times. Valerie Austin taught me computers and baseball, and coached me through the entire first draft.

The example of other speakers inspired me often. Among many, two stand out — the late Roy Smith of Parry Sound, an outspoken champion of working people's rights, a man who went from the logging camps to the provincial legislature and who loved politics with his whole being, and Heather Bishop who never fails to be there when honesty and gentleness are needed. Jane Rounthwaite, Vicki P. McConnell and Joan Jamieson helped me to go cosmic.

To these people I offer my sincere appreciation. And I am heartened by the example of all who speak out for the world and for the rights they hold dear. Last of all, my thanks to Annie and Wilf who reviewed each new page, and Kodiak who hatched the chapters.

Jump In: Getting Started

TIPS FOR SPEAKERS

1. The determination to speak your mind will give you the courage to do well.
2. Jitters are nervous energy; channel them to work for you.
3. The audience is your safety net. In a learning situation, you need each other.
4. Energy flows between the speaker and the audience. Good listeners pay attention to your message and your intent.
5. Make real eye contact; speakers and listeners need it.

Speaking Our Minds: A Canadian Tradition

Audacity is not usually associated with the Canadian temperament, yet we have a long history of speaking out when conscience requires it. From William Lyon Mackenzie's battles against the suffocating grip of the Family Compact in 1837, to David Suzuki's championing of the earth's resources, people of integrity have spoken out. Often, they have done so at great cost to themselves. Nellie McClung, famous as a dauntless, controversial speaker, left her family to tour the country on behalf of women's rights, legal reform, and factory safety legislation. Doris Anderson said that after she spoke out in the struggle to get sexual equality written into the Charter of Rights and Freedoms in 1980, she was a pariah for several years.

Anderson, Mackenzie, McClung, Suzuki—all demonstrate a belief in standing up for their convictions, in speaking with reason and compassion.

What compels ordinary citizens to speak out? A former student of mine lives in a small town that was trying to fight a proposed chemical dump. Outside of oral presentations in high school, she had never spoken publicly; however, she decided it was time:

I knew that if I didn't speak up for our town, something I loved very much would be lost. I think the need gave me courage.

Never throw away an opportunity to speak. When you talk to people, you can affect their lives. You may not think you're doing it, but a brief remark can give someone a new idea, advice they need that very day, the courage to go on. Speaking is extraordinarily important.

The next time you need courage to speak out, remember that it's part of our tradition:

 The next time a cabinet minister in the government tries to tell women to go home and shut up, he'll think twice about it.
(DORIS ANDERSON)

 Not one word do I retract; I offer no apology!
(WILLIAM LYON MACKENZIE)

 For the first time I knew I had the power of speech. I saw faces brighten, eyes glisten, and felt the atmosphere crackle with a new power.
(NELLIE McCLUNG)

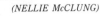 *Why else do we live if we don't struggle for things that matter to us.*
(DAVID SUZUKI)

Expert Advice: The Real Stuff

Whom would you ask for advice on speaking? Speakers, of course. To prepare this book, I questioned outstanding speakers from all parts of the country. In the interviews that conclude the chapters, people such as June Callwood, Eddie Greenspan, and Rick Hansen share their strategies for preparation and delivery: yet, they are not the only people who know how to prepare and speak under pressure. Over the years, my students have made suggestions that I have incorporated in this text. Here then, is the real stuff, expert advice from professionals, and my own list of rules for good speeches, arrived at after making and hearing thousands of them.

Advice from the experts

A good speech must entertain. It is pointless to make an important point in a boring fashion because it may be lost. It has to be made in an entertaining and dramatic way.
   (EDDIE GREENSPAN)

I prepare by giving a lot of hard thought to the audience, what experience they've got, and where they're at. I don't want to patronize people with information they already have....What would be useful to them....for you to talk about.
   (JUNE CALLWOOD)

People should be nervous; if you're not scared to death before you give that speech, chances are it's going to be a bomb. Don't be afraid of the fear. Use it to your advantage. All of that fear gets the adrenalin going and you use it.
   (DAVID NICHOL)

Don't adjust your underwear in public!
   (GAIL HEASLIP— Communications consultant)

They [academics] tend to talk down to people and use jargon to cover up their inadequacies. That's total crap. Anybody who can't speak in very simple language is trying to cover something up.
   (DAVID SUZUKI)

I always use slides; I like talking to people as though we're watching home movies....You have to look at the audience as you speak, because if they're not looking at you, you might as well walk away, turn the slides off.
   (ROBERTA BONDAR)

When you're tired and at the edge, and you don't think you have any more to give, sometimes you come up with your best performances.
   (RICK HANSEN)

Making an analogy is vitally important to making your ideas understood. It helps people know precisely what you mean; i.e., cabby to Justice Berger of U.S. Supreme Court: "Putting people in prison is like putting clothes in the wash without any soap. The clothes get wet but no dirt comes out."
   (EDDIE GREENSPAN)

Be well prepared. Rehearse your speech out loud to yourself, or a spouse, or a colleague a few times before you deliver it. Try as much as possible to be yourself at the podium. You are usually your own

worst critic so don't let every little slip throw you. Just relax and enjoy your audience.
    (Her Excellency the Right Honourable JEANNE SAUVÉ)

Don't read to people! Don't stand up in front of four people or 400 and read to them. It's insulting. Have notes—don't get lost but whatever you do—don't read to me!! I know how to read. Talk to me.
    (JOHN De SHANO)

I write in note form, sometimes full sentences, on folded pieces of white paper. Never any longer than five sides of notes. Just one word will sometimes remind me of a story. I take care with the opening and with the end.
    (JUNE CALLWOOD)

So much depends on the crowd and the atmosphere. You have to be organized...but you also have to leave room to react spontaneously.
    (RICK HANSEN)

I try to talk with emotion, to get excited, and to get others excited. Most people are afraid of dying during their speech. And most people are afraid to let emotion enter into it. So they hang onto that script, they read it—I mean, they shouldn't have chairs, they should have beds for the audience.
    (DAVID NICHOL)

Keep the level of enthusiasm up throughout the whole speech—there's somebody out there who is as interested in minute fifteen of your speech as in minute one.
    (ROBERTA BONDAR)

Be prepared. Know the content. The most nerve-wracking thing in the world is not being sure of what you're doing. Be absolutely comfortable with the material.
    (JUNE CALLWOOD)

I think it's important to be controversial and to cause an audience to think about how they truly feel about the subject matter. I will never hold back from an audience my true feelings on a subject, and I will not tone down my language to the point where my beliefs are not crystal clear. I will call it as I see it. I owe that much to my audience.
    (EDDIE GREENSPAN)

Suggestions for the Best Speech Possible

Value It

1. Never miss an opportunity.
2. Explore the topic as if it were a gold mine: sift through all the possibilities until you find the really valuable material.
3. Know your audience. What do you have to offer them?
4. Research. Research. Research. Know the topic well and get excited about it.

Plan It
{
5. Stop researching and plan.
6. Get your thesis down to one simple, clear-cut statement. Apply the One-Sentence Shower Test.
7. Hammer out an overview—a three-part proof that makes the direction of your speech clear to you and your audience.
8. *Test* the thesis and overview. Can you state them clearly? If you are still wallowing in mushy generalities, go back to Step 2 and get a new angle.
9. Add colour—stories and examples that speak to the heart *and* mind.
10. Make clear *notes* in point form.
}

Do It
{
11. Practise, by yourself at first. Then persuade your friends and family to listen. Experiment with various inflections and gestures. Know your speech and enjoy it.
12. Get psyched up. A healthy amount of nervousness gets the adrenalin flowing.
13. Arrive on time and take some private time to calm yourself.
14. Get a feel for the audience and the occasion.
15. Pause...
16. Make eye contact and—
17. *Go for it!* Connect with your audience; get right out there on the edge and give it everything you've got.
}

Conviction

The first rule of public speaking is to have something to say. Believe in what you're saying—speak from the heart. If your commitment to a subject is strong, that energy and enthusiasm shows in your delivery. Even nervous speakers can move their listeners when it is apparent that the importance of their message has given them the courage to speak.

Speaking from the Heart

Language

Have you heard the story about two students talking about a visiting lecturer?

"Wow! That was an incredible speech!"
"Yeah, it was so significant."
"What statistics! What proofs!"
"Yeah!—did you understand it?"
"No—did you?"

**"Stop trying to
sound like the
speakers you
admire. Sound like
yourself—your
voice has never
been heard
before."**
(Vicki P. McConnell)

David Suzuki, in the interview that concludes this chapter, says "anyone who can't speak in very simple language is trying to cover something up." Find your own words, your own examples. Avoid glib generalities, and find specifics that interest and excite you. When a student uses the example of Alvin Law, a talented and practical thalidomide survivor, it means a lot more than a vague discussion of the government's responsibility in the introduction of new drugs.

When you practise, listen for your own voice, your own words.

Voice

Put your hand over your heart. Can you get your voice to come from that spot in your body? If you do the breathing excercises in Chapter Five, and if you *consciously* try to get your voice to come from your heart, you will sound warm, convincing, and in control. Basically your voice is **the barometer of your self-confidence.** If the sound is coming from high inside your head, you *sound* (and probably *are*) nervous. You've stopped breathing.

If the sound is coming from your chest, near your heart, you are breathing well. You are in control and sound confident. It is a voice that encourages trust. In most situations, speak from the heart.

If you need to be very even, very sincere, breathe even deeper, and get the air to come from your diaphragm. In times of great stress, this tone can change the mood.

Getting Ready

You're ready to start. In this chapter you will find sections on dealing with jitters, the importance of a good audience, the basic design of a speech, coaching yourself to success, and finally, the directions for your first solos—the mini-speeches.

Jitters

> Look at me. Knots in my stomach....My throat tightens....My heart hammers so loud in my ears I sometimes miss my first cue.
> (DAVID FRENCH, *Jitters*, Talonbooks, 1980)

Most beginners are afraid of the big three; they are sure they will panic, puke, or perspire. Some people blush; the rosy colour (always a bright red on fairskinned people) starts at neck level and rises steadily, like a gas gauge. I was once so nervous that my stomach knotted into balls of fire and I had to lie down flat in an empty cloakroom. I prayed the pain would go away in time for me to make the after-dinner speech. A famous publisher is convinced that his throat is dry whenever he has to speak because all the water in his body has gone to his hands and armpits. The best way to handle the nervousness is to **jump in.**

Nervous energy is useful. Actors call it getting up for a performance; athletes need to be on the edge for a big meet. Speakers need that same high, the rush of adrenalin that gives them extra drive. In this chapter, you'll learn to channel it.

EXERCISE: Truth and Consequences

Take a piece of paper and jot down

  a) *three* things you hope to gain from the course;
  b) *three* things you dread about it.

The instructor gathers all the papers and reads them aloud, mentioning no names.

  Let's look at the results of this exercise. Some of the most common fears are

  "blanking out";

  "making a fool of myself in front of others";

  "shaking and turning red in the face";

  "boring people, putting them to sleep";

  "my voice shaking and stopping";

  "not knowing what to say."

Once you've read your list you'll know that most people share the same fears, and we are going to deal with those immediately:

  You will *not* blank out in the first exercises because they are short and on a specific topic.

  You are *not* going to make a fool of yourself. You are going to look like someone who is trying very hard, and everyone's sympathy will be with you.

  If you shake, no one will notice unless you try to turn over a scrap of paper.

  If you turn red in the face, you will have the class's sympathy, and they'll be pulling for you.

  You will *not* bore people. They are all in the same boat and know that if they are to succeed, you must as well.

  Your voice *may* shake but that is natural. This is a class for people to learn and shaking is allowed within the class.

The things that you want from the course will vary. Some will want to get a few laughs; others will want to learn how to organize and present material in a way that is convincing or even thought-provoking. Some need organizational skills and others want to work on their voice. As long as you follow the lessons, everything is possible.

"Years of actually getting up in front of audiences have taught me only three lessons: 1) you don't die; 2) there's no right way to speak, only *your* way; and 3) it's worth it."
(Gloria Steinem)

Your Safety Net: The Audience

Once you get to the front of the room you will have to look at the people in front of you, and that is when you realize *everyone matters*. Are they judgmental? Bored? Are they helping you? In a learning situation, it is everyone's responsibility to help. Everyone is noticed.

If you are sitting in the audience, you may think it is like being in high school. No one notices if you read a newspaper, eat your lunch, turn around to borrow a pencil, or change your shoelaces. However, as soon as you are up front you will see that *everyone* matters. As a member of the audience in a public speaking group, it is your job to help one another. You require a good audience to help you through your speeches, so you had better learn to listen well and help others. This is teamwork.

EXERCISE: The Slouch Versus the Real Listener

One member of the class goes to the front of the room. Everyone else then adopts typical postures of a bored or hostile group: slouching, tilting their chairs back, chewing gum, talking, filing their nails, yawning, glaring at the speaker, and mentally directing hideous insults his or her way. Exaggerate your pose as much as you can. Then, on a signal, sit up, lean slightly forward, make genuine eye contact, smile, and look forward to what the speaker has to say.

   a) What sort of message did your postures convey?
   b) How much can an audience affect a speaker?

The diagram opposite of energy exchange shows you the importance of the audience and the enormous impact it can have on the speaker. By applying yourself, by being attentive, you can improve the quality of the speech you are hearing.

Eye Contact: Fake or Real?

Have you ever fallen asleep in class and had your elbow slip off the desk? Have you gazed aimlessly in front of you while you planned your shopping list, reviewed your finances, or resolved

The slouch versus the real listener

never to procrastinate again? We all know what fake eye contact is. Slouch back and gaze aimlessly at the wall in front of you; your eyes are open but glazed over. You are totally lost to the situation. This is fake eye contact and it happens when people are bored or uninterested. Although it is commonly seen in classrooms, it is unnerving for speakers.

Simply by knowing this, you can correct it. Sit up and look at the speaker, really look. Genuine eye contact will help that person; it gives her or him a sense that the audience is supportive and interested in the content of the speech. Practise real eye contact. It works.

EXERCISE: See Me, Hear Me: Real Eye Contact

Two or three people go to the front of the group, one at a time. As each attempts to talk about the importance of sleep (or money, food, etc.) the rest of the class engages in fake eye contact. On a signal, give real eye contact. What's the difference?

What Happens If No One Listens?

Why is so much emphasis placed on you as a listener? Suppose the first volunteer from your group goes forward to make a speech and you give that person the same look you would give an instructor lecturing on the "The Effects of the White Pine Weevil on the Canadian Lumbering Industry" or "The Use of the First-Person Narrative in Anglo-Saxon Poetry." That person is going to be finished before he or she starts. You are necessary: speakers need the support of their listeners.

Beginning, Middle, and End: Listening for Information

If you know how a speech is organized, you'll know when to listen and when to relax. The old formula for an essay or a speech holds true:

- Tell them what you are going to say;
- Say it;
- Tell them what you've said.

Generally, this follows the plan you've already learned elsewhere as introduction, body, and conclusion. We will now look briefly at the organization of a speech (the topic is covered in detail in Chapter Two).

Some people use elaborate outlines with headings and subheadings. Others prefer to work with scraps of paper and old envelopes. Organization does not need to be elaborate to be effective, but clear organization is vital. The introduction should have a brilliant grabber that seizes the audience's attention and

Energy Cycle

Speakers and listeners *share* energy. Whatever energy a speaker generates reaches the audience and they, in turn, contribute excitement and strength to the event.

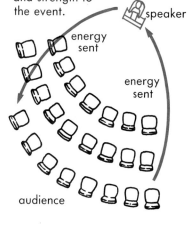

leads them to your thesis—the main argument or point of your speech. It includes an overview of your three to five main supporting statements. This flows to the body of your speech in which you give the main arguments in the order you listed them. Then, in the conclusion, you clearly summarize your points and drive them home with a zinger, which leaves your audience convinced of your argument and admiring your technique. The plan looks like this:

I
Introduction
(Beginning)
{
a) Grabber: a hook to seize audience attention
b) Thesis: a precise statement of your main idea or argument
c) Overview: an outline of your major supporting points

II
Body
(Middle)
{
Main Point One
plus supporting statements
Main Point Two
plus supporting statements
Main Point Three
plus supporting statements

III
Conclusion
(End)
{
a) Reference to Thesis
b) Review of Main Points (if necessary)
c) Strong finish

Good listeners zero in on the thesis and the main points of the overview; then they can relax. The speaker, if he or she is good, will give those main points in order; listen to each one. Make notes of the thesis and supporting arguments. Write down any examples that appeal to you or that may be useful, and wait for the conclusion. A good speaker will reinforce his or her argument. If both speaker and audience know and make use of a similar structuring principle, everyone *should* know what is happening and arrive at the same conclusion.

Active and Encouraging Listening

Real or active listening involves more than hearing. We hear many things; we listen to few. We may hear but not understand. We may hear but reject. We may hear and forget. What's the reason for not listening effectively? Is there a vocabulary difficulty, or can you not hear properly? If you are not familiar with a specialized term like RRSP, you may not be interested. Perhaps an accent stands in the way. If an Australian says what sounds like "clear the table, we need spice," he doesn't mean cinnamon or nutmeg: he needs space.

Can you teach yourself to listen well and get involved so that you learn from the speech and encourage the speaker? Here are some well-known strategies:

1. **Prepare yourself mentally.** Set yourself up for the chance to hear another person's opinion, to learn a technique, to receive helpful information, or to enjoy yourself.

2. **Get past blockades.** A person's clothing may not be your idea of fashionable, mannerisms may get in the way, or an introduction may be trite or exaggerated. Your willingness to listen should overcome these obstacles.

3. **Adopt a listening posture.** Lean forward slightly, sit up straight, and look directly at the speaker. Make real eye contact and try to show with your own expressions that you are actively involved in the speech. You are both putting yourself in the right frame of mind and helping the speaker.

4. **Attune your ears.** What happens when a speaker has a soft voice? Often, people call out ''speak louder'' or ''we can't hear you.'' Listeners need to practise attuning themselves to different voices; if you give your full attention to others, you will hear them. People don't need to speak louder; we need to listen better, to concentrate on making a connection. Obviously there may be problems in larger auditoriums, but we should make an effort to hear since softer voices and different accents are part of our world.

5. **Withhold judgment.** If someone is going to speak on ''The Use of Laser Beam Technology in Optical Surgery,'' do you expect to be bored? Remember, it is the mark of an intelligent person to want to stretch his or her intellectual capacity, and to give new ideas a chance. What if a speaker is going to talk on unions, and in your home the attitude has always been anti-union? This is the hardest part: to listen and to reserve judgment until you have heard that speaker.

6. **Anticipate main points and reflect on the ideas.** Follow the speech and make mental comments.

7. **Take notes.** Speeches are an entertaining way of learning new material. Take notes; they will help you remember. You can make files on the speeches you have heard: if you date the notes and get the speaker's name down correctly you may be able to use those speeches as part of primary research for essays or projects. If you know how the speech is structured, then taking notes is not complicated, but rather a simple matter of thesis, overview, main points, and conclusion.

8. **Listen to the tone of the speaker for the real meaning.** Remember, a speaker uses more than words; he or she also uses tone and gesture to convey the message.

The Speaker's Responsibility to be Heard

Automotive technology students identified three things for a speaker to consider:

1. Are there shop noises interfering with your talk?
2. Does your listener trust you? Can you use diagrams, models, or old parts to explain what must be done?
3. Does your listener understand you? Are you using terms your client doesn't know? If you don't share a common language, yelling won't help. Again, use diagrams and parts to help in the demonstration. Talk calmly. Don't put others down and don't put yourself down.

EXERCISE: Mystery Sounds

The following exercise is designed to sharpen your hearing skills and develop your listening ability.

Identifying random sounds. Turn your back on the instructor and try to identify a variety of everyday noises such as

  a) a pop-up tissue being pulled out of the box;
  b) the click of a ballpoint pen;
  c) the sound of a zipper;
  d) the ripping of paper;
  e) the whoosh of a can of pop being opened;
  f) velcro being unfastened.

EXERCISE: Surprise Quiz

Without previously notifying you, the instructor gives a brief and informative talk on anything she or he is interested in: a topic in the news, the National Park system, credit-card buying, whale-watching off the Pacific coast. You then have to answer ten specific questions. How well were you listening?

Speaking and Skiing: Coaching Yourself to Success

Good speakers are like good skiers: they make it look so easy. They also know about the hours of practice, the rush of excitement, and the need for good coaching. Coaching for speakers? Of course. Whenever I ski down a hill, I can hear my instructor's voice: "Crouch, relax." It took me years to get it right but one day it finally happened and I flew down the hill.

How can you coach yourself in speaking? Some people talk to themselves before they start; others write cues on their note cards:

pause
count to 3
eye contact
breathe
relax

To achieve the technique and maintain it, you need to practise. Designing a good speech is half your job; delivering it well is the other. Some people worry so much about their speeches, they end up without enough time to rehearse, and try to read disorganized notes. Why should the audience have to listen to a speaker who didn't care enough to practise? When you read your notes over, your mind interprets words that were meant to be read. The same words sound very different when they are spoken. **Practise your speech and listen to yourself.**

This book offers you more than 17 specific speaking opportunities; that's more times before an audience than most people experience in five years. As you follow the exercises, remember that technique, coaching, and practice are all part of your training. After 17 practice runs, you'll be great!

TAMING THE JITTERS

Channel your nervous energy by

1. Knowing your material well.
2. Practising at home—out loud.
3. Having a friend in the audience for support.
4. Speaking on something you know well.
5. Pampering yourself. Will a new shirt or hair cut make you feel better? How about a cup of cappucino or some herbal tea?
6. Breathing deeply before you start (In-2-3-4; Out-2-3-4). This helps calm your nerves, and lowers your voice almost an octave. It's reassuring to sound in control. (For breathing exercises, see Chapter Five.)
7. Putting your notes on the podium. *Never* hold them in your hand; the shaking will give you away.
8. Holding on to something if you need to—the edge of the podium, a tissue in your pocket, a lucky stone in your hand.
9. Knowing that your nervousness is not only normal, it's an ally.
10. Remembering the advice of Nellie McClung, writer, reformer, and politician: the surest cure for nervousness is to have something important to say, and concentrate on getting it across.

Speech Assignment: Jump In

You are ready now; the audience is geared up and should be aware of positive listening strategies. You can handle your jitters and use them well. Try one of these mini-speeches:

1. One-Minute Exercises

With one or two days to prepare, develop a one-minute speech on either

a) A great Canadian: this person can be a well-known public figure, a person in history, a family member or someone you admire;

b) An introduction of yourself using a line drawing depicting your secret talent or special interests (e.g., a picture of a ballet dancer, a water skier, a musical instrument).

You are allowed brief notes.

2. Desert Island Semi-Impromptu

Your instructor announces that he or she has won a million dollars and is sending each of you on a special trip to a desert island. You have no idea of what the island will be like but your instructor promises you creature comforts: food, water, various facilities. What is the one thing you are going to take with you? Avoid something all-inclusive such as your wallet or knapsack. You have 15 minutes to leave the room to find the one essential thing, and develop a mini-talk on its importance and the three reasons you chose it. You are allowed brief notes.

3. Alternative Semi-Impromptu: The Perfect Gift

Instead of finding the one necessity to take to a desert island, use your time to find a gift for the Prime Minister of Canada that would make your political concerns obvious. Outline why your gift would be effective.

Good luck with your first real speech.

DELIVERY TECHNIQUES TO REMEMBER

1. When you reach the podium, pause, count to three mentally.
2. Make eye contact. At the very least look once to the left, once to the right, and once to the centre back.
3. Pause at the end before you leave the podium. Stop, count to three, make eye contact and then leave. This helps you look more like a speaker and less like a sprinter.

INTERVIEW
David Suzuki

Jan. 5, 1988

Dr. David Takayoshi Suzuki is a world renowned geneticist, a television and radio show host, and a university professor. He speaks unceasingly for the things in which he believes, and the combination of his integrity, scientific ability, and personal

Geneticist, Professor, Radio and Television Host

warmth makes him a popular speaker worldwide. As host of *The Nature of Things with David Suzuki* on CBC television, he makes Canadians more aware of science and its moral implications.

Q
How do you make a speech interesting for such diverse audiences?

A
I think of an audience in terms of my father. He was a labourer and I pitch my speeches to him. When I taught I found I had a talent for translating esoteric material into terms that everyone could understand and get excited about.

One of the problems we have today is that people think if you don't have an education, you can't understand what's being discussed. In my shows, we assume that the audience, anybody, can understand the material.

Q
Do we use jargon too much?

A
Academics tend to talk down to people and use jargon to cover up their inadequacies. That's total crap. Anybody who can't speak in very simple language is trying to cover something up.

Q
Have you heard a good speech lately?

A
The greatest speaker I've heard recently is George Wald at Harvard. He gave a lecture on the Origin of Life and it was so wonderful that I could have wept with enjoyment. It's a great subject and he used good visual images. He shared his personal philosophy and

made it seem he was talking to you personally.

Q
What speech are you proudest of?

A
In a subtle way my speeches evolve and change from week to week; they are constantly undergoing a process of growth. Really, I'm fondest of the latest one.

Q
As Canadians, how could we improve our skills as speakers?

A
Discourse is not part of our culture; we have no love of give and take, of really debating. When I was young, I used to go to dinner at my girlfriend's house, and

her father loved to debate and argue. I enjoyed it and got right into it.

I also think that television is an alienating medium in terms of conversation. There's an emotional response to pictures but very little thinking involved.

Q
You give generously of yourself to so many issues. Why do you take the time to speak about difficult issues [e.g., South Moresby Island, protecting the environment, preservation of a distinct Canadian culture]?

A
Why take the trouble to speak up? Because you care, because it matters to you as a human being. You have to stand up and fight for the things you believe in. Why else do we live if we don't struggle for things that matter to us?

David Suzuki

Speech: The Good Old Days

As part of Patrick Watson's Struggle for Democracy *series, outstanding Canadians, including David Suzuki, commented on their perspectives of this country.*

You know, I hear a lot of people who say they wish we could go back to the good old days when people were more honest, and society was a better place to live. I think there's another way of looking at it. I think Canada has changed immensely in the past few decades but it is a much richer, more vibrant, and, I think, a far more preferable society today.

When my parents grew up in the '20s and '30s, it was inconceivable that some one with slant eyes like mine or skin colour like mine could ever be an entertainer, or be on television in prime time. The notion that Canadians would look to people like Adrienne Clarkson or myself, or that British Columbia would have a premier, Dave Barrett, who is Jewish, or that P.E.I. would have a premier of Lebanese background, or that we would have a black lieutenant-governor in Ontario—those ideas are very recent, and, I think, a reflection of the extent to which Canada is a much greater multi-ethnic society. And, I think, a richer and a far better one.

The good old days really exist in people's heads; the good old days are now.

January, 1989

OUTLINE OF A ONE-MINUTE SPEECH

Name: _____

Date of Speech: _____

Purpose Statement: _____

INTRODUCTION

    Grabber:

    Thesis:

    Overview:

BODY

    Supporting Argument #1

    Supporting Argument #2

    Supporting Argument #3

CONCLUSION

    Reference to purpose (thesis):

    Summary of main steps:

    Zinger:

SELF-EVALUATION FORM

This form is to help you evaluate your own speech. It can be kept private or shared with your instructor or peers.

Type of Speech: _____

Name: _____

Title: _____

Date: _____

DELIVERY
Physical Presence

Did I make eye contact with others?

Was my posture natural and appropriate?

Was I aware of my facial expressions and hand gestures?

Were there any distracting mannerisms that I was aware of?

Did I feel good?

Could I feel an energy exchange with my audience?

VOCAL DELIVERY

Was my voice under control?

Did I sound confident?

Was I aware of breathing calmly?

How was my enunciation?

Did I manage to avoid um's and ah's?

Did I sound interested/excited/ committed?

How did my voice sound to me?

DESIGN AND CONTENT

How well did the introduction and conclusion work?

Did the framework unify my speech?

Was there a natural progression from point to point?

Did my notes keep me on track? Did I use them?

Did the audience seem to understand the organization of my speech?

Was the information clear?

What was the energy level of the conclusion?

What would I change the next time?

What worked very well?

OVERALL EFFECTIVENESS

Did I connect with this audience?

Did I achieve my purpose?

What do I remember most about making the speech?

What unexpected or unforeseen things happened?

What am I most pleased about?

OTHER COMMENTS   Grade:

PEER EVALUATION FORM

Peer evaluation should be done in a constructive and supportive fashion. The speaker may choose people to do assessments or they may be assigned alphabetically. Some groups maintain the same speaker/assessor teams for the entire course; others change for each speech. The instructor may wish to see this evaluation before it goes to the speaker.

Type of Speech: _____

Speaker: _____

Title: _____

Assessor: _____

Date: _____

DELIVERY

Physical Presence

Did the speaker maintain eye contact?

Did she or he establish a rapport with the audience?

Were gestures natural and effective?

VOCAL DELIVERY

Did the speaker sound convincing/spontaneous/excited?

Was his or her voice clear and loud enough?

How did you respond to the speaker's mood?

DESIGN AND CONTENT

Did the introduction interest you?

Did the overview give you an indication of the main proofs?

Did the speech flow easily and logically from one point to another?

Was the conclusion strong and memorable?

Did the conclusion reinforce the thesis and main points?

What was the thesis of the speech?

OVERALL EFFECTIVENESS

Did you learn something new or worthwhile from the speech?

Were you moved by it?

What was the most outstanding part of the speech?

What changes do you recommend?

What parts should the speaker definitely keep?

OTHER COMMENTS

Grade:

EVALUATION FORM

Type of Speech: _____

Name: _____

Title: _____

Length of Speech: _____

Date: _____

Legend: S = SUPERIOR   E = EFFECTIVE   NW = NEEDS WORK

DELIVERY
Physical Presence
- Eye Contact
- Rapport with Audience
- Posture
- Gestures
- Use of Notes
- Appropriate Use of Audio-Visual Support Material

VOCAL DELIVERY
- Naturalness/Spontaneity/Enthusiasm
- Clarity
- Variety (Tone, Pitch, Pace)
- Volume
- Absence of Verbal Tics (um, ah, okay, like)
- Sense of Control and Calm

DESIGN AND CONTENT
- Use of Framework for Introduction and Conclusion
- Clear Thesis and Overview
- Coherence/Use of Transitions
- New/Interesting Information
- Strong Finish

LANGUAGE
- Word Choice
- Impact on Audience
- Grammar

OVERALL EFFECTIVENESS
- Treatment of Topic
- Intelligent Awareness of Audience
- Achievement of Purpose
- Impact on/Connection with Audience

OTHER COMMENTS

Grade:

Watch Closely Now: The Demonstration

> *Every speech is different—different environment, different people. You have to come from the heart...make them feel they're the most important people in your day, in your life, at that time.*
>
> *(RICK HANSEN)*

TIPS FOR SPEAKERS

1. Brainstorm for ideas, for a topic that you are interested in or feel strongly about.
2. Trust yourself: offbeat ideas may lead you to exciting topics.
3. Audience analysis is essential for every speech. Learn as much as you can about the audience: their background, attitudes, knowledge of the topic.
4. Mapping your Success. With a Three-Part Plan, everyone will know where your speech is headed.
5. A good thesis should pass the "One-Sentence Shower Test."
6. Prepare a Seven-Day countdown and stick to it.
7. Practise your delivery. Get comfortable with your material and avoid distracting mannerisms.

**How to throw a cream pie
How to change a tire
How to organize a speech**

This chapter has two functions:

1. To demonstrate how to organize and prepare a speech;
2. To outline the techniques involved in delivering a competent demonstration.

Like every good demonstration, the section on organizing a speech has a natural progression:

1. How to find a topic;
2. How to build a speech;
3. Zeroing in on a thesis;
4. Matching your speech and your audience;
5. Putting you and your audience at ease.

If you follow the steps, your speeches will be well constructed. The process starts with a three-part plan, the nuts and bolts of speech preparation.

The Plan That Works

Why do you need a plan? You've just spent 14 hours researching bats. You've been to the Ministry of Natural Resources, the library, the museum, and the local pest-control office. You know everything about bats: how to remove them from old buildings, plans for bat houses, how the brown bat reproduces, the mythology of bats, the use of bat droppings for fertilizer. You are brimming with bat lore and bat stories.

Indeed, you know so much about bats that you could talk for hours, and *that's where the danger lies*. What do you hope to accomplish? Will people be able to follow you? How should you organize the material?

Organize In Threes

The three parts of the plan you use are simple.

Introduction: Grab the audience's attention and tell them what you're going to tell them;
Body: Tell them;
Conclusion: Tell them what you've told them and leave them with a powerful finish.

Not only does your speech have three main sections—introduction, body, and conclusion—you should also arrange your main arguments, reasons, steps, or challenges, in *three* clear sections. Why three? The human brain cannot absorb and *remember* more; the audience does not have written backup. Although your speech is well researched, dynamic, and logical, the audience is listening, not reading. They need very precise statements of your argument, your reasons, and your summary.

"I feel a recipe is only a theme, which an intelligent cook can play each time with a variation."
(Madame Jehane Benoit)

If you prepare a speech on how to catch and release a bat without harming it in thirteen easy steps, no one will be able to remember more than four. By the time you get to the crucial step ten, no one will retain the information.

Organize in threes: stoplights have three colours; baseball has three outs. Three is a magic number in western society—use it as an organizing principle.

In an expanded form, the plan looks like this.

The Three-Part Plan That Always Works
I. Introduction

The introduction itself has three parts.

a) *Grabber:* Why should anyone listen to you? The grabber answers that question. It captures the attention of the audience and makes them *want* to listen to you.

b) *Thesis:* Why are you speaking? The thesis is a clear and precise statement of the point you wish to make, the explanation you have to offer, the argument you seek to present.

c) *Overview:* Where is the speech going? The overview is a preview of the three main points you will use to support the thesis.

II. Body

Present the main supporting arguments outlined in the overview *in the order you gave them.*

Supporting Argument #1
    plus back-up and examples
Supporting Argument #2
    plus back-up and examples
Supporting Argument #3
    plus back-up and examples
Remember, pare down your reasons to three strong points.

Throw out your weak ideas.

III. Conclusion

The conclusion also has three main functions.

a) It rounds out the speech and adds a sense of completion;
b) It reinforces the thesis, and reviews main arguments (if necessary);
c) It jolts the audience with a strong final statement. If appropriate, it urges them to action. The conclusion should be so dynamic that everyone remembers it.

The following outline of a demonstration speech shows how to apply the three-part plan.

Sample Speech: The South Magnetawan Bat Brigade
Purpose: After hearing my speech, the audience will know how
to remove a bat from a house without injuring it.

I. Introduction

   a) *Grabber:* A personal story:
               "Imagine waking up at night to the flutter of
               a bat's wings as it swoops just above your
               face."
   b) *Thesis:* How to remove the bat from the room with-
               out hurting it or frightening yourself.
   c) *Overview:* Three main sections:
               a) equipment
               b) capture
               c) release

II. Body

Equipment:
- bat hat with wide brim for protection
- bright flashlight
- sieve and sturdy cardboard

Capture
- forcing yourself to get up off the floor
- finding the bat
- putting the sieve over the bat and the cardboard behind to make a cage

Release:
- carrying the sieve cage gently to a door
- releasing the bat with a gentle swooping motion in order to avoid hurting its wings
- shutting the door quickly to avoid re-entry

III. Conclusion

- Refer to purpose and the main steps—equipment, capture, and release.
- Clincher: "This humane way of getting rid of bats really works. The only problem is that bats have excellent memories and may live for 20 years. Sooner or later, they'll remember the entrance and visit you again."

This, then, is the framework of a speech. By using this simple and dependable outline, you will be able to build your argument, no matter how complex, and know that the structure is sound. You will not get bogged down in detail, and your audience will be able to understand and follow you.

Once you understand the process, the next step is to find a topic.

Mental agility, emotional calm, and steely discipline are what you need to find a topic, narrow it down, and hammer out a thesis that will work.

There are three scenarios in getting a speech topic:
1. Your instructor tells you what the topic is;
2. You are given a wide-open assignment—make a speech on anything;
3. The double flip: start with a given topic, and using free association, arrive at an offbeat but workable topic.

Scenario One: Your Instructor Sets the Topic

Your first assignment is a brief speech on "Successful Management Strategies", "How to Help the Homeless," "The Best Children's Book on the Market", or "Resource Management." What is your first reaction to these topics? Do you like any of them? Do any of them mean anything to you?

First Steps

1. What does the instructor mean? Are there limits?
2. Clear up any difficulties of vocabulary. What is meant by "management strategy"? How old is a child? If your instructor sets a limit, you have to follow it. If she does not, you can take an open approach to the whole topic. Of course, your instructor is going to deal with the most obvious questions: how long does the speech have to be? when do you have to speak? Remember, if you have questions at this point, either ask them in class or go right to your instructor.

Scenario Two: The Wide-Open Topic

Make a three-minute speech "on anything that you find interesting," or "on anything you think is of significant interest to your class." If you get a wide-open assignment, STOP, and remember what I am going to say.

Do not try to find your final topic immediately. Students worry unnecessarily when they insist that the perfect topic spring complete into their minds. If that perfect topic, complete with thesis, method of organization and examples does not *immediately* drop, do not say, "I can't do it, I can't think of a thing." You can; here's how.

The Secret of Finding a Topic

EXERCISE: Brainstorming

a) Write a word on a piece of paper: shoe, microphone, kayak, purple, money, maple syrup, video shops, swimming, banks, cow, cornflakes, etc.
b) Choose one of these words and for the next 60 seconds write down as many things associated with that topic as you can.

This is brainstorming. There are only three rules:

1. Don't stop writing things down;
2. Don't think;
3. Don't evaluate.

You are after quantity, so don't say, ''this is stupid,'' or ''this won't work,'' or ''I've already done this.'' Give yourself one minute and write.

If you took the word *shoe*, your list might look like this:

socks
running shoes
types of running shoes
styles of running shoes
prices of running shoes
deck shoes
hiking boots
construction boots
shoes as weapons
dancing shoes, ballet shoes
cost
materials
style
shoes as accessories
import/export market
uncomfortable shoes
bare feet
cowboy boots
blisters

If you're new to brainstorming, you will need practice to develop speed. Take another word and repeat the process. Time yourself for one minute. Do not stop; do not think; do not evaluate.

Experienced speakers brainstorm all the time to find an idea or fresh approach that they like and that the audience will enjoy. *Do not ignore this step!* In order to get truly involved in your speech, you need to have a handle on it, an approach that you're comfortable with and that excites you. Whether you are passionately arguing why adopted children should be helped to find their birth parents or more calmly discussing the quintessential Canadian sport, make sure you know the topic, and have the interest, energy and conviction to follow it through.

I think that's the whole secret. If you are going to be bored, your audience is going to be bored. The secret is finding a topic that interests you.
   (SHERI ALEXANDER—Hospitality student)

What are the criteria of a good topic?

1. It meets the requirements of the assignment.
2. It interests you.
3. It interests your audience.
4. There is research material available.
5. You can organize it and develop it within the time available.

EXERCISE: Pub Practice

In your class or at a pub have different people write down single words and brainstorm each one. When you are standing at the bus stop, concentrate on a passerby and rhyme off all the things you associate with that person.

Emotional Calm: Free Floating

Instead of desperation, try this calm, free-floating approach to your subject. Let's say you tried to brainstorm on management strategies but could only think of managers:

boss
raise
inventories
personnel
success
unemployment
three-piece suits
Lamborghini
interviews
motivating employees
teams
beast
fire
promote

It is a good list. Which topic intrigues you the most? Remember, the topic is "Successful Management Strategies." What if you don't know any? The boss as a beast appeals to you because you have a particular person in mind. This is where relaxation is needed. Daydream for a minute. Take a bath. Go into a reverie at the bus stop. Lie down on the couch and tell your family you're thinking.

Scenario Three: The Double Flip

In the tub you think of extinct animals like the dinosaur, vicious ones like the hyena or weasel, and loyal pack leaders like the wolf. Eureka! You have your topic—the boss as an animal: the dinosaur, out of date; the weasel, cut-throat; or the wolf, a team leader—you have narrowed it down, you have your examples.

This example demonstrates that you do not have to worry about always staying exactly within the topic as it was first suggested: you can think of offbeat ideas. If you have any doubts about this, take the topic to your instructor and see how it works. Look at the criteria. Will it interest your audience? Will it interest you? Do you know enough about it? Can you find research material?

Now we can try this with the topic "Resource Management." Wood is a resource, iron ore is a resource, minerals are a resource, but time is a resource too, as are people and money. What else is a resource? Suppose one of your friends is a bird watcher keen on birds of prey, such as eagles, owls, falcons, or hawks. She has told you about Canadian efforts to raise bald eagles and ship them to the United States where loss of habitat has resulted in dangerously low numbers. Can you talk on the need to manage wildlife, especially birds?

You remember a newspaper article in which Canadians are trying to crack down on illegal smuggling of the peregrine falcon. What other bird needs managing? If you live in the city, you know about pigeons; they certainly need regulating. This could be a good speech. This is an unorthodox but innovative way of getting a topic—the double flip. Take an idea, do some mental somersaults and come up with a new twist. Instead of water or minerals you will discuss "Wildlife Resources: Managing Canadian Birds."

Priming the Pump

Crisis scenario: What happens if you brainstorm and still can't find a thing to talk about? What else can you do? You have around you all the resources you need: your friends, the radio, television. Make sure you check the news and issue programs on television. Newspapers and magazines are jammed with interesting, current stories. You local library has a selection of national and local magazines—scan the headings and the articles that appeal to you.

EXERCISE: Finding Ideas

This is a list of topics covered in national magazines for one month. Is there something here that you could use or brainstorm with in order to get a topic that you can use?

Scan these titles and circle at least five that you could develop.

Maclean's

René Lévesque: a Quebec hero and
  Canadian patriot
stock market panic
apartheid
  economic sanctions against South
  Africa
  Canada's role in the Common-
  wealth
free trade and the wine, lumber,
  and clothing industries
Farley Mowat's book *Virunga*, an
  account of Diane Fossey's work
  with the rare mountain gorillas
  of Central Africa's Virunga range
endangered species
  grizzly bears and the B.C. forest
  industry
Niagara Falls
increase in crimes against the
  elderly
World Series
  will the Blue Jays ever do it?
  the best domed stadiums
Nobel Prize winners
miracles of transplants in infants
  organ donors
best movies
best all-round running shoe (an
  advertisement)
growing occurrence of dioxin, a
  cancer-causing agent, in everyday household products like
  paper towels.

Destinations

Grenada—a great holiday spot
Jamaican resorts catering to genera-
  tions of Hollywood stars
the Epcott centre
great cities of the world

Canadian Consumer

soaps: are laundry detergents really
  new, improved and soft?
insect repellent: aerosols, lotions,
  and sticks—repellents that get
  rid of bugs and several layers of
  skin
small claims court
car insurance

Lemon-Aid

New car guide
Used car guide

Byte: The Small Systems Journal

laser printers and what they do

Canadian Geographic

Niagara Falls-world wonder or
  chemical dump?
bald eagle—transplanting them from
  Saskatchewan to the U.S.
whale watching in the St. Lawrence
the Gang Ranch—Canada's largest
  ranch
a world heritage site—Head
  Smashed In Buffalo Jump in
  Alberta
Bruce Peninsula, Canada's newest
  national park, part mainland and
  part marine

Harrowsmith

log-house building
wild-flower cultivation

Chatelaine

Couch Potato's Guide to Life
collecting antiques
wise driver's emergency car kit
death penalty
Pierre Berton
rice is a great food
should victims of crime get to speak
    in court?
militant animal rights activist, Vicki
    Miller
money as an emotional issue

Rolling Stone

continuing popularity of *Sgt. Pepper*
sound systems for pickups, vans,
    and jeeps
karaoke (empty orchestra) Japanese
    entertainment made popular
    worldwide. People sing to taped
    accompaniment. Now there are
    karaoke machines as well as
    bars
great college hangouts
Mikhail Baryshnikov—ballet
    star/movie star
Pop artist performers: Suzanne
    Vega, Bono, Tracy Chapman,
    Glass Tiger, Los Lobos

The Financial Post: Moneywise

self-employment, advantages and
    disadvantages
prefab housing market
accessories for oenophiles—the
    world's best corkscrew
pulp and paper exports
should rich parents help their off-
    spring get started in business or
    let them do it alone?
managing farms in bad times

miscellaneous

5 handiest carpentry tools
how to build a stereo stand
how to judge good furniture
compact discs: advantages and dis-
    advantages
who is the queen of country
    music—k.d. lang or Anne
    Murray?
making beer
the best wine to order
removing a cork
real Buffalo chicken wings
acupuncture for your pet

high performance cars
pet peeves: telephones that accept
    only computerized
    phone cards
people who ask for
    credit card numbers
    over the phone
cash machines that run
    out
telephone answering
    machines

Steely Resolution

Now is the time to control yourself, stop worrying and *stop researching*. Make a list of the five best possibilities and choose one. The most common error beginners make is to worry and research until the night before. It does not work. You need to spend time on the delivery of your speech. After a day and a half, choose the topic; it may not be perfect but it will make a good speech if you work at it.

Assuming you have a week to research, organize and practise your speech, your schedule should look like this:

THE SEVEN-DAY COUNTDOWN

Day 1: check details
talk to friends
brainstorm
Day 2: brainstorm and research
formulate a thesis
Day 3: design speech—work on thesis and overview
of main points
Day 4: add supporting arguments, examples,
details, etc.
make notes and start to practise
Day 5: revise notes: practise aloud
Day 6: PRACTISE! PRACTISE! PRACTISE! (aloud)
Day 7: Relax! Review notes one last time.
Practise once more aloud.

This plan divides your time almost equally into time to plan and time to practise. You *need* the chance to rehearse.

EXERCISE: Brainstorming in Action

(allow 30 minutes)
This exercise gives you practice in finding suitable topics, and narrowing them down to specific ideas for speeches. Imagine a city skyline, one part of which you may isolate in a telescopic sight. Imagine the cityscape as the topic, and the specific building as the subject you will discuss.
a) Choose *two* of the following topics and brainstorm one minute on each. Try to get a list of ten things for each:

tattoos
bush fever
atomic energy

black flies
student loans
sound systems
fast-food outlets
acupuncture
high-speed police chases
water sports

b) From each of the lists, select the *two* best suggestions.
c) You have before you *four* ideas; for each one make a statement that you can explain, prove, or demonstrate.
d) Choose the best one.

If your topic is too vast for a short speech, concentrate on one specific aspect of it and use it as the focal point of your presentation.

GREAT CANADIAN QUIZ I

How good are you at Canadian place names, holidays, history, folklore, and political institutions. Here's a quick quiz to get your mind alert.

1. When is Groundhog Day?
2. What is screech?
3. When is Canada Day?
4. Who invented basketball?
5. What team was named the greatest Canadian basketball team of the first half of this century?
6. What did Pierre Elliot Trudeau always wear in his lapel?
7. What province was the last to join Confederation and in what year did it enter?
8. What city was know as Pile of Bones?
9. What are the first names of the beer-guzzling McKenzie brothers, eh?

(Continued)

10. What is the more popular name of Anne Shirley?
11. Santa Claus's address is the North Pole, Canada. What is the postal code?
12. In what year was the present Canadian flag adopted?
13. Name the political confederacy operating before Europeans came to this country, and still working.
14. The three main transportation passes through the Rockies are named after a bird, an animal and the hair of a person. What are they?
15. Where and what was Africville?

To test yourself further, consult:
John Robert Colombo, *Colombo's Canadiana Quiz Book* (Western Producer Prairie Books, 1983).
John Fisher, *The Complete Cross-Canada Quiz and Game Book* (McClelland and Stewart, 1978).
Sandra Martin, *Quizzing Canada* (Dundurn Press, 1987).

Answers: Great Canadian Quiz I

1. February 2
2. a powerful Newfoundland rum
3. July 1
4. James A. Naismith
5. The Edmonton Grads, a women's team
6. a rose
7. Newfoundland, 1949
8. Regina
9. Bob and Doug
10. Anne of Green Gables
11. HOH OHO
12. 1965
13. League of the Five Nations or League of the Iroquois, now know as the Six Nations
14. Crow's Nest Pass, Kicking Horse Pass, Yellowhead Pass
15. a black section of Halifax, razed in 1969

The Thesis—The Heart of the Plan

The next step in organizing a speech is zeroing in on the specific point you wish to make—your thesis. If you are going to do a speech on the boss as an animal, (dinosaur, weasel, or wolf), you require a basic idea of what you're going to prove: your theme, or thesis, is the heart of your speech.

What is a possible thesis for a speech on the manager as animal? How about "Tyrant or team leader? Managers are like animals: dinosaurs, weasels, and wolves. The successful ones are team leaders and, like wolves, their loyalty is to the pack." That is a great thesis, but does it have to be so long? No, it can be very short. Here is a student's thesis on hamburger places: "The things I look for in a burger restaurant are friendliness, atmosphere, and hot peppers." A nursing student doing a speech on palliative care had this thesis: "Palliative care attempts to reassure the patient, ease his or her suffering, and help the patient face impending death."

Mapping Your Success: More on the Thesis and Overview

The perfect plan is like a road map: the **thesis,** or main idea, is your destination; the supporting ideas outlined in the overview are the details of your route. Look at the examples just given. Can you identify the main supporting points in each case?

The preview makes it clear where your speech is going. Have you ever tried to drive someone home and been forced to follow terse commands: ''Turn right here! Now left! Quick, left again here! Okay, stop!'' Isn't it easier to have someone say, ''Go along Burrard Street, and turn right on Pender. Stay on Pender and merge with Georgia at the intersection of Georgia and Pender. Then continue west on Georgia, and you'll run right into Stanley Park.''

That is what the overview does: it lets the audience know the main turns the speech will take as you drive home your thesis. They can anticipate your reasons and work with you instead of wondering where you're heading. To continue the analogy of a journey, a speech with a definite thesis and precise overview enables the audience to recognize the landmarks and appreciate the route.

The overview also makes things clear for *you*, the speaker, so that you can devote your efforts to addressing your audience directly, to appear to be winging it and speaking from a need to communicate your ideas to that particular group.

Putting It All Together

How well do you understand the process of preparing a speech? If you understood the first three sections on organization, finding a topic, and formulating a thesis and overview, you should be able to demonstrate the technique yourself.

Imagine you have been assigned a two-minute speech on high-rise apartments. You don't live in one but you have visited several. Your brainstorming might produce this:

neighbours
condominiums
subsidized housing
high rent
no yard work
rent review board
slow elevators
great view
party rooms
sauna and weight rooms
few play areas for children
security problems
excessive noise

finding a roommate
fear of heights
fire safety
the pool
good location

(Can you see the various points of view reflected in this list?) These are all good topics; however, you have to choose one. You decide on security because you have a friend who has had security problems in a high-rise; he will provide excellent first-hand information.

Once you do some preliminary research, you realize that security is still a general heading and you have to brainstorm again. This is an informed list; it reflects the work you have done:

need for better peepholes in doors
cheap locks
keys kept by former tenants
elevators
main foyer door too accessible to strangers
parking garages
poor lighting
theft
muggings
loud fights
balconies dangerous on lower levels
mailbox theft

Finding the Thesis

You need to refine exactly what you want to prove or outline. The thesis is your precise statement of where the speech is headed or what it will demonstrate.

Considering the topic, you have at least two routes: ''Why are there so many security problems?'' or ''what are the major danger areas?'' The student who did this speech identified the foyer, the elevators and parking garage as the major danger areas. She also figured out why they were so dangerous. Owing to time limitations, she had to make a choice: to discuss the reasons for the lack of security in high-rises or the main danger areas.

These are the thesis statements she considered; remember, they were prefaced by the grabbers.

Thesis Statement A

''Security problems in high-rise apartments are the result of shortsighted or incorrect attitudes on the part of designers, owners and tenants.''

This thesis statement almost has the overview in place. The following statement is even more specific. It classifies the danger areas.

Thesis Statement B

"The areas of greatest risk in highrise apartments are the foyer, the elevator and the parking garages."

The student went on to discuss the three danger areas in the order given in the overview.

In each case the thesis and overview give the audience an exact outline of the purpose of the speech and the major points. The audience knows where the speech is going and how it will get there.

The One-Sentence Shower Test

How do you know if your thesis is clear? Take the one-sentence shower test. You've worked hard on your speech and you're in the shower. Challenge yourself: **"Can I state in one sentence what my whole speech is supposed to prove?"**

Pass the test and you have a thesis and a speech. Mumble and ramble until the water runs cold and you had better start narrowing things down and hammering out one precise idea.

WHO? WHAT? WHEN? TESTING YOUR TOPIC

Before you go any farther, ask yourself if your topic is appropriate

for the audience,

for the occasion,

for the time allotted.

Matching Your Speech and Your Listeners: The Need for Audience Analysis

When Rick Hansen went round the world on his Man in Motion tour, he spoke to hundreds of groups of people. Although exhausted, he always took the time to make his remarks special for each audience. He has a knack for reaching out to establish a link. More than that, he takes instant notice of people and circumstances. When he visited Bawden Correctional Institute in Alberta, he began his speech like this:

We are all imprisoned in different ways.

The speech was obviously a success: the inmates presented him with a ball and chain.

You too must adapt your speech to each audience and each occasion. An audience analysis is *essential* each time you speak; it is part of your preparation. In most cases, it is also your responsibility. You can do an informal analysis by telephone, asking whoever contacted you about the group. In your class, you

can make observations and ask questions to add to your knowledge of your classmates and instructor.

Consider these situations:

1. You have prepared a speech on the superiority of country inns and why they are better than large hotel chains. Your audience is a group of managers from several chains. How can you adapt your topic? Would it not be better to speak on the qualities of country inns that are found (or you would like to find) in larger hotels?
2. You are asked to speak to a community group on the life of a college student. Do they know what a community college is? Are they more interested in courses, vocational possibilities, costs, and the level of instruction, or in the personal development you experience while in college?
3. You are a street worker going to the municipal council to ask for funds for shelters for street kids. Will they be more convinced by a discussion of the needs of your clients, or proof that it is cheaper to care for them before they are perpetrators or victims of crime?

Often, you do not have to change your speech as much as your examples. Let's say you're talking about investing money and you have used a hunting analogy to explain the difference between safe investments and speculation. When you discover

Rick Hansen in Australia

During the Man in Motion tour, Hansen tried to make each audience feel they were the most important people in his day.

that your audience consists of naturalists, changing the analogy to conservation will make your presentation more effective.

Analysis Checklist

Here are some of the things to check when you do an audience analysis. They may help you to get a clearer picture of the group and the situation. You must guard against making unfair assumptions based on age, income, or education, while at the same time determining how those factors affect the speaking occasion.

Age

Occupational background

Gender

Rural or urban experience

Parents or non-parents

Traditional or alternative family groups

Race or nationality

Disposable income

Level of education

Interests and hobbies

Knowledge of the subject

Warning: Derogatory remarks about race, religion, gender, disability, size, or sexual preference are unacceptable everywhere. Such slurs undermine your credibility and insult your listeners by assuming they would accept such remarks.

Exercises on Audience Analysis

EXERCISE: Asking the Right Questions

You are speaking on a) airline deregulation;
                      b) the spread of crack in high schools.

What would you want to know about your audience in order to prepare a good speech?

EXERCISE: Class Analysis

Jan MacLeod, a speaker from St. John, New Brunswick, is coming to speak to your class on "The Deaf Community." Prepare a two- or three-paragraph analysis of your class to send to her. (You may compile your own list of speakers and topics.)

EXERCISE: Winning and Losing Topics

Based on your analysis of your class prepare a list of

a) three topics to generate maximum audience *interest*;
b) three topics to generate maximum audience *boredom*.

To see how accurate you are, do a survey. Ask ten classmates how interesting or boring they find your topics.

Putting Yourself and Others at Ease
Fulfilling Basic Needs

As you know from your other studies, Abraham H. Maslow classifies basic human needs in an ascending order (see illustration). You must make sure those needs are met, that your listeners feel worthwhile and respected, in order for them to get the most out of your speech. You should pay attention to the speaking environment:

- Is there enough air in the room?
- Is it too cold or too hot?
- Can everyone see and hear? Are there appropriate arrangements for the hearing impaired?
- If it is evening, did someone arrange for coffee and tea for those arriving directly from another meeting?

Maslow's Hierarchy of Basic Human Needs

As well as being comfortable, people need to feel worthwhile and respected, according to Maslow. A good speaker pays attention to *all* levels.

Self-actualization needs: to fulfill one's potential as a unique person

The Highest and Most Human Need

Aesthetic needs: to find order and beauty
Esteem needs: to be competent and gain approval
Cognitive needs: to know and understand
Belonging and love needs: to be with others and be accepted

Human Psychological Needs

Safety needs: to be physically secure and out of danger
Physiological needs: to satisfy hunger, thirst, and the need for warmth

Basic Survival Needs

- Do people feel secure? If there is a disturbance outside your room that sounds threatening, ask someone to investigate. Your audience will be concentrating more on the outside noise than on you.

Higher level needs can be met by

- referring to the audience as a group of interested, motivated people;
- acknowledging their intelligence by such remarks as "let me refresh your memory of Maslow's Hierarchy";
- respecting their position on a subject;
- making them feel that they matter. As Rick Hansen says, "You want to make those people feel important; they're the most important people in your day."

When Are You Speaking?

If you speak first, you may have latecomers entering the room. If you speak last, you may face a tired or hungry group. After a meal, you will need a high energy approach to revitalize a mellow group.

Often, you are one of several speakers. In that case, find out their approaches to the subject in advance. You can then plan a complementary or contrasting position, rather than repeating what has already been said. That way the audience will be enriched rather than bored.

EXERCISE: "You Have To Be Good"

An experienced speaker suggested the following exercise. Match the time with the degree of brilliance required.

You have to be good	on Friday afternoon before a long weekend
You have to be even better	at 9:30 a.m.
You have to be dynamite	after lunch
Almost anybody can do it	after a lunch with wine

What Method of Presentation Suits the Audience?

Depending on the size of the group, their level of understanding of the topic, and their reasons for coming to hear you, various types of presentation are possible. Your skills and knowledge of the subject will also influence your choice. When and why would you use the following:

- a straightforward presentation?
- speech and question period?
- short introduction to a question and answer session?

Talk Without Speaking: What Your Body Language Tells Others

We communicate with our words, our eyes, our bodies. Audiences notice the way you walk to the front of the room, and the facial expressions you use. Although listeners make predictions about your speech from the way you look, they generally withhold judgment until after the first few minutes; your words, after all, are what count.

Books on body language in your library will give examples of speakers who clench their fists when they lie, assume aggressive postures when dealing with people they dislike, or adopt a closed posture when anxious. The following suggestions will help you look good and establish credibility before you speak.

1. **Psych yourself up.** Bring a sense of anticipation to the experience—it shows in your eyes and face.

2. **Breathe deeply.** You will look and feel calmer.

3. **Wear appropriate clothing.** It should be comfortable and send the right signals to the audience.

4. **Practise rising from your chair and walking to the front.** Rise quietly, and walk carefully with your eyes on your destination.

5. **Watch out for stairs.** Those people who run up them in an exaggerated display of eagerness often make spectacular entrances.

6. **Walk confidently to the lectern, keep your posture erect, and acknowledge other speakers naturally.**

7. **Establish eye contact.** Make the audience feel that they are special. Find a receptive person to the left, right, and centre of the group and speak to them in turn.

8. **Make your gestures natural.** They should be determined by the content of your speech, and not by nervousness.

9. **Do not dress yourself on stage.** The checklist "On Arrival" (in Chapter Eight) suggests you have some private time as soon as you arrive to check buttons and belts, to tuck in your shirt, etc. New speakers, with 45 pairs of eyes on them, are often seized with the urge to fix their clothes. Control yourself.

10. **Trust your audience.** They want you to do well.

EXERCISE: Weird Postures to Avoid

This exercise is fun. It is designed to make you aware of quirky postures or gestures caused by nervousness. Speakers are often unaware that they are making them. You may work alone or in small groups, one person performing and the others providing feedback and encouragement.

a) Choose a card. On each is the name of a weird posture or gesture that nervous speakers use *frequently* (see following list).
b) Take three minutes to practise the posture and prepare a 30-second speech of your choice (e.g., "junk food I love"). Exaggerate the posture and get feedback from your partners.
c) One at a time, go to the podium. A classmate reads the title of the quirk and you demonstrate it during your 30-second talk.
d) Get these postures out of your system *before* your next speech. The video tape *A Class Act* includes this exercise and all the following postures:

key jangler	one-legged crane
ballet position	the snob
toe tickler	gum chomper
hip shifter	abdominal cramps
dancer	clothes hitcher
tilter	

Weird Postures To Avoid

Abdominal cramps

Tongue-rolling

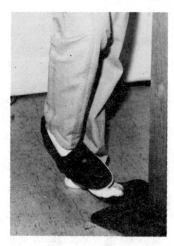
Toe-tickling

Demonstrations: The Real Thing

The real test of a chapter on organizing and preparing a speech is for you to use what you have learned. Demonstrations are a good, non-threatening way to experiment; the audience concentrates on the materials instead of you.

A demonstration speech is instructive and interesting if

1. the subject matches the audience, the time allotted and the space available;

2. you know the subject well and have a genuine interest in sharing it;
3. you organize clearly;
4. you rehearse until the demonstration and delivery are smooth.

We often make demonstration speeches as part of our jobs. Cooks and bakers show assistants how to make a creole sauce or crème caramel. A technician for the Ministry of Natural Resources helps others make a walkway through a bog. A salesperson sells different lighting systems by demonstrating the advantages of each. A veterinarian shows a group of assistants how to prepare an animal for anaesthetic. **The purpose of the speech is *not* to talk about a subject, but to explain it so clearly as you demonstrate that the audience learns the procedure and remembers it.** After your presentation, the audience should remember the main steps, and be able to work on their own.

Actual Topics Used for Demonstration Speeches

How to

paint clown faces
cut glass
pot a plant
execute a good golf swing
pour beer
do a Greek dance step
tie a bow tie
change a tire
use a haki sak
choose a ski boot
uncork wine
read palms
buy a good amplifier
spike hair
stop on roller skates
eat spaghetti
prepare squid
boost a car battery
cast: jig bait casting, imitation bait casting, live bait casting
twirl a pen
install a light switch
adjust bindings on ski boots
bone chicken breasts
throw a cream pie
diaper a baby
give a massage

Glass-cutting in the classroom

How to apply army-issue camouflage make-up

tie-dye material
hand-paint T-shirts
change a washer
clean a chimney
choose a canoe paddle

How to make

a simple table
duck decoys
tea
espresso
popcorn
the ultimate milkshake
the perfect peanut butter and jam sandwich
Irish cream liqueur
various exotic drinks
vegetable dip
carrot cake
fudge brownies
carrot juice
Caesar salad
paper roses
paper
decorator bows

How to use

underwater breathing apparatus
instant cash machines
correct cycling procedures
a 35 mm camera
a formal place setting
army issue camouflage make-up

Demonstration speeches add excitement to the class; you never know what will happen. The smell of garlic draws you to some exotic concoction; speakers in costume intrigue you; clusters of equipment promise hours of variety and interest. I still use recipes I learned from students; in my classes I learned how to prepare squid, use professional corkscrews, and make simple tables.

A Note on Ethical Responsibility
If you demonstrate a procedure involving health or safety—boosting a car battery, or helping a choking victim—you must be properly trained. Showing an incorrect cable connection may cause an accident. A responsible speaker does not alarm or frighten his audience: a student once caused an uproar when he suddenly produced a gun (a starter's pistol) during a speech. The class was so unnerved that they couldn't concentrate.

Make the Topic Specific

Limit your demonstration to one procedure, such as spiking your hair or using a microphone. If you choose taking a good picture, there are too many variables. Limit yourself to framing your subject, using different settings, or choosing background. Once you have your topic, list all the steps and *discard non-essential ones*.

The Three-Part Plan

Imagine a before-and-after situation: before your speech, the audience knows little about throwing a cream pie; after you're finished, they'll know how to throw the pie, and how to escape.

Your Speech Outline

I. **Introduction**

> *Grabber:* arouse curiosity
> *Thesis:* state what you are going to demonstrate and its importance
> *Overview:* outline the major steps—road map to competence

II. **Body**

> Show the steps in order

III. **Conclusion**

> Summary of major steps and a zinger to round off the presentation

But a Demonstration Has more than Three Steps.
Stephanie Auld, a junior ranger, was planning to demonstrate a graceful canoe stroke, the solo running pry. She had outlined eight steps:

1. Lean the canoe to the paddling side;
2. Approach the turning point;
3. Change the position of the paddling hand;
4. Insert the paddle blade under the canoe on the paddling side at a 45 degree angle and place the opposite hand on the gunwale for balance;
5. Hold the paddle in position until turn is half done;
6. Remove paddle from water;
7. Adjust weight to stop turn;
8. Resume paddling position.

When she realized that no one would remember all those steps, she organized them in three major sections: position, stroke, and follow-through.

PUTTING THE DEMONSTRA-TION TOGETHER

1. Make the topic specific
2. Follow the Three-Part Plan
3. Rehearse

Her friend, Fred Heidema, on the other hand, needed four major sections for his messy demonstration of cream pie throwing: selecting the pie, approach, delivery, and escape.

EXERCISE: Making It All Seem Simple

Choose one of the following topics, list all the steps involved, and organize them into three main sections:

    a) Building a simple stereo stand;
    b) Blowing bubble gum;
    c) Opening a door silently;
    d) An easy stretching exercise.

Modified Demonstrations

Demonstration speeches are usually done in chronological order, from beginning to end. However, what if there is a time lapse while the cookies bake or the glue dries? Will a boring repetitive action like accordion pleating a piece of paper turn your audience off? The modified demonstration is a technique to use in these cases.

If you plan to bake in class, bring the ingredients to be mixed in front of the group, *and* samples of the finished product. The components of a birdhouse can be assembled up to the stage of glueing, the next example can be worked on until it is time to paint, and then the third complete model is shown. There is nothing more boring than watching someone pleat kleenexes to use for pompons; make sure to use a modified demonstration for any action that involves a series of repetitive actions.

Rehearse

Rehearsing with props is essential to a smooth performance. Actors are meticulous about the placing and use of props, and speakers should be too. Your credibility will be enhanced if you know your subject well and can handle your materials confidently. Use the following checklist as you rehearse your speech; imagine your audience in the room.

1. **Rehearse with the materials until you are familiar with them.** This will allow you to give more eye contact to your audience when you actually do the speech.
2. **Have interesting props.** If you have a collection of materials—ingredients for a recipe, or pots of sequins or nails, put them in separate containers with large, colourful labels. Make the setup interesting.

HAVE INTERESTING PROPS

3. **Check your sightlines.** Set the demonstration up at home, *exactly* as you will do it. Then, walk from your position as speaker to where the audience will be. Is anything blocking your view? Are there bags or materials in the way? This is the most common problem with demonstration speeches. Make sure the audience's view is unobstructed.
4. **Can your notecards be seen at a distance?** Many things require your attention. Practise handling the materials, connecting with the audience, and checking notes all at once.
5. **Practise your movements often.** Can you pour liquids, fold paper, join pieces of wood, or slice mushrooms without your hands trembling?
6. **Repeat key ideas** and include a summary.
7. **Use the audience, involve them, appeal to them.** Make sure they understand.

Speech Assignment: The Demonstration

Choose a topic and prepare a three-part plan to include all the necessary

steps. Be prepared to enjoy and learn much during this assignment.

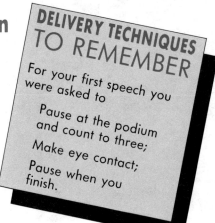

DELIVERY TECHNIQUES TO REMEMBER

For your first speech you were asked to

Pause at the podium and count to three;

Make eye contact;

Pause when you finish.

Now, add the following:

1. Assume a confident posture;
2. Breathe before you start. You will have better control of your voice;
3. Eliminate verbal tics (okay, um, ah).

INTERVIEW

Rick Hansen
Man in Motion

March 30, 1988
Ottawa

Rick Hansen is a wheelchair athlete, writer, and speaker. Inspired by the example of his friend, Terry Fox, Hansen embarked on the Man in Motion tour around the world in a wheelchair. He covered 24,901 miles (40,073 kilometres) and wheeled through 34 countries. The tour lasted from March 21, 1985 to May 22, 1987, a total of 792 days.

THE END IS JUST THE BEGINNING
Welcome Home Rick

In 1983, he shared athlete of the year honours with Wayne Gretzky; in 1987 he became a Companion of the Order of Canada, and he was the commissioner general for the Canadian Pavilion for the 1988 World Expo in Australia. He is now married to Amanda Reid, living in Richmond B.C., and working as a consultant on disability to the president of U.B.C.

Q

During the Man in Motion tour, you spoke many times each day, and yet you made each group and each speech special. How did you do it?

A

When I am speaking to the public, whether it's one person or 100 000 people, I want them to perceive me as I am feeling. I try to wipe the slate clean of the last speech because every speech is different— different environment, different people. What you have to do is come from the heart, speak from the heart in a way that allows people to gain a sense of what you feel, as well as what you think. They must know that you care about them, that you think they are important.

These days, so many people are getting into public speaking, and becoming proficient at it, even slick. They get mechanical and monotonous or repetitious, sometimes losing the life, and the feeling and the essence of what speaking is all about. It's storytelling, and communicating, and educating. (I think that part of public speaking has got to be preserved.)

Q

Even when you were exhausted, you made that kind of an effort?

A

No doubt about it. There were times when I came in from the road and I was just fried. I'd wheeled 70 miles that day, dealing with headwinds and shoulder injuries, and perhaps be cold and wet. We'd also have to deal with logistical matters and crew problems. Then, I had to turn around, and go out into a town hall where there were 300 people waiting, and they'd been there for four hours. The last thing you feel like doing is trying to overcome what you're feeling—which is a lot of depression, anguish, and pain.

You have to dig down very deep within you, to the essence of what drives you, and come up with not the image of somebody who's hurting, but the image of somebody who is positive, who has a wonderful message that's important for people to listen to. You want to make those people feel important; they're the most important people in your day, in your life, at that time.

Q

What inspired you on the tough days?

A

It's the sum of all the people on the tour that made it the success that it was. No one individual or group was more important than the other, including myself. We were all important, integral parts; we were a team. I had to come up with that. And I think it was my inherent belief in the dream, my commitment to it, and the teamwork around me, that allowed me to perform on those tough days when I didn't think I could.

When you're tired and at the edge, and you don't think you have any more to give, sometimes that's when you come up with your best performances.

Q

How did people respond?

A

That was the magic of the tour. People could relate to it in normal life; it leapt the bounds of disability. Anyone who is setting goals, chasing dreams, dealing with adversity and setbacks along the way, could relate to the message. They realized the value of teamwork, of cooperative endeavour, of the results possible when they challenge themselves.

Q

When you spoke at the Bowden Correctional Centre in Alberta, you started your speech with the line, "We are all imprisoned in different ways." That was a great way to establish a bond. How do you do that?

A

I treat each crowd differently. I never say the same thing. My words reflect a lot of the crowd I'm with. At Bowden, I wanted to say something those guys could relate to. It was important to find an analogy. They have their own personal battles to deal with, and I wanted them to be able to relate to the message, and perhaps, in turn, find inspiration for their own lives.

Q

How long did it take to find that opening?

A

It was spontaneous. I don't like to come into a place with set lines because so much depends on the crowd and the atmosphere. You have to be organized, don't get me wrong, but you also have to leave room to react spontaneously.

Q

What was your message? What were you out there to tell us?

A

What inspired me on my journey was not trying to raise funds for spinal cord injury research, but the inherent message Terry Fox delivered. Terry was a good friend of mine and although he was trying to raise money for cancer research, he created so much awareness of the potential of disabled persons. He brought the country together; he made people feel a way they had perhaps never felt before.

That message of awareness of disabled persons was so important. I thought if I could challenge myself to fulfil an old dream of physically wheeling around the world, and bring that message with me, that I could be a catalyst. I could be a messenger for a better understanding of disabled persons.

Q

What challenges did you issue?

A

I wanted to challenge people in their communities to see how they could remove the many barriers that still remain in the way of disabled persons achieving their potential. Outdated attitudes and physical obstacles have to be removed. We need to instill the idea that it's a community effort. Sometimes people want to slough it off; it's not their responsibility. But it's only a split second away from happening to anyone of us.
[Rick Hansen was 15 when the truck in which he was riding was involved in an accident. As a result of the injuries he received he is a paraplegic.]

We have to take that responsibility. We don't want to hand things out to people, but we do want to be compassionate. We want to know how we can help them achieve their potential, to get out and be successful in life again, be productive citizens, enjoy what they can in their own lives. That's the inherent message of my journey.

Q
Did you see evidence of change in your travels?

A
Yes, it was wonderful to see improved facilities, better funding, educational programmes, new legislation, and changed attitudes on the part of the government and the public.

Q
Do you get nervous when you speak?

A
I get nervous when I have to be organized for an extended speech. I don't get nervous when I speak from the heart, but I'm also trying to learn to be organized for a longer presentation. The combination of being organized and maintaining sincerity means so much to me that I get nervous.

I'm new to a more formal speaking style. The message or vision is always clear, but I'm always tired and in a hurry. I want to have enough control so that I can get off a plane and *know* I can always come through. I don't want to rely on having a good day, but be sure I can do it.

Last week, I spoke to an IBM conference; I was well organized and decided to break from the set speech and expand personally on a few points. I expanded from 35 minutes to 50 minutes. It was still quite successful I think.

Q
What speech of yours sticks in your mind?

A
My little speech in B.C. Place. I was home in Vancouver in a stadium and I thought a lot about what I wanted to say. I just didn't want to tell them about Rick Hansen, I wanted to tell them about our dream, the vision that we worked for as a team. My tour is over and yet the challenge is still there. I wanted them to know, and I want each person out there to realize that it's their turn to carry on. I'll be there to support them.

Q
What advice do you have for people who want to speak well?

A
Organize yourselves. Speak from the heart. Be sincere. Give the audience everything that's in you, just like it's your first speech. Have a feeling for the audience and a sense of being with them. If you're speaking to kids, don't revert to old ideas of "adults and kids." Just talk to them so they understand you, and so that you have a feeling for them and what they face.

Rick Hansen

Speech: The Dream is Just Beginning

Rick Hansen and his team took his message to the entire world. These are excerpts taken from his remarks on the road. They show the determination and faith in people that took him 24,901 miles around the globe.

I see myself only as a catalyst. I want to deliver a message to the world, to challenge people to have positive attitudes about disabled persons, and to take action to break down barriers standing in the way of their potential.

We all have perceived disabilities of one kind or another. There are many setbacks in life and I'm wheeling to show that these setbacks *can* be overcome. So never give up on your dreams.

I believe there is a direct link between the physical and emotional rebuilding of one's body. Through rehabilitation, sports, and recreation programmes, not only will disabled people be able to get on with their lives, they will be able to re-enter the community and make their own dreams come true.

I'm hoping disabled people will be treated with respect for what they *can* do, rather than what they can't do. We all deserve the right to live, to be the best we can be. The tour will end in Vancouver but *the dream is just beginning*.

1987 Man in Motion tour

OUTLINE OF A DEMONSTRATION SPEECH

Name: _____

Date of Speech: _____

Purpose Statement: _____

INTRODUCTION

    Grabber:

    Thesis:

    Overview:

BODY

    Step #1

    Step #2

    Step #3

CONCLUSION

    Reference to purpose (thesis):

    Summary of main steps:

    Zinger:

SELF-EVALUATION FORM

This form is to help you evaluate your own speech. It can be kept private or shared with your instructor or peers.

Type of Speech: _____

Name: _____

Title: _____

Date: _____

DELIVERY

Physical Presence

Did I make eye contact with others?

Was my posture natural and appropriate?

Was I aware of my facial expressions and hand gestures?

Were there any distracting mannerisms that I was aware of?

Did I feel good?

Could I feel an energy exchange with my audience?

VOCAL DELIVERY

Was my voice under control?

Did I sound confident?

Was I aware of breathing calmly?

How was my enunciation?

Did I manage to avoid um's and ah's?

Did I sound interested/excited/committed?

How did my voice sound to me?

DESIGN AND CONTENT

How well did the introduction and conclusion work?

Did the framework unify my speech?

Was there a natural progression from point to point?

Did my notes keep me on track? Did I use them?

Did the audience seem to understand the organization of my speech?

Was the information clear?

What was the energy level of the conclusion?

What would I change the next time?

What worked very well?

OVERALL EFFECTIVENESS

Did I connect with this audience?

Did I achieve my purpose?

What do I remember most about making the speech?

What unexpected or unforeseen things happened?

What am I most pleased about?

OTHER COMMENTS

Grade:

PEER EVALUATION FORM

Peer evaluation should be done in a constructive and supportive fashion. The speaker may choose people to do assessments or they may be assigned alphabetically. Some groups maintain the same speaker/assessor teams for the entire course; others change for each speech. The instructor may wish to see this evaluation before it goes to the speaker.

Type of Speech: _____

Speaker: _____

Title: _____

Assessor: _____

Date: _____

DELIVERY

Physical Presence

> Did the speaker maintain eye contact?

> Did she or he establish a rapport with the audience?

> Were gestures natural and effective?

VOCAL DELIVERY

> Did the speaker sound convincing/spontaneous/excited?

> Was his or her voice clear and loud enough?

> How did you respond to the speaker's mood?

DESIGN AND CONTENT

> Did the introduction interest you?

> Did the overview give you an indication of the main proofs?

> Did the speech flow easily and logically from one point to another?

> Was the conclusion strong and memorable?

> Did the conclusion reinforce the thesis and main points?

> What was the thesis of the speech?

OVERALL EFFECTIVENESS

> Did you learn something new or worthwhile from the speech?

> Were you moved by it?

> What was the most outstanding part of the speech?

> What changes do you recommend?

> What parts should the speaker definitely keep?

OTHER COMMENTS

Grade:

EVALUATION FORM

Type of Speech: _____

Name: _____

Title: _____

Length of Speech: _____

Date: _____

Legend: S = SUPERIOR   E = EFFECTIVE   NW = NEEDS WORK

DELIVERY

Physical Presence

   Eye Contact

   Rapport with Audience

   Posture

   Gestures

   Use of Notes

   Appropriate Use of Audio-Visual
Support Material

VOCAL DELIVERY

   Naturalness/Spontaneity/Enthusiasm

   Clarity

   Variety (Tone, Pitch, Pace)

   Volume

   Absence of Verbal Tics (um, ah,
okay, like)

   Sense of Control and Calm

DESIGN AND CONTENT

   Use of Framework for Introduction
and Conclusion

   Clear Thesis and Overview

   Coherence/Use of Transitions

   New/Interesting Information

   Strong Finish

LANGUAGE

   Word Choice

   Impact on Audience

   Grammar

OVERALL EFFECTIVENESS

   Treatment of Topic

   Intelligent Awareness of Audience

   Achievement of Purpose

   Impact on/Connection with Audience

OTHER COMMENTS

Grade:

Think It Over: The Informative Speech

TIPS FOR SPEAKERS

1. Use the library and firsthand interviews as research sources.
2. Information is obtained through a *process* by which facts are gathered, organized, compared, and balanced in a logical manner.
3. Train yourself in speed planning for any topic. A three-part plan always works.
4. A good introduction has a grabber, a clear thesis, and an overview of major points. Save enough energy for a STRONG FINISH.
5. Visual and audio aids can enhance your speech. They should communicate immediately.
6. Note cards should be in point form and legible at a distance. Highlighting helps you find important information at a glance.
7. Aim your speech at an intelligent teenager. Don't hide behind an inflated vocabulary.

- *Where is the best place in Halifax to get a charbroiled burger with guacamole and cheddar cheese toppings?*
- *How can you tell the difference between fox tracks and wolf tracks?*
- *What childhood game had the most influence on your social life? (or social awareness?)*
- *Do you consider the city morgue a possible tourist attraction?*

Any one of the above is a good topic for an informative speech, the purpose of which is to share knowledge and create understanding. If you can find, sort, analyze, simplify, organize, and present your material, you'll be the hit of your company or seminar group. First, there are a few things to learn.

Getting Your Speech in Shape

Start by brainstorming the topic and exploring available research resources. Then, move to the general purpose and design of the speech. When you have a firm thesis and outline, concentrate on the introduction and conclusion. They form the framework of your speech and need clarity, drama, and impact.

The accompanying flowchart, ''Charting Your Success: Preparing a Speech,'' outlines this process; in this chapter you will learn more of the skills necessary to complete the following steps:

1. Researching;
2. Organizing your materials;
3. Devising memorable introductions and conclusions;
4. Making things clearer by using statistics, analogies and audio-visual aids;
5. Keeping on topic with effective note cards.

As you work through these sections, remember that speeches must be lively as well as informative. As Eddie Greenspan states in the interview that concludes this chapter:

> [*A good speech*] *must entertain. It is pointless to make an important point in a boring fashion because it may be lost. It has to be made in an entertaining and dramatic way.*

Research

Research gives your speech the solidity it needs to be useful and convincing. Once you have a topic, your research will help you discover the *essential* information you need to know and all the exciting details that will give your work direction and emphasis. There is one warning: **Don't go off the deep end!** We all know research fanatics who put their anxiety about the speech into library hours. They have pages of notes and hundreds of

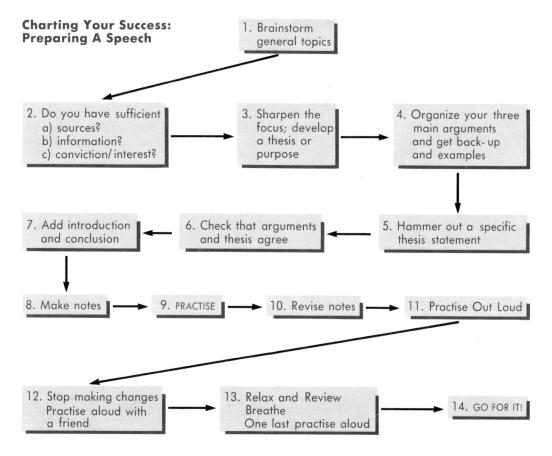

**Charting Your Success:
Preparing A Speech**

1. Brainstorm general topics

2. Do you have sufficient
   a) sources?
   b) information?
   c) conviction/ interest?

3. Sharpen the focus; develop a thesis or purpose

4. Organize your three main arguments and get back- up and examples

7. Add introduction and conclusion

6. Check that arguments and thesis agree

5. Hammer out a specific thesis statement

8. Make notes

9. PRACTISE

10. Revise notes

11. Practise Out Loud

12. Stop making changes Practise aloud with a friend

13. Relax and Review Breathe One last practise aloud

14. GO FOR IT!

details but no time to practise. Stick to your schedule and control yourself.

Primary Research

Primary research is information you gather yourself. It involves interviews, visits, observation, reading unedited written material (such as scientific reports, trial transcripts, financial reviews). If you are interested in acupuncture, the interviews you do with acupuncturists, doctors, patients, advocates and critics of the procedure, are primary research. If you have had acupuncture treatments yourself, you are a good source of information.

Secondary Research

The finding, reading, and analyzing of written (or taped) material will most often lead you to the library. Stephen Overbury, the consummate Canadian researcher and teacher of research, considers our libraries the best, although most often overlooked, sources of information. In his book, *Finding Canadian Facts Fast,* he writes:

There are at least three things you can be sure of about libraries: they collect information on every subject; the information can always be located; and the librarians who run them have been trained to meet your information needs.

(STEPHEN OVERBURY, *Finding Canadian Facts Fast.* Toronto: Methuen, 1985. p. 85)

Using the card catalogue or microfiche to search for information by author, title, or subject is a starting point. Once you consult these, it may be appropriate to check periodical indexes to obtain the most current information. Your search might proceed like this:

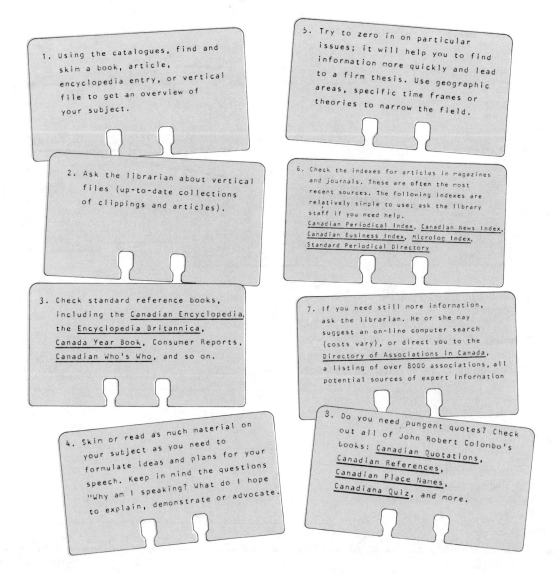

1. Using the catalogues, find and skim a book, article, encyclopedia entry, or vertical file to get an overview of your subject.

2. Ask the librarian about vertical files (up-to-date collections of clippings and articles).

3. Check standard reference books, including the Canadian Encyclopedia, the Encyclopedia Britannica, Canada Year Book, Consumer Reports, Canadian Who's Who, and so on.

4. Skim or read as much material on your subject as you need to formulate ideas and plans for your speech. Keep in mind the questions "Why am I speaking? What do I hope to explain, demonstrate or advocate.

5. Try to zero in on particular issues; it will help you to find information more quickly and lead to a firm thesis. Use geographic areas, specific time frames or theories to narrow the field.

6. Check the indexes for articles in magazines and journals. These are often the most recent sources. The following indexes are relatively simple to use; ask the library staff if you need help. Canadian Periodical Index, Canadian News Index, Canadian Business Index, Microlog Index, Standard Periodical Directory

7. If you need still more information, ask the librarian. He or she may suggest an on-line computer search (costs vary), or direct you to the Directory of Associations in Canada, a listing of over 8000 associations, all potential sources of expert information

8. Do you need pungent quotes? Check out all of John Robert Colombo's books: Canadian Quotations, Canadian References, Canadian Place Names, Canadiana Quiz, and more.

In all cases, make sure to get the bibliographical details as you work: author, title, date and place of publication or broadcast. You may not be asked for this information but you must have it.

Evaluate Your Sources

> There is no such thing as objective reality. We each select our experiences through the filters of our genes, values and belief systems. Ask a logger from B.C. and a Haida Indian to talk about the importance of a virgin stand of cedar trees or a Bay Street businessman and a person on welfare about taxes and social services. You would swear from their responses that they come from different worlds.
>
> (DAVID SUZUKI, *Metamorphosis*. Toronto: Stoddart, 1987. p. 5)

Evaluate your material as you work; you may reject a book or article without wasting time making notes, or you may decide to read the work and check it against other sources. As you gather and organize your material, you must evaluate constantly: you will eventually have to make the decision whether to use the material or not.

"My nation was ignored in your history textbooks."
(Chief Dan George)

For example, Canadian history books written in English before 1960 state that Louis Riel was a traitor; present texts describe him as a leader of the Métis, and a Canadian hero. What accounts for difference?

Anyone researching AIDS will run into a similar dilemma; various sources will advocate differing, even conflicting suggestions. Take, for example, the question of introducing needle exchange programs for intravenous drug users, a high-risk group. When you read articles or hear debates on this issue, what factors would you need to consider in order to test the validity of the argument?

You will often have to compare one source to another. This cross-testing will help you make an informed judgment. In deciding whether to accept or reject information, you should start by examining the following:

1. **The author.** Is the author an expert in that field? Does he or she have suitable credentials? A member of the National Council on the study of AIDS or a member of a local AIDS group may have a better grasp of the situation than a right-wing tabloid that opposes all help for, or understanding of, minority groups.
2. **The tone.** Is the tone reasonable? Is there evidence of scientific proof and fair investigation? Does the author show more interest in solving the problem, or avoiding political and social controversy?
3. **The publication.** Is the publisher well-known, with a reputation for fairness? Does the material come from a professional journal or an inflammatory magazine? What

newspapers, magazines, radio and television shows in your area are

- fair?
- known for balanced reporting?
- biased?
- more interested in mass appeal or sensationalism?

As Overbury states: "slanted material is not necessarily unusable—it may be used in context—but you must be aware of the bias in order to make good use of it", (Overbury, p. 7).

4. **Date and place of the report or publication.** Time can make substantial differences in research results, public attitudes and views concerning social and health issues. Big cities will often pioneer techniques that affect large numbers of their population long before smaller centres feel the pressure to concern themselves. On the other hand, local newspapers highlight issues, such as the closing of rural post offices, that national journals overlook.

EXERCISE: Balancing Your Sources

Where would you go to find a *fair* and balanced evaluation of the following?

How to finance a car
The contribution of René Lévesque to Canada
Importance of k.d. lang to Canadian music
The housing situation in your city or province
Whether to increase or cut the amount of money available for student loans.

Using Research Correctly
Completing the Process

Gathering the facts does *not* mean you have finished your research; you must now classify and weigh the material. Stephen Overbury tells of selling a potentially explosive article on the exporting of tank engines to South Africa, a violation of the United Nations arms embargo. Unfortunately for the article, the engines were for trucks, not tanks, and although Overbury salvaged the story, he warns of the danger of faulty assumptions and incomplete research:

> Gathering random facts does not necessarily mean obtaining information. Information is obtained through a process by which facts are gathered, organized, compared, and balanced in a logical manner.
>   (OVERBURY, p.xii)

Avoiding Plagiarism

If you are preparing a speech about the responsibilities of a fire crew boss working for the Ministry of Natural Resources, much of what you learn may be new to you. All information considered public knowledge can be used without specific acknowledgment. However, if you get into value judgments about techniques used, whether or not there is enough regulation of fire crews, or sufficient on-the-job training, you must be prepared to acknowledge your sources and give them credit (and blame) for your statements.

Similarly, if you use other people's *ideas*, even if you do not quote directly, you should give them credit. Although it is hard to know when to acknowledge sources, you should be very careful in this area and err on the side of caution.

Plagiarism occurs when you knowingly pass off the work, words, or ideas of others as your own. It is a mean-spirited thing to do. And it's illegal.

Organizing Your Information: The Principle of Three

*Organize your observations, arguments, steps, explanations, and exhortations into **three** manageable, memorable segments.*

This organizational method is clear, it's simple, and it works for anything. Are you going to praise the attractions of Peggy's Cove? How will you organize your mass of enthusiastic observations? Try three main categories:

1. The beauty of the Nova Scotian coast;
2. The richness of local folklore;
3. The superb seafood.

This same system will work for the mountain of information you have on the Chilkoot Pass, the gateway to the fabled Klondike Gold Rush Route. If you want to convey the thrill of hiking the Chilkoot you can concentrate on

1. The history of the Klondike Rush of 1898;
2. Scenery;
3. Climbing adventures.

Each major section has subsections so that you can work a considerable amount of information into your speech and present it so clearly that your audience will remember what you have to say. To do this, jot down significant points for each main section, look for ideas or themes that go together, experiment with mini-plans, and you're ready.

This takes practice; once you are used to taking an idea and breaking it into main ideas and supporting subsections, you'll be able to do it in seconds.

What Determines the Order of Your Main Points?

The nature of your speech, the occasion, and your common sense will tell you how to order the various sections. Your aim is to approach the subject in a way that you and your audience will enjoy pursuing.

1. **Chronological order.** Events that have a certain sequence, such as a marketing strategy or medical procedure, should be outlined in the order they occur. Reverse chronological order is also a clear way to organize your points.
2. **Flashback or flashforward.** Add a little drama by starting at one point, and casting forward or back in time to present the material.
3. **Spatial order.** If you're discussing the design of a recreation centre or the safest, most efficient arrangement of machinery in a small manufacturing plant, spatial ordering is most logical. Geographical order is easy to follow if you're outlining national concerns like weather or trade patterns, or tourist concentrations.

The principle of three: Environmentalists ask people to "Reduce, Re-use, Recycle."

4. **Cause-and-effect order.** Do you want to illustrate the unquestionable link between a smoke-free workplace and the reduction of employee sick days? Are you advocating the use of incentives to increase productivity or performance? How about free trips to Hawaii guaranteeing better examination results? Audiences are intrigued by this very clear and interesting approach.
5. **All-things-being-equal order.** Sometimes all the factors are equal and anything will work. It's up to you to decide on an approach that will be logical and interesting. If you're giving the orientation speech for new counsellors at a drug rehabilitation centre and you want to talk about the major times for vigilance, you might decide to work from the most to least obvious times of stress. Use the approach that makes sense and interests you.
6. **Climatic order.** Saving the best for last is a method you've used many times. Whenever you argued with a younger brother or sister about whose turn it was to clean up, the arguments went: "it's only fair to share the job; most of this is your stuff; if you don't do it, I'm going to tell you came home late on Saturday." That's climatic order; choose the most convincing reason and save it for a strong, energetic finish.
7. **When you're desperate.** If nothing works, remember you can always discuss anything using the categories physical, emotional and psychological. It's an overused strategy, but you may need it as a last resort. For example, the physical, emotional, and psychological

- appeal of colour on cereal boxes;
- impact of portable radio headsets in the workplace;
- benefits of pets in senior citizens' centres.

Smooth Transitions

How do you move from point to point smoothly? If you watch a relay race, you'll see that the switch-over is a crucial moment that runners practise often. In your speech, you need that same grace to move naturally from one idea to the next. If your overview is clear, your audience will know your main arguments and be ready for the switch. Here are words speakers use to make clear, logical transitions.

TRANSITIONAL DEVICES

Adding a point

and	another	furthermore
also	a second point	in the same way
besides	likewise	in addition
next	too	
or	as well as	
again	in addition	
further	by comparison	
moreover		

Emphasizing a point

above all	in fact	especially
certainly	to be sure	in particular
chiefly	without doubt	even more important
doubtless	unquestionably	to repeat
indeed	for sure	

Showing similarity

in like manner
in the same way
similarly

Introducing examples or details

for example	namely	specifically
for instance	such as	in particular
as you can see	that is	for one thing
to illustrate	the following	in fact

(Continued)

Restating a point

in other words	to put it another way
in effect	in short
similarly	that is to say
that is	if we look at it from a different perspective

Introducing a contrast or qualification

although	unlike	whereas
but	while	after all
conversely	yet	admittedly
however	despite	in spite of
in contrast	surely	if
nevertheless	unfortunately	
nonetheless	conversely	
on the contrary	granted	
on the other hand	even if	
otherwise	occasionally	
still		

Showing result/cause and effect

as	then
because	therefore
for	thus
for that reason	it follows that
since	
accordingly	
as a result	
consequently	
hence	
so	

Showing connections in time

before	next	when
previously	tomorrow	thereafter
formerly	immediately	lately
once	soon	eventually
earlier	in the future	subsequently
now	shortly	ultimately
presently	at the same time	final
meanwhile	simultaneously	in the past
at this time	at this time	
at present	after	
nowadays	afterward	
	then	

(Continued)

Indicating chronology or sequence
finally
first, second, third...
first, secondly, thirdly...
   (do not use firstly)
next
in the first place, second place...
at first
to begin with
next, also, then, moving along
at the end, at last, finally

Concluding
(try to aim for something more original than "in conclusion.")

in brief	as a result
to sum up	therefore
on the whole	consequently
finally	accordingly
all together	to conclude
as we have seen	thus
lastly	

With thanks to Robyn Knapp, Centennial College

EXERCISE: Group Speed Planning

1. To develop your skills in breaking down a topic, any topic, into sections and subsections, convince your friends to play this game. Make sure that everyone understands the three-part, step-by-step method outlined in this chapter and make a list of topics. You can do this by brainstorming together, using the first five ideas you see in the newspaper, or covering your eyes and pointing at part of a list in this exercise. Remember, all topics are fair game. Everyone gets the same number of topics and the same amount of time.

2. Now, spend five or ten minutes working up plans and then read them to each other asking for comments, criticism, and praise. The criteria for evaluating a plan are the same you would apply to any speech:

    a) Is it clear?
    b) Is it complete?
    c) Is it coherent?
    d) Is it convincing?

3. Ready for a practice? Take an example from a social service worker's speech on the correct response to an abused child. The three main sections are attitude, tone, and words. In two minutes, think up the subsections for each. Attitude might include respect, care, belief; tone will include caring, reassurance, encouragement, protection; words will tell the child that the worker is sorry that it happened, that it isn't the child's fault, and that help is on the way.
4. Need topics to start you off? Try these:

VCR	parent abuse
birth control	junk food
minimum wages	domed cities
running shoes	Star Wars
tanning salons	fixed link from P.E.I.
domed stadiums	to mainland
diet centres	student discounts for
importance of sunlight	travel
high-performance cars	
"hot" vacation spots	

EXERCISE: Thesis Olympics

By now, you should be ready to challenge the other members of the class. Your instructor provides suitable prizes: stale doughnuts are the favourite.

a) Divide the class into four even groups, sitting in clusters.
b) You are given *one minute* to choose a general topic.
c) Write the topic on a piece of paper.
d) On a given signal, pass the paper clockwise to the next group. At the same time, you will receive your topic.
e) Take two minutes to hammer out a thesis statement and an overview of three main points. The instructor may award bonus marks for a precise, complete thesis and overview.
f) Once you are accomplished at this game, step (e) can be amended so that the first group finished, in whatever amount of time, wins.

Students quickly learn to give their competitors challenging topics. Recent games have yielded the following subjects: eyewear, volcanoes, guaranteed minimum income, nuclear submarines, female police officers, gasoline, endangered species, daycare for farm families, radioactivity, centrifugal force, and monkeys.

Street Practice

Use the time walking or driving to work or school to practise on your own. Whatever you pass, whatever comes to mind, chart it into a workable plan. Is there a street musician on the corner?

Instruments: guitar, accordian, saxophone.
Success: money, crowds, general appearance.

Did someone cut you off at the intersection?

Reasons: Type A, fatigue, mindless wonder.
Personality changes in a car:
                mean machine, ruthless competition, status.

Having coffee in a doughnut shop?

Doughnuts: calories, freshness, sugar powder on your face.
Sociological studies possible:
                workers getting a sugar boost for the drive ahead, the aimless and homeless putting in time, the regulars gathering for gossip and neighbourhood analysis.

Eventually, you'll be so good at this that the division of major topics will go smoothly.

Once your thesis and overview are in place, and the order of your supporting arguments established, you can add examples. Then it's time to design a framework for the speech: the introduction and conclusion.

Great Intros and Dynamic Conclusions

A powerful introduction starts with a hook or grabber. Grabbers seize the attention of the audience and make them want to listen. If you work to develop a great grabber suitable for your speech, you can intrigue your audience and make them impatient for the rest. If you link your grabber to the conclusion, your speech will have a framework that gives it a sense of wholeness. Be sure to choose a grabber that is appropriate for your speech and the audience, and remember to connect it to the rest of your material at some point.

Some grabbers that work well are:

Stories and Examples

We are a nation of storytellers. Listen to your neighbours relate details of a near miss with a chain saw, their latest search for an apartment, or their surprise at seeing Anne Murray in a neighbourhood restaurant. Narratives touch your listeners, make your speech more real. One student's presentation on child abuse began with a brief history of Elena, a small girl who would not speak to anyone until a teacher at the day-care centre triggered a response when she was doing a puppet play; the story was a quick way to introduce the topic and engage the sympathy and interest of the audience.

Diane Francis, a business commentator and analyst, knows the value of using anecdotes to explain things to the general public.

> *Business is as interesting as watching paint dry. It's full of details and numbers. But it's the people who do business that are interesting. ...Business is like sport—it involves people and action.*
> (CBC, As It Happens. *July 7, 1987*)

Where do you find these stories? Research, of course. As you read, interview, or listen, take down the anecdotes that will add life and emphasis to your speech. Your friends and family will be good sources, and the media are usually reliable. Eddie Greenspan, outstanding criminal lawyer, author, and speaker maintains a large file of stories and examples:

> *Because I speak often, if I am attracted to an analogy that I read in the press or in a book, or if I hear it on the radio or on television, I will make a note of it. I collect what I think are good examples of whatever point is being made.*

Urban legends are popular and exciting stories to use. They are a type of city dweller's folklore, widely known and *always* supposed to be true. You may know the stories of alligators (and grass) in the sewers of New York, the poodle in the microwave, the disappearing hitchhiker. "The Choking Doberman" was an urban legend popular in the mid-1980's. My students even heard it on several news reports and one of them used it as the grabber for her speech on safety in highrise apartments.

THE CHOKING DOBERMAN: AN URBAN LEGEND

A woman living in North Vancouver came home to her apartment after work one day. As she opened the door, she spied her Doberman Pinscher lying on the floor choking and nearly unconscious. Grabbing the dog, she rushed to her car and drove him to the vet. There the vet took the dog to the surgery and told the woman to go home and wait for her report. As soon as the woman returned to her apartment, the phone rang and when she picked it up, the vet said: "Get out of your apartment immediately. You are in great danger. I've called the police and they'll be right there."

The woman ran from her home and met the police outside. When they opened the woman's bedroom cupboard, they found a man crouching on the floor, faint from loss of blood and in great pain. When the vet had examined the dog, she found two fingers stuck in his throat; guessing that the dog had attacked an intruder she called the police and the woman to warn her.

(You can find many more urban legends in Edith Fowke; *Folklore of Canada*, (Toronto: McClelland and Stewart.))

Quotations

Here are six quotations. For what speeches and audiences are they appropriate?

> *Friends take you along but they don't always bring you back. Miss Eva John always said that.*
> (GARTH JOHN — Student in Fluid Power and Robotics, Centennial College)

> *I want to do something where I know there's a chance of failing. ...I'm not going to put out stuff that comes from a bored mind.*
> (NEIL YOUNG)

> *You've got to be right on. [Colour is] like skipping rope; if you're off a skip, you're out of luck.*
> (MARILYN BROOKS — Fashion designer)

> *What Canadian retailer advised: "Early to bed, early to rise, never get tight and advertise"? [answer: Timothy Eaton]*
> (Trivial Pursuit, Genus Edition)

> *Women have cleaned up things since time began, and if women get into politics there will be a cleaning up of pigeon-holes and forgotten corners. ...The sound of the political carpet-beater will be heard in the land.*
> (NELLIE L. McCLUNG)

> *Float like a butterfly, sting like a bee, His hands can't hit what his eyes can't see.*
> (MUHAMMAD ALI)

Historical References

Events in the lives of great world leaders, such as Martin Luther King, Jr., or Norman Bethune, can provide a good starting point for your talk. You may refer instead to specific national events: the driving of the last spike to complete the Canadian Pacific Railway in 1885, the use of the War Measures Act to deal with the FLQ crisis in 1971, the relocation of Japanese Canadians in World War II, the entry of Newfoundland into Confederation in 1949, the Olympic Winter Games in Calgary in 1988. One student used the example of Bethune to open a speech on inventiveness: Bethune was so determined to cure his own case of tuberculosis that he pioneered a new surgical procedure and experimented on himself.

"What we do not have is a lot of time but we do have enough time to do things fairly."
(Martin Luther King Jr.)

Humour

> *Why is six afraid of seven?...*
> *Because seven eight nine.*

> *What's yellow and goes around?....*
> *A long-playing omelette.*

Humour is a hard thing to define and an even harder technique to perfect. If you have a gift for humour, if it's appropriate for the occasion, and if you practise, it can break the ice and quickly get your audience on your side. Banish from your repertoire any joke that is racist, sexist, or pokes fun at minorities. Tellers of bad jokes insult themselves and their audience.

In Canada, we're fond of a self-deprecating type of humour, one that drily pokes fun at our regional foibles. We are all familiar with jokes about Maritimers, but lately prairie humour has become increasingly more widespread. Connie Kaldor, a Saskatchewan-born singer, is fond of a tongue-in-cheek way of drawling on about the glitter of prairie social life. To introduce a song about a truck stop, she describes a small arborite counter-topped wayside where the waitress doesn't get many tips " 'cause in Saskatchewan they don't believe in leaving spare money just lying around.''

The Honourable Mr. Justice Willard "Bud" Estey, formerly of the Supreme Court of Canada, born in the same province, has a similar wit: "I grew up on the Prairies where everybody was equal; we were all broke.''

Music
Books are not your only source of quotations; ''Give Peace a Chance'' and ''We Shall Overcome'' are familiar to all of us. From Jane Siberry to Rita MacNeil, from Stan Rogers to Corey Hart, from Spirit of the West to Glass Tiger, music can enliven a speech and provide just the right words. Quote the lyrics or put the song on a tape (consult the checklist on using tapes) and watch the look of delight and surprise on the faces of your listeners. Be sure to clarify how the words and music relate to your topic.

Unusual or Startling Statement
To startle your audience to attention requires an element of surprise in your grabber. Sheri Alexander, a student in a travel counsellor course, began this way:

> If malaria, yellow fever, and hepatitis don't mean anything to you, maybe the words ''lawsuit,'' ''reputation,'' and ''unemployment'' do. It is your legal responsibility as travel agents, to make sure that the health requirements of your clients have been met before their departure.

Her classmate, Diane Lynch, caught everyone's attention immediately when she announced that stopping was the hardest part of roller skating. She said this from the back of the room, skated between the aisles to the front of the room where she smacked into the front wall. We were instantly alert. Your statement may be challenging or unusual but it cannot be insulting or your listeners will retaliate by closing their minds.

THE SETTING AS GRABBER

What could be more appropriate for a speech about the close ties between rural and urban Canadians than a herd of bronze cows? Cynthia Patterson used these sculptures, located in an IBM tower complex, to act as a grabber. Her championing of rural concerns is discussed further in Chapter Six.

Cynthia Patterson A Message from Rural Canada, October 1987

Thank you all for coming to our rural meeting in the city, among the cows. These beautiful cows, cast by Joe Fafard, a Saskatchewan artist, help to make us feel at home in this large city. Sometimes, when I'm talking with Rural Dignity volunteers on the telephone, I hear the unmistakeable sound of mooing in the background. Then I realize the other person is speaking from an extension phone in the barn. Many of us enjoy a close companionship with cows.

But, quite apart from feeling comfortable with these animals, we chose this site for another reason. I think Joe Fafard, IBM, and Rural Dignity might share a few ideas on the relation between village and city.

These cows, planted firmly here in the centre of one of North America's largest cities, make a strong statement. Their presence is a visible reminder of the connection between town and country. Urban and rural Canadians *are* interdependent. We rely on one another for food, for work, and for the variety of experience that makes life rich. The sight of cows in downtown Toronto should not strike us as strange, but remind us of how things really are. The cows in front of the IBM building are especially appropriate because the wise application of new technology allows city and country to communicate as never before. Decentralization need not mean isolation. We can look forward to more people being able to live a relaxed, healthy, rural life while doing their work with the aid of computers, and communications equipment.

It is not an exaggeration to say that never before in our history has the connection between rural and urban areas been more important or held more potential. And we believe that if only you knew some of the problems we are up against, you'd share our concern, and want to help.

Cynthia Patterson used her setting as a grabber.

Grabbers change with your topic, your style, and your audience. As a class or group, decide on a single topic. Every member of the group then has eight minutes to decide on a profile of his or her audience and a great grabber. The time allotment includes practice. At the end of eight minutes everyone stands and delivers; the audience provides encouragement and helpful feedback. (This is a good exercise to videotape).

The Rule for Conclusions: A Strong Finish

Distance runners know the secret of a good finish: save enough energy to put on a burst of strength at the end. If you've watched a 1500-metre race, you'll see the strong runners work for a position at the front of the pack; they hold that spot until the last lap when they give a final great push to pull ahead and fly to the finish line. It's a wonderful thing so see and a good strategy to adopt. With planning, you can be sure your entire speech is full of energy; with training you can learn to save enough good material, enough conviction, and enough personal dynamism to avoid petering out and **finish strong.**

Sheri Alexander's conclusion tied in well with her grabber, *and* packed a punch:

> *Dr. Azouz is here today to make you aware of what you and your clients may be up against once they leave the country. And how you can save their lives, and your neck.*

EXERCISE: Finishing Strong

"Where does the power come from to see the race to its end? From within."
(Chariots Of Fire)

Using the same topic you prepared for the exercise on grabbers, prepare a strong finishing statement. Together the introduction and conclusion should form a framework that strengthens your speech. If you need new topics, you might consider:

the importance of water
the fitness level of Canadians
are steroids banned substances or part of every athlete's training?
what's wrong with caffeine?
chocolate is my downfall
a personal hero

EXERCISE: The SQSQS Formula for Introductions and Conclusions

Jack David, speaker, publisher, and teacher, uses the SQSQS method of remembering five kinds of grabbers:

Statistic
Quotation
Story
Question
Startling statement

Take one topic and see if you can develop five grabbers, one of each type. Decide which is most effective. You should then be able to devise a conclusion that refers to the grabber, and frames your speech neatly.

Statistics are numerical facts; they can be clinchers or clunkers in your presentations.

Making Things Clear: Statistics, Analogies, and Visual Aids

1. **Make sure statistics are accurate.** Check different sources to make sure that the statistics you are using are fair and unbiased.
2. **Use statistics comparatively whenever possible.** If you want to stress the plight of the beluga whales found in the Saguenay River northeast of Quebec City, it is not enough to say that there are fewer than 500 left in this area, unless you point out that a century ago there were 5000.
3. **Use familiar parallels.** Good comparisons also make statistics approachable; in the case of the belugas, a marine mammal at the top of the food chain, recent autopsies have shown very high levels of PCBs, cancer-causing agents. How high are the levels? There are so many dangerous contaminants in the beluga corpses that, according to our laws, they should be considered hazardous wastes.
4. **Statistics should mean something to the audience.** Isolated numbers will not make an impression, but examples or stories will. For example, the Northwest Territories has one-third of all Canada's territory but a population smaller than the crowd in Calgary that watched the opening of the 1988 Winter Olympics. There were almost 60 000 people at McMahon Stadium, and there are only 52 000 people in all of the NWT.

   Eddie Greenspan conveys the inadequacy of the amount of money spent on the Ontario Justice System with this anecdote:

   > My mother used to drive from Niagara Falls to Toronto to see her grandchildren. When the government built the Burlington Skyway she was very pleased and was sure they had done it just to make her visits to her grandchildren that much easier. They spent more money on that skyway so that my mother could drive to Toronto than they spent on the entire Ontario justice system in ten years.

5. **Do not overuse statistics.** In her book *Outrageous Acts and Everyday Rebellions,* Gloria Steinem confesses to "a habit that might be okay in articles but is death in speeches: citing a lot of facts and statistics." Her friend and lecture partner Florynce Kennedy told her kindly: "Look, if you're lying in the ditch with a truck on your ankle, you don't send somebody to the library to find out how much the truck weighs. You get it *off.*"

Analogies

Analogies help to make a point by offering the audience a parallel example and asking them to make logical connections. In a speech about the criminal justice system and whether or not it should rehabilitate criminals or just warehouse them, Greenspan used the lesson given Warren Burger, former Chief Justice of the U.S. Supreme Court. Burger was in a cab and the driver recognized him and offered his opinion of the prison system: "putting people in prison is like putting clothes in the wash without any soap. The clothes get wet but no dirt comes out." (Interview, January, 1988)

A sports analogy works very well for public speaking. Good skiing and speaking have a lot in common; it looks so easy when you do it well. Only the speaker or skier knows the importance of practice, technique, coaching, and pacing. Only she or he appreciates the rush of adrenalin just before you start. It's that rush that gives you the edge, the desire to go for it and win.

EXERCISE: A Sports Analogy

Using any sport, develop an analogy to convey how you feel about speaking in public and how you prepare yourself to do well.

Audio and Visual Aids

Imagine a world without television, radio or movies. We've become used to the vibrancy of media, and have libraries of sopisticated audio and visual resources. Speakers can use anything from the clunk-clunk, one-at-a-time slide show, to multi projector images synchronized with music, to short video clips. Whatever you choose, remember that **back-up material can never replace a good speaker.**

Be careful about the support materials you select. Gail Heaslip, a communications consultant who specializes in staging conferences, emphasizes the following point:

The graph ⎫ must **say** something. It
The overhead ⎪ must communicate to the
The object ⎬ mind, or to emotions, or to
The video/audio clip ⎭ b o t h .

> "The whole process [political activity] is sort of like doing dishes. They're never done— there's *always another dirty dish.* And it never stops. We have to continue to be vigilant."
> (Gerry Rogers)

Visual aids are used to imprint an image so strongly in the minds of an audience that both the picture and the statement are unforgettable.

The usual advice to beginners is to concentrate on your speech and don't get caught up in the preparation of extravagant audio-visual material (A-V); the temptation is great to vent your nervousness by expending your energy in getting just the right slide or making the lettering perfect on a diagram. A good rule is to make sure you spend most of your time designing and practising a clear, coherent, thoughtful speech. Then, if support A-V would *enhance* your delivery, there is an unprecedented amount of superb material available. Choose carefully and sparingly.

You are the best judges of good A-V: ask yourselves if the material you are considering fulfils the following criteria:

1. Is it necessary?   3. Is it clear and colourful?
2. Is it big enough?   4. Is it a grabber?

Materials that are poorly produced, hard to see, used as fillers rather than reinforcement, can detract from your speech.

Types of Visual Aids

1. **Graph, map, or chart.** Line graphs, pie graphs and bar graphs are good ways of illustrating a speech in which numbers are used; they transmit information with immediacy and ease. Look at the examples to see what subjects go well with the different types. Some graphs also make use of pictures to add drama and interest to the presentation; good examples are in all major magazines and newspapers.

   Charts are graphic representations of material that compress much information into a form that is easily read and understood. You might use a chart to show the organizational plan of a group or company, or to illustrate the steps in the manufacture of a product. The flowchart that introduces this chapter was devised in response to a student's request for a simple, easy-to-follow outline of the speech-making process.

   Maps are often used to indicate patterns: weather movement, immigration, import/export trends, tourism. If you draw your own map, or use one already available, make sure that the information you wish to convey is emphasized, that you colour the map to focus on selected detail.

   When using graphs, charts and maps be sure that the colours are sufficiently vivid and contrasting to communicate easily, that the size of the letters is adequate for viewing from a distance, and that you provide clear, interesting, lively interpretation.

2. **Slides and overhead projectors.** Many topics, especially those related to tourism, or to a process or a product, are naturals for slide back-up. Use your own, or part of a collection provided by a resource library. Make sure the slides you use are simple and uncluttered. It is more effective to use several, vivid pictures to get the message across than to rely on a dense, confusing shot. For all presentations involving A-V equipment, consult the checklists. For now, remember only the most important advice.

   - Practise your speech with the slides several times in advance;
   - *Never* use material you've never seen or rehearsed with;
   - Always carry an extra bulb, your own extension cord, and, unless you really trust the contact person, your own projector;
   - If you're the sort who likes to inflict upside-down or out-of-focus pictures on people, stick to your own family, and avoid giving pain to your audience.

   For some inexplicable reason, people refuse to arrive early or to carry spare parts and extensions. Often the first part of any speech requiring slides, done by a novice, involves protracted and painful apologies, pleas for parts, and general bumbling. **Do it well or skip it!**

   Overhead projectors are portable and easy to use. By combining computer graphics, good colour, and clear lettering, you can create excellent transparencies. Many photocopying machines can produce transparencies directly from printed material and will enlarge or reduce the size. Used in moderation, overhead projectors are helpful. Remember, however, that your face is far more interesting than an endless repetition of diagrams and charts.

3. **Pictures and sketches.** If you can't bring your Clydesdale to school to demonstrate how to shoe a horse, the next best thing is a sketch or diagram. These take work, and the person who holds up a tiny, smudged drawing immediately loses credibility. Make a clear, colourful drawing and then, just as in your demonstration speech, put the picture at the front of your room and go to the back to check its effectiveness. Can you see it? Can you read it? Never, never be guilty of introducing an obviously inadequate scrap of paper with the apology: "I know you can't see this very well at the back but...."

4. **The blackboard (or whiteboard)** is a standard piece of equipment in most lecture and board rooms. Before you use it, ask yourself whether your speech really needs it. Will

"IF YOU CAN'T BRING YOUR CLYDESDALE TO SCHOOL"

you spend more time talking to the board as you work than you will explaining things to your audience? Would a chart or picture prepared ahead be better? Can you get to the room ahead of time to put your material on the board before you start? If you use the board, make it brief, and face the audience at least some of the time.

5. **Actual objects.** You will use objects, such as ski boots, for your informative speech on how to buy downhill equipment to add interest and appeal to your presentation. Make sure they are large enough to be seen by all and can be carried and handled easily.

6. **Video tapes and music.** Music can change the pace of your speech as well as make a point. The audience doesn't expect it and are delighted to recognize songs or musicians. **Use only as much as you need.** To attract attention or reinforce your argument, you need 20-30 *seconds* of a song; don't give in to audience pleas to "play the whole thing."

   Well-produced video tapes can also add an extra dimension to your presentation. Again, figure out *why* you are using it and show only as much of the tape as you need.

Hospitality students use a model to point out the features of the CN tower.

Your audience will always catch you if you try to fill dead space with second-rate video clips.

Video tapes are used to reinforce your ideas, to accentuate your speech. **They are *not* used to provide a break from a boring experience.** You, the speaker, and your message are most important—the visual and audio aids are back-up.

7. **Storyboarding a speech.** Storyboarding is a technique used in film to note the shots required for the script; in speaking it refers to matching the key points of the spoken material with slides—dramatic, clear, lively, funny, poignant pictures. An example would be a talk on how to use T-cells to combat leukemia and other forms of cancer, or the use of puppets to explain surgical procedures to children. If you are speaking about management's effort to improve employee relations in your company, try to arrange enough lead time to enable you to take slides of the actual people you'll be talking about. Audiences delight in seeing themselves, although in some cases, discretion is required.

    Storyboarding requires several advance run-throughs and an experienced assistant, but if you follow the advice given in the checklist, your speech will be convincing.

8. **Human assistants.** As sophisticated as we are, an audience is always intrigued by the use of a group member to demonstrate a technique. If you rehearse thoroughly so that the demonstration and the message are clear, and your assistant uses expressions appropriate to the moment, your audience will remember your speech for some time. (See the video *A Class Act* for the demonstration speech in which a class member was used as a door.) A human model can be very helpful when the subject is complicated; one student showed how to check the breathing apparatus on scuba equipment while the other talked. It can add suspense: for instance when a WEN-DO (women's self-defense) instructor uses a large male attacker to demonstrate holds and releases, the audience is concerned. Human models also add a sense of theatre: when two helpers act out, for example, effective counselling techniques, the speaker can get the message home far more emphatically than is possible with a straight how-to lecture. This approach gives your audience the information they need, and adds drama and the unexpected to your speech.

    Keep this type of back-up short. **Make the point with the demonstration and stop.** It is your job as speaker to outline, clarify, and review. The technique is good as long as it is not overused.

Final Reminders About Audio and Visual Aids

1. Use speaker back-up materials only when necessary, and then only as long as you are talking about them. Sometimes an audience will catch sight of a visual aid before it is used and focus attention on it instead of you. If you aren't using it, keep it covered or out of view.
2. Use your aids to improve pacing as well as understanding.
3. Do not overuse speaker back-up—too much of anything becomes predictable and boring.
4. Explain the visual aid as you use it. The audience may not automatically understand it.
5. Talk to your audience, not the object or picture. If you're using a ski boot, make sure your eyes are directed on the audience, not the inside of the boot. This is harder than it sounds.
6. Make sure that everyone can hear, see, and understand.
7. Move to the screen to point out something on a slide, overhead, or film clip. Don't fumble with pointers or little flashlight arrows; the audience wants to see more than the top of your head as you bend over the work.
8. If you have an assistant to help with the projector, make sure that she or he knows the material and is familiar with the equipment.
9. Are you sure you want to pass material around the room? What happens to the pacing of your speech? The time for the visual has passed and people are still moving, poking each other or whispering as they pass the object. Just as you want complete eye contact for your dynamic conclusion, four people have their heads down looking at the visual you gave out five minutes ago. If you are going to pass something around, make sure you consider it carefully.
10. Does the back-up material add clarity, colour, and impact to your presentation?

EXERCISE: Evaluating Audio-Visual Material

a) Divide into small groups.
b) Choose one or two types of visual aids described in this chapter.
c) Draw up a list of criteria for good examples of the back-up material you selected.
d) Search the building and return with a good example of the material you have chosen. (You may also wish to bring a bad one.)
e) Prepare a presentation using the example(s) you have found.
f) Present criteria for a good example of the back-up material your group has concentrated on.

Notes That Help

Good notes make the difference between speakers and ramblers. And good notes are ones that people *use*. Whenever I speak, people come to me and say, "I don't know how you do that. I'm always afraid I'll forget what I'm trying to say." When I ask if the person practises, he or she invariably says, "Oh yes, but then I just get going and, most of the time, I forget the point I was trying to make."

You have to discipline yourself to check your notes—keep on course. You wouldn't understand a skier who wiped out because she decided to shut her eyes. How can a speaker expect to keep on track without checking her notes?

The ideal notes are the ones that work for *you*. They may vary in style, but you *must* have them. Notes consist of the main details of your speech written in **brief point form.** They

- keep you on course;
- provide reassurance;
- rescue you from total blanks. (Have you ever seen a speaker look up at a full auditorium or a video camera and go blank? It won't happen to you.)

Speaking to people means creating the impression that you are talking to them directly and are intent on communicating an important idea. Eye contact and better audience rapport can be achieved if you have good insurance: clear, brief, pre-tested notes.

Why Notes?

Why use a point-form outline instead of reading from a thick bundle of papers? A speech is a speech; it is not a memorized piece, nor is it a reading—you are talking to the audience, and should sound fluent *and* natural. If you have the entire speech written out, you *have* to read it. Few people can resist the temptation to look down when the entire speech is right before them. Once they start to read, they can't look up, or they'll lose their place on the page of print. **Do not write out your speech. You will lose your place and your audience.**

June Callwood, an extremely popular and very moving speaker, describes an early disaster in the interview in Chapter Seven:

> *The second speech I gave was entirely written, and I nervously read every word. I found that I'd left the last page on the seat where I'd been sitting. I had to leave my seat and come down the stairs to get the page, and I've never had a written speech since.*

Some speakers don't have notes because they researched for so long, they didn't have time to make notes and rehearse; you aren't a good speaker until you have the discipline to do the job right. Others think that a big sheaf of papers looks impressive; generally the audience stares glumly at the stack of paper, counting how many sheets are left until the end. Here are basic criteria for effective note cards. Experiment and discover what works for you.

MAKING CLEAR SPEECH NOTES

- These are notes, not novels; have a maximum of five to seven cards.
- Put the notes on heavy paper or cards to eliminate shaking.
- The size is up to you—larger cards cut down on the number required.
- Writing must be large and legible—visible at a glance from at least 50 centimetres away.
- Use point form.
- Number your arguments. Use a highlighter or coloured pen to highlight key words and arguments.
- You may wish to write essential lines out in full.

   (I like to write out my conclusion and any line I worked hard on and consider *essential*, perhaps two or three of these per speech, maximum. When I reach these lines, I *don't* read them. I make a natural pause, review the exact phrasing, then look directly at the audience, and give them my best shot.)
- Include statistics you might forget.
- Write out punchlines to jokes.
- Number your speech cards.
- Use *one side only*. (When some people get nervous, they have a tendancy to shuffle the cards as they use them. Their careful ordering goes haywire and they *never* find side seven.)
- Don't have too many cards—know your speech better or use bigger cards to eliminate a constant turning of notes. Your eyes should be on the audience.
- Keep an emergency set at home or in your car.
- Give yourself delivery cues at the sides of the card:

   pause
   relax
   slow down
   smile
   eye contact
   stop dancing
   use visual
   breathe!

- Improvise a podium at home by putting a box on the kitchen table and practise your speech *with* the cards. Do they work? Is the print large enough? Is revision necessary?

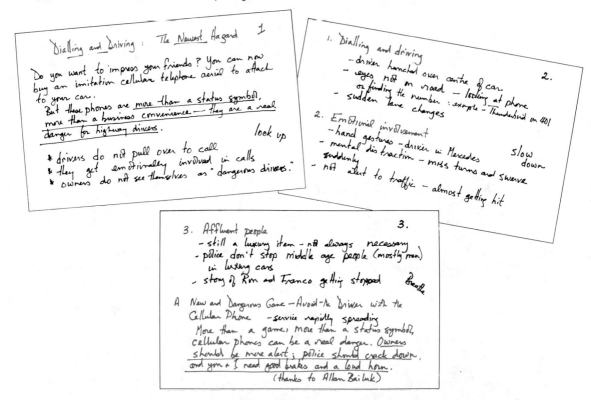

Dialling and Driving : The _Newest_ Hazard   1

Do you want to impress your friends? You can now buy an imitation cellular telephone aerial to attach to your car.
But these phones are _more than a status symbol_, more than a business convenience — _they are a real danger for highway drivers_.

look up

* drivers do not pull over to call
* they get emotionally involved in calls
* owners do not see themselves as "dangerous drivers."

1. Dialling and driving
- driver hunched over centre of car
- eyes not on road — looking at phone or finding the number : example — Thunderbird on 401
- sudden lane changes

2.

2. Emotional involvement
- hand gestures — driver in Mercedes
- mental distraction — miss turns and swerve suddenly
- not alert to traffic — almost getting hit

slow down

3. Affluent people
- still a luxury item — not always necessary
- police don't stop middle age people (mostly men) in luxury cars
- story of Ron and Franco getting stopped

breathe

3.

A New and Dangerous Game — Avoid-the Driver with the Cellular Phone   — service rapidly spreading
More than a game, more than a status symbol, cellular phones can be a real danger. Owners should be more alert; police should crack down, and you + I need good brakes and a loud horn.
(thanks to Allan Bailuk)

A Note to the Nervous and the Very Confident

If you know your speech cold and want to dazzle your audience by appearing to wing it, go ahead, but tuck in a set of notes, just in case. Sometimes overconfidence can trip up a good speaker. You may know your speech well when you rehearse it the night before, but the day of your speech may be hectic. You may have to

- take your sick dog to the vet;
- settle a family argument on the way out;
- do a last-minute review for a test;
- go to lunch to celebrate a friend's new job;
- check with the A-V technician that the equipment you need is ready.

Everyone's day is busy; you need good notes. They give reassurance.

What happens if the opposite is true—you're so anxious you can't remember a thing? Mirella, a hospitality student, was so nervous that she often stopped speaking, unsure of what she wanted to say. Her long written pages were a trap. Whenever she tried to look up, she lost her place in the jumble of words. When she learned to make careful notes and rehearse with them, she could *always* find her place. When she got distressed, she would pause, look at her notes, and resume. She was a quiet, shy speaker whose very determination enlisted the support of her audience.

Questions To Ask Yourself

1. When do you make your notes? How important is it that you practise with the very same notes you will use for the speech?
2. Can you see the cards when they're on a lectern 50 to 60 centimetres from your eyes?
3. Can you find the main points and important examples and statistics when you're excited?
4. Have you used colour to accentuate key ideas?

Use Your Own Language

As you prepare your speech, you should be able to hear yourself talking. Do you sound natural? Whether you are describing the operation of a commercial snowmaking machine, explaining a simple process to assistant bakers, or outlining the various options for building an investment plan, you want your audience to understand. That depends on your language. You need to be precise, and use terms correctly. However, do not turn a good talk into a boring lecture full of jargon, careful qualifications, and gutless abstractions.

Use your own language; you should be able to deliver your speech and *feel* it at the same time. Find your own words; if anything is forced or stagey, alter it so that your personality comes through. Remember that speaking from the heart means using words you understand and mean.

Here is advice from the best:

> I would try to think of how I would explain it [a scientific paper] to my parents so they could see why it was exciting or important. It's very simple really, but scientists tend to get caught up in fine details and try to qualify everything to be accurate. Too often, the central question and the passion and excitement are drained away.
> (DAVID SUZUKI, *Metamorphosis*, p. 133; see also interview)

> *Speakers...use those words to impress others with their knowledge and erudition, and it's absolutely ineffective. Lawyers do it; they love to use words like "purport." Now, I've never sat in a bar and heard anyone use the word "purport" in general banter. And so, I never use that word. I don't need to hide behind my words, to say words that make me sound smart.*
> *(EDDIE GREENSPAN)*

> But up to now you have been briefed by officials, and officials always know how to take the blood out of a story. So now I believe you have a better understanding in your heart, which is where you make decisions.
> (PATRICK WATSON, *Zero to Airtime* p. 147)

Be Specific: Bring Your Words Alive

When Alberto Tomba, "La Bomba," won two gold medals in downhill skiing at the 1988 Winter Olympics in Calgary he told a reporter that his father had promised him a car. Was it any car? No—it was a Red Ferrari. When my neighbour invites me for lunch, he tempts me with fresh bread. Any bread off the shelf? No—we have nine-grain bread spread with fresh apple butter from the Kitchener market. A student of mine boasts that she's from the Acadian heartland of Canada. Is it sufficient to say the Annapolis Valley in Nova Scotia? Not for her—she's from Wolfville, next to Grand Pré.

Your speech will be far more immediate if you take the time to find nouns, colours, verbs, references that are accurate. Our conversations are loaded with specific words: we don't wear running shoes, we wear Nikes or Reeboks; we can't challenge all of the government's policy, but we can concentrate on drought relief, or housing policies. When you practise your speech, use the liveliness of your daily conversation, and search for words that accurately describe ideas, actions, and feelings.

EXERCISE: Win, Lose or Tie

Laurence Pengelly, a musician with an avid interest in word usage, is also a sports fan. In the month of April 1989, he read three large metropolitan dailies and listed all the synonyms for "winning," "losing," and "tying" that he found on the sports pages. His list is given below.

annihilated	demolished	hammered
ate up (pitching)	demoralized	helped
	destroyed	humbled
battered	devastated	humiliated
beat	doubled	hurled past
blasted	downed	
blew	drowned	jolted
bowed under to	drubbed	jumped on
bulldozed	dumped	
buried		killed
	edged	
cleaned up	embarrassed	levelled
crucified	equalled	
crumbled	erased	manhandled
crunched	evened	massacred
crushed		matched
	faltered under	mauled
dampened	feasted on	mockery
dazzled	flattened	(made a)
defeated	folded under	murdered

nudged by	rifled past	squeezed by
	ripped apart	stampeded
ousted	roared past	steamrolled
over the	robbed	stifled
("It was the	rolled over	stole
Jays *over the*		stopped
Yankees.")	scrambled	stymied
	scraped by	swept
paced	shot down	
plastered	shut down	tarred
plowed	skinned	thumped
pounced all over	slammed	tied
pounded	slapped	topped
pulverized	slaughtered	tore up
pummelled	slipped by	tortured
punished	slumped	trampled
	smothered	
rallied over	snatched	walked over
rampaged	(snow) plowed	walloped
ran over	snuffed out	whipped
ransacked	squeaked by	won over

Check the pages of your own newspapers. How many synonyms can you find for "said," "financial hard times," "car," "prejudice," "old," "expensive."

EXERCISE: How Do You Feel Today?

When people meet you in the hall and say "how are you doing," do you tell them the truth? How often do we all mumble "okay?" **How do you feel today?** Choose an adjective and surprise the next person who asks.

What Can You Learn from a Video Tape of Your Speech?

It's time to see what you do and how you do it. A video tape will show you how you look and sound. Students generally make the following statements: "Is that me?", "I never noticed that I...stood on one foot...said 'um' that many times...looked that confident." You will notice that you look calmer than you often feel; the tape will establish some of your strengths. It is *your* voice that you hear and it is different from the voice you normally consider yours, because of the sound reverberations in your head. Accept it and find the good aspects of it to emphasize and the weaker ones to correct. Some of you may prefer to start with an audio tape and progress to video. Either way

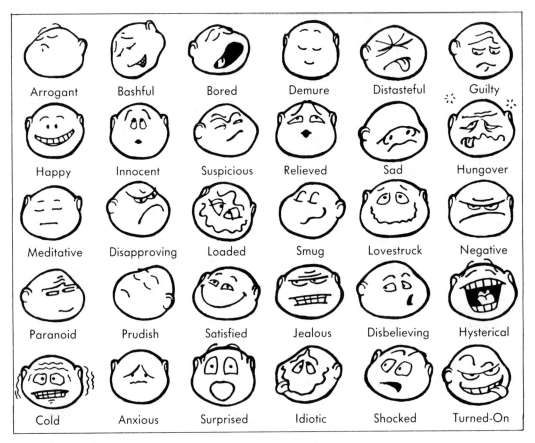

Arrogant · Bashful · Bored · Demure · Distasteful · Guilty
Happy · Innocent · Suspicious · Relieved · Sad · Hungover
Meditative · Disapproving · Loaded · Smug · Lovestruck · Negative
Paranoid · Prudish · Satisfied · Jealous · Disbelieving · Hysterical
Cold · Anxious · Surprised · Idiotic · Shocked · Turned-On

How Do You Feel Today?

you will be able to assess your voice and pacing as well as the content. Concentrate on what you want to say and the taping will be less obvious.

TAPING EXERCISE: Dynamic Intros and Strong Conclusions

Prepare a dynamic and complete introduction (grabber, thesis, and overview) and a convincing conclusion for *one* of the following topics:

a) Canada's National Animal Should Be....
b) The Biggest Rip-Off....

Omit the body of the speech; your overview will outline the main supporting reasons for your choice. When you replay the tape you can assess the clarity of your organization and your delivery.

Suggestions for Taping

The taping should be a positive experience. The camera operator can place the video camera at the back or side of the room and use a good microphone closer to the speaker, but not at the lectern. Try to include close-ups and distance shots, and views of the speaker's hands and face and even feet. If you use an audio tape recorder, the microphone should be as inconspicuous as possible and the tape long enough so that no one has to interrupt the speaker to flip a tape.

The exercise is short, and if the class is supportive it can be taped, and played back in one session. It is important that class members identify with each other and offer praise and encouragement. The individual student can be left to select the details he or she would like to improve. Some people like to review the tape in private and submit an evaluation sheet, but at this stage, working and reviewing as a group can be instructive, and fun.

It's time to combine research skills, delivery techniques, and good design in an informative speech. Plan your speech so that your audience will understand and remember your presentation. These guidelines should help:

1. **Generate interest.** Devise a good grabber. Follow it with convincing reasons why people should listen to you.
2. **Make sure the audience understands.** If the material is new or complicated, you should check that your listeners are comprehending. Are they nodding their heads in agreement? Are there rumblings of confusion? Ask if you need to clarify a point. Precise suggestions about the application of the information will help.
3. **Answer all the basic questions.** Who? What? Where? When? Why? How? How much?
4. **Emphasize your main ideas.** Organize your speech according to the principle of three and make sure your audience follows your progression from point to point. Use transitional remarks such as "having dealt with the need for more jelly in the doughnut, we can examine the third and final problem, messy sugar coatings."
5. **Repeat the key ideas.** Most teachers know that the secret of getting people to remember is to repeat key ideas three times in different ways: "if you breathe calmly and deeply just before you speak, you'll avoid embarrassing squeaks and breaks in your voice;" "we've all run to the telephone first thing in the morning and, without taking a breath, have answered. What an embarrassing sound comes out." And a few minutes later: "the impression you make will be much better if you remember to take several slow, deep breaths just before you start to speak."

The Informative Speech

6. **Are you excited about your own topic?** If you did research that opened up fresh possibilities, or thought of an entirely new approach to a familiar subject, your energy will attract and engage your audience. If you are interested in your material, your enthusiasm will give liveliness and conviction to your performance. That in turn will help your audience get interested, absorb the information, and remember it. The test of a good speech, its organization, research, and delivery, is to see whether or not the audience can remember the main points the day after they heard it.

7. **Are you on schedule?** In Chapter Two, there is a seven-day countdown; here is a 24-hour countdown. Let's assume you are speaking at 10:00 on *Wednesday* morning.

24-HOUR COUNTDOWN

24 hrs. to go	Tuesday	10 a.m.	— make a final copy of notes
		11 a.m.	— rehearse with those notes — make sure of examples — wow your partner, friend or cat with your delivery
		11:30 a.m.	— STOP CHANGING THINGS! — experimenting's over: this is it! — concentrate on delivery
22 hrs. to go		12 noon	— daily living — take care of yourself
14 hrs. to go		8 p.m.	— your lucky friend hears the speech again — which anecdotes work best? — can he or she identify thesis and overview? — you need *praise* and feedback
12 hrs. to go		10 p.m.	— relax—STOP PRACTISING!
2 hrs. to go	Wednesday	8 a.m.	— get ready: check notes are in order
1 hr. to go		9 a.m.	— start deep breathing for control — if speech is short, have a quick run-through; if it's long, just rehearse the introduction, conclusion, and any hard spots.
BLASTOFF!		10 a.m.	— BREATHE. RELAX. GOOD LUCK.

Prepare a three-to-five-minute informative speech.

You may generate the topics yourself or use one of the following suggestions:

1. Child's Play

Choose a childhood game such as "Capture the Flag," "Red Rover, Red Rover," "Categories," "Spin the Bottle," "Nicky-Nicky Nine Doors," "Jumpsies," or "Fox and Geese." Describe the game and its social function.

2. Praise or Pan: A Review

Visit a restaurant or hotel in your town or city and prepare a review. The restaurant may be a gourmet palace or the local fish-and-chip place, but your review must be thorough and organized according to the Principle of Three outlined in this chapter.

You do not need to stay at the hotel, but can review its public rooms on the basis of decor, atmosphere, etc. Be sure to include all the basic information (location, cost, etc.) your audience will want.

3. A Local Treasure

Visit a local spot that is significant for its social, cultural, environmental, historic, or entertainment value. Describe it and outline its worth.

To prepare for this last assignment, brainstorm with a group to get ideas; one group extolled the pleasures of such diverse attractions as a romantic skating rink at the local park, Kensington Market, and the former morgue now used as a police museum.

Brainstorming will help you to develop thoughtful questions:

- When is the spot open?
- When is the best time to visit?
- What group of people would enjoy it most?
- Do you need tickets?
- Is it suitable for all age groups?
- Is it safe? What about fire exits?
- Is it physically demanding?
- Is it suitable for the differently abled?
- Is it wheelchair accessible? Completely or partially?

Speech Assignment: The Informative Speech

DELIVERY TECHNIQUES TO REMEMBER

1. Psych yourself up: take deep breaths, anticipate the challenge.
2. Use audio-visual aids naturally: handle them gracefully but address your remarks to the audience.
3. Use energy to build to a STRONG FINISH.

INTERVIEW

Eddie Greenspan

Lawyer and Author

Jan. 21, 1988
Toronto

Edward Greenspan, Q.C., is a defence lawyer renowned for his championing of the underdog and his outspoken opinions of the Canadian justice system. In 1987, he undertook a nationwide tour, speaking against the reinstatement of the death penalty. He is an entertaining speaker, and his clarity and wit make him a favorite as the host/narrator of "The Scales of Justice," a CBC docu-drama on famous Canadian Criminal Trials.

Q
What makes a good speech?

A
It must entertain. It is pointless to make an important point in a boring fashion because it may be lost. It has to be made in an entertaining and dramatic way.

A good speech must be made in fairly simple language. It's senseless to use words that are not generally understood. Maybe it's my training as a lawyer; I recall using the word "surreptitiously" when I was addressing a jury, and I saw glazed looks on the faces of the jury that caused me to conclude that they didn't understand what I meant by that word.

When I'm addressing a gathering, I assume that I'm talking to bright high-school students, always. In law school, in writing law exams, we're told to write as though we were trying to explain complicated legal principles to a bright thirteen-year-old. That's a good rule when you're speaking—speak to a bright thirteen-year-old. Don't talk down to an audience but don't speak in such complex language or leave the ideas hanging in so complicated a fashion that people simply won't understand your meaning.

Making an analogy is vitally important to making your idea understood. It helps people know precisely what you mean.

Humour is something I always try to inject. No matter how serious the speech, even when I was debating the death penalty, *if it was apropos* I would make a humorous reference. In the case of topics that are simply not funny, like the prosecution of a hatemonger like Ernst Zundel, no jokes. There are things that are too serious for any levity at all. For some reason, occasional jokes during the death penalty debate were acceptable. But wherever humour can be injected, I will take advantage of it. I won't use constant one-liners, but I will inject humorous remarks to lighten the seriousness of what I am saying in order to keep my audience listening. If you lose your audience, speaking is a waste of everybody's time. When I structure my public speeches, I often begin with three or four humorous anecdotes, to put the audience in a good and receptive mood.

But if you're going to use humour, the depth of the rest of your speech has to be that much better. You cannot keep the speech at a superficial level or you're under-estimating your audience.

Q
How do you prepare for a major speech?

A
Because I speak often, if I am attracted to an analogy that I read in the press or in a book, or if I hear it on the radio or on television, I will make a note of it. I collect what I think are good examples of whatever point is being made. Of course, it is always on legal matters. If I am given the task of addressing a group on a certain subject, the first thing I do is gather up the major works on that subject and I read them, so that I'm not missing some issue or point relevant to that topic. I also read minor works or essays so that I am fully aware of competing or opposing views, and take from that material quotes that best

sum up what the writers are trying to say. I dictate a summary of my interpretation of what I have read. Then I outline in point form, what the key issues in the area are, pro and con, and from that, I determine what my views are relative to all views on the subject. That is, I look at the popular position on any issue and look to the position of its detractors and dissenters and I try to determine where I stand. I end up with a summary of the main issues and a clear statement of what my views are on the subject. I then go to the material I have collected to see if I can find any quote or story that is appropriate and then I sit down and dictate my speech.

Q
Do you like to know about your audience in advance?

A
I like to know the type of people I'm speaking to, in a general way, so that I know where their interests lie and what part of the community they reflect. Oftentimes while I'm there and I sense the mood of the audience, I may change some of the examples that I intended to use. I always speak to the head-table guests to get

a flavour of the organization and the audience.

Q
Why did you spend all that time and energy going around the country in 1987 speaking against capital punishment?

A
It happened to be an issue that I was vitally concerned about as a Canadian; it went to the very heart of what I believe. The death penalty was a moral and social issue that I could not remain silent on. Had I done nothing and the death penalty been restored, then I would have been a party by my silence to a significant legislative change that would have been, in my view, a serious step backward. I could not sit silent.

I happen to believe that Canadians are just and decent; the death penalty is neither a just nor appropriate measure for a civilized state to take against crime. Canadians did not seem to know that the death penalty would do nothing to decrease our murder rate.

Q
How do you explain unfamiliar terms?

A
If I'm talking about a concept, like a

rehabilitation model of punishment, I won't use any expression unfamiliar to the general public. Or, I'll stop and explain, I'll go back historically. If I'm talking about the rehabilitation model, I'll go back and explain how prisons began and why we have them. For a long time, we thought prisoners were sick and needed to get better. Those theories have been questioned over time. I don't assume that the audience is familiar with the subject of the speech.

Q
What errors do speakers make?

A
Speakers often use terminology that they *assume* the audience understands when, in fact, they don't. Speakers lose their audiences that way. They use those words to impress others with their knowledge and erudition, and it's absolutely ineffective. Lawyers do it; they love to use words like ''purport.'' Now, I've never sat in a bar and heard anyone use the word ''purport'' in general banter. And so, I never use that word. I don't need to hide behind my words, to say words that make me sound smart.

Q
Do you get nervous?

A
I get anxious every time I speak. When I stand up, it's a question of trying to win the audience. For the first five minutes of my speech, I run the big risk of telling jokes; there's nothing worse than a joke falling flat; recovering from it is very difficult. Yes, I'm apprehensive about every public speech I give. I want the audience to be entertained and informed. Working towards that, I will always look at my entire audience as often as I can, trying to bring them all into the speech.

Q
Do you have notes?

A
I have notes. I write my speeches out in longhand or dictate them and they may go through two or three revisions. I learn my speeches. I also have very good peripheral vision; I can look at an audience and see my notes at the same time.

Q
Can you tell if a person is telling the truth?

A
No better and no worse than anybody else. I don't think that I'm any

better or any worse than anybody else at the difficult task of trying to figure out who is telling the truth. Every person has to make those decisions every day; if you talk to a car salesman, you have to determine if he's telling the truth or not; if you ask a waitress or waiter what's good on the menu, you have to decide if they're telling the truth or not. You have to learn to trust or not to trust what's being said to you by the demeanor of a person or other things that help you in your truth-seeking mission. When you watch television, you have to decide if you're being told the truth or not during every news report.

Q
Have you heard a good speech or speaker lately?

A
Nice question. I am impressed by a device that Conrad Black uses when he introduces speakers; his knowledge of the speaker's background including pertinent years, dates, positions, titles, events, all given without reliance on a single note, truly impresses me. It is a very effective device; he obviously has a magnificent memory and

he utilizes it effectively and absolutely wows the audience. He works without a single note and without ever looking down. Very, very impressive.

Q
What don't you like?

A

I don't like the heaviness of some speeches in which people wade through statistics. If you can't prove your point simply by making an analogy from the statistics, and you go on and on, the audience just listens to large numbers.

Q
What are the qualities of a good speaker?

A

In terms of a dazzling speech, the Diefenbaker form of address is the very best. But who has it today? I think Trudeau had it; he was a marvellous, effective, at times spellbinding speaker. Stephen Lewis is an excellent speaker. You have to have something you can't learn or acquire: charisma.

Q
What speech did you enjoy giving?

A

I enjoyed speaking to the Empire Club about the role of the defence lawyer. There was a good feeling in the room, and the Empire Club is the World Series for a speaker. In fact, I said that to them, that I could now die and go to heaven having reached the height of a speaker's goal, addressing the very prestigious Empire Club. I think people really liked that. They like honesty, humility, sincerity and self-deprecation, a very Canadian characteristic. I think it's important to make the audience happy and feel good.

But let me also point out that I've said things to audiences that they clearly don't like; in fact, I may infuriate and I may upset. But they don't walk away not liking me or not talking about what I've said. I think it's important to be controversial and to cause an audience to think about how they feel about the subject matter. I will never hold back from my audience my true feelings on a subject and I will not tone down my language to the point where my beliefs are not crystal clear. I will call it as I see it. I owe that much to my audience.

Eddie Greenspan

Speech: The Futility of the Death Penalty

In 1987 Eddie Greenspan spoke out against the death penalty in a series of nationwide appearances. This is an edited version of that speech. Note especially the power of the conclusion.

In Canada, capital punishment was abolished in 1976, but it has never lain still in its grave, and continues still to raise its ugly head from time to time. Each time a police officer or prison guard is killed, we hear a clamour for its return. After little Alison Parrot's death, the Toronto Sun had a front page editorial calling for the return of the death penalty.

It is my purpose to hopefully persuade you first, that capital punishment is *no* deterrent to crime and therefore an unjustifiable weapon to deter potential murderers, and second, that the state wants to continue to kill its victims, not so much to defend society against them—for it could do that equally well by imprisonment—but to appease the mob's emotions of hatred and revenge.

...To attempt to abolish crime by killing the criminal is the easy and foolish way out of a serious situation. Unless a remedy deals with the conditions which foster crime, criminals will breed faster than the hangman can spring his trap. Capital punishment ignores the causes of crime just as completely as the primitive witch doctor ignored the causes of disease; and like the methods of the witch doctor, it is not only ineffective as a remedy, but is positively vicious in at least two ways. In the first place, the spectacle of state executions feeds the basest passions of the mob. And in the second place, so long as the state rests content to deal with crime in this barbaric and futile

manner, society will be lulled by a false sense of security, and effective methods of dealing with crime will be discouraged.

Even now, are not all imaginative and humane people shocked at the spectacle of a killing by the state? How many men and women would be willing to act as executioners? How many fathers and mothers would want their children to witness an official killing?

I have always hated capital punishment. To me it seems a cruel, brutal, useless barbarism. The killing of one individual by another always shows real or fancied excuse or reason. The cause, however poor, was enough to induce the act. But the killing of an individual by the state is so deliberate and cold, without any personal grievance or feeling. It is the outcome of long premeditated hatred. It does not happen suddenly and without warning, without time for the emotions to cool and subside, but a day is fixed a long way ahead and the victim is kept in continued, prolonged torture up to the moment of execution.

...And yet some people misperceive rising crime rates and say that if we had capital punishment—if we could literally put the fear of death into these criminals—the problem would all go away. Now that doesn't make sense, of course. Crime rates have nothing to do with capital punishment. In this capital punishment debate you will hear lots of statistics. You will hear people talking about crime going up and crime going down when there is or is not capital punishment. This is not a topic where it is possible to find the one definitive study which concludes, once and for all, that capital punishment is a deterrent, has no effect, or, indeed, that it cheapens life and encourages people to kill.

...It is easy to be in favour of

revenge in the abstract. But if something happened to someone you know, and that person got angry with another family member, went out and purchased a weapon and killed his victim, would you really want that person—automatically—to be hanged? Don't think about it in the abstract; think about a real person. We don't hang abstractions, we hang real people.

...Now some people say capital punishment is justified because it prevents a murderer from ever again committing the same crime. In Canada, less than 10 people who have been found guilty of murder by a Canadian Court, were ever convicted of murder again. Former Prime Minister Trudeau, in the debate of Parliament to abolish the death penalty, said "in order to be absolutely sure that no murderer would murder again, we would have to take the lives of all persons convicted of either 1st or 2nd degree murder, even though the probability is that an infinitesimal percent of them would ever commit murder again if allowed to live. That's an unacceptably high price to pay in human lives for a sense of security insignificantly greater than we have now." No one knows whether visualizing and hearing of the effects of punishment of one deters others or induces others; or whether, even if it served to deter in this particular way, it might not render men, women, and children callous to human distress.

Only one thing is certain about capital punishment or its effect—that it is administered for no reason but deep and fixed hatred of the individual and an abiding thirst for revenge. Are we so lacking in hope for the human race that we are ready to accept state-sanctioned vengeance as our penal philosophy? Capital punishment is too horrible a thing for a state to undertake. We are

told, "Oh, the killer does it, why shouldn't the state?" I would hate to live in a state that I didn't think was better than a murderer.

There isn't, I submit, a single admissible argument in favour of it. Nature loves life. We believe that life should be protected and preserved. The thing that keeps one from killing is the emotion they have against it; and the greater the sanctity that the state pays to life, the greater the feeling of sanctity the individual has for life.

We stopped taking human life in 1962—24 years ago. That's the last time the hangman in Canada practised his terrible trade. And for those of you who regret that situation—who lust for the return of that rope, let me remind you of this: Donald Marshall was convicted for a crime he did not commit. Which of you, sitting here today, could have pulled the bag over his head? Which of you could have fastened the rope around his neck? Which of you could have sprung the trap door which sent Donald Marshall to his death? Because that is what capital punishment is all about. It's not just another news story on page 10 of your newspaper. It's the coldblooded killing of a human being. The next time you hear that bloodthirsty cry for revenge, I ask you to remember that.

1987

OUTLINE OF AN INFORMATIVE SPEECH

Name: _____

Date of Speech: _____

Purpose Statement: _____

INTRODUCTION
    Grabber:

    Thesis:

    Overview:

BODY
    Supporting Argument #1

    Supporting Argument #2

    Supporting Argument #3

CONCLUSION
    Reference to purpose (thesis):

    Summary of main steps:

    Zinger:

SELF-EVALUATION FORM

This form is to help you evaluate your own speech. It can be kept private or shared with your instructor or peers.

Type of Speech: _____

Name: _____

Title: _____

Date: _____

DELIVERY
Physical Presence

Did I make eye contact with others?

Was my posture natural and appropriate?

Was I aware of my facial expressions and hand gestures?

Were there any distracting mannerisms that I was aware of?

Did I feel good?

Could I feel an energy exchange with my audience?

VOCAL DELIVERY

Was my voice under control?

Did I sound confident?

Was I aware of breathing calmly?

How was my enunciation?

Did I manage to avoid um's and ah's?

Did I sound interested/excited/committed?

How did my voice sound to me?

DESIGN AND CONTENT

How well did the introduction and conclusion work?

Did the framework unify my speech?

Was there a natural progression from point to point?

Did my notes keep me on track? Did I use them?

Did the audience seem to understand the organization of my speech?

Was the information clear?

What was the energy level of the conclusion?

What would I change the next time?

What worked very well?

OVERALL EFFECTIVENESS

Did I connect with this audience?

Did I achieve my purpose?

What do I remember most about making the speech?

What unexpected or unforeseen things happened?

What am I most pleased about?

OTHER COMMENTS

Grade:

PEER EVALUATION FORM

Peer evaluation should be done in a constructive and supportive fashion. The speaker may choose people to do assessments or they may be assigned alphabetically. Some groups maintain the same speaker/assessor teams for the entire course; others change for each speech. The instructor may wish to see this evaluation before it goes to the speaker.

Type of Speech: _____

Speaker: _____

Title: _____

Assessor: _____

Date: _____

DELIVERY

Physical Presence

Did the speaker maintain eye contact?

Did she or he establish a rapport with the audience?

Were gestures natural and effective?

VOCAL DELIVERY

Did the speaker sound convincing/ spontaneous/excited?

Was his or her voice clear and loud enough?

How did you respond to the speaker's mood?

DESIGN AND CONTENT

Did the introduction interest you?

Did the overview give you an indication of the main proofs?

Did the speech flow easily and logically from one point to another?

Was the conclusion strong and memorable?

Did the conclusion reinforce the thesis and main points?

What was the thesis of the speech?

OVERALL EFFECTIVENESS

Did you learn something new or worthwhile from the speech?

Were you moved by it?

What was the most outstanding part of the speech?

What changes do you recommend?

What parts should the speaker definitely keep?

OTHER COMMENTS

Grade:

EVALUATION FORM

Type of Speech: _____

Name: _____

Title: _____

Length of Speech: _____

Date: _____

Legend: S = SUPERIOR   E = EFFECTIVE   NW = NEEDS WORK

DELIVERY
Physical Presence
Eye Contact

Rapport with Audience

Posture

Gestures

Use of Notes

Appropriate Use of Audio-Visual
Support Material

VOCAL DELIVERY
Naturalness/Spontaneity/Enthusiasm

Clarity

Variety (Tone, Pitch, Pace)

Volume

Absence of Verbal Tics (um, ah,
okay, like)

Sense of Control and Calm

DESIGN AND CONTENT
Use of Framework for Introduction
and Conclusion

Clear Thesis and Overview

Coherence/Use of Transitions

New/Interesting Information

Strong Finish

LANGUAGE
Word Choice

Impact on Audience

Grammar

OVERALL EFFECTIVENESS
Treatment of Topic

Intelligent Awareness of Audience

Achievement of Purpose

Impact on/Connection with Audience

OTHER COMMENTS   Grade:

We Can Work It Out: Small Group Communication

TIPS FOR SPEAKERS

1. Skill-Drill-Grill: speaking in small groups requires specific techniques. Be aware.
2. Talk Without Speaking: *how* you speak to others is as important as *what* you say. Your tone has a direct bearing on the group's success.
3. Team Positions: The role you have varies according to the situation.
4. Taking Your Turn: leadership is fluid. A good chairperson or manager utilizes everyone's leadership skills.
5. The Game Plan: Decision-making varies according to the situation. Good speakers can help their groups achieve consensus.
6. Time Out: In order to resolve conflict, you have to talk about it openly. That's the hardest part.
7. Signals: Inclusive language respects everyone.

What groups do you remember best—your sports team, a seminar group, camp or counselling staff, a neighbourhood action committee? Can you recall how good it felt to be able to really talk to each other? If you learn how to communicate well, your group will have a two-fold success:

1. Group members will feel valued and productive;
2. The task will be accomplished.

Small groups are like teams—two or more people with a common goal. If you recall your experience on a successful team, you'll remember the feeling of commitment to your goal and to each other, the camaraderie and trust you shared, and your determination to do difficult things to help the team succeed.

Sports teams, businesses, ski patrols, paramedics, astronauts, production groups, and community organizations all require the communication skills outlined in this chapter. However, the skills don't exist in a vacuum; they are an outward manifestation of your internal commitment and belief in your group or team. You'll care enough to speak well only if you believe in your group and its goal.

Most people would rather play baseball than read about it. Similarly, it's more fun to participate in small group activities than to study them. This is, therefore, a do-it-yourself chapter. For each of the major sections—**positions to play, leadership, making decisions,** and **resolving conflict**—there is an outline of the skills involved. It is followed by a drill or exercise, and some time to grill yourself, to evaluate your experience. Finally, there is a section about the words, tone, and vocabulary that will support or undermine your group efforts, and a new challenge—the impromptu.

This chapter's interview is with Dr. Roberta Bondar, one of six astronauts in Canada's Space Programme. As a physician and space pioneer, she understands the need to work efficiently in small groups.

Before you start to build your understanding and skills of the group experience, read this:

Skill, Drill, Grill: The Do-It-Yourself Chapter

Note on Small Groups

FOUR   *tradespeople, a contractor, a plumber, an electrician, and a carpenter, are planning a bathroom renovation.*

SEVEN   *family members are having a loud dinner-table discussion regarding the wedding plans of Avis, the second child in a family of two daughters and one son. Her fiancé and a brother-in-law are also present.*

EIGHT   *friends are making plans to travel the Trail of '98, the Klondike Gold Rush Route. They will travel up the*

**This group climbed the
Chilkoot Trail. Here
they celebrate at the
border of Alaska and
British Columbia.**

*Alaska coast, hike the arduous Chilkoot Trail, canoe 500
miles from Whitehorse to Dawson.*

THREE   *people, a travel counsellor and two clients, are trying to
finalize plans for a late summer trip to Austria, Hun-
gary, and Bulgaria.*

FOURTEEN *employees of a leading jeans producer engage in a year
long series of discussions to plan their new building.*

The success of these small groups depends on whether they

- **realize they are a working *group*.** People often meet
  to work together without taking notice that the process
  may be in any way different than working alone or working as one of 80 people directed anonymously.
- **understand the working of a group and the value
  of each person in it.** People in groups need to know
  they are important, that what they have to contribute is
  valuable. They need to be heard and valued.
- **determine that the *way* a group works is as important as the job it has to do.** That is, the task and the
  method or process, are interrelated. If you concentrate
  only on getting the job done as fast as possible, your group
  will not be as efficient. If the cook for the Klondike group
  orders all the food without any group interaction, she may
  have to do a lot of reordering once she knows their health
  and dietary needs.
- **deal with conflict and controversy.** Conflict is normal in groups and it should be admitted and discussed
  openly. Most unsuccessful groups fall apart because members keep resentment bottled up inside. Eventually the
  pressure is too great; the situation explodes and the group
  may not recover.

- **talk to each other.** *How* you speak to people is as important as what you say; it has a direct bearing on the group's success. The phrase "good communication skills" is such a cliché that few people know what is required. You need the desire and ability to talk honestly and kindly to other people. It's not always easy to do. Your words, tone, facial expressions and body language are talking all the time; they reveal your attitudes and feelings, and directly affect the other people in your group.

Skill

The role you have in a group is not static; it varies according to the situation. If the tradespeople discuss the job of renovating a bathroom, each of them—the contractor, the plumber, the electrician, and the carpenter—is an expert. Therefore, according to the task at hand, each will assume some leadership. At other times, they will be group members whose functions will range from giver of information to seeker of information.

How do you assess what the group is doing and what it requires? Roberta Bondar, a knowledgeable and articulate scientist, has a very energetic style of dealing with others. However, she uses listening as the basis for her group work:

> I'm a listener; I observe how people are interacting, I try to figure out where they're coming from, what they're trying to get out of the group, or what points they are trying to get across. And I adjust my level of contribution to that.

The most important thing a group needs is a purpose or a contract. If the purpose or reason for the group is clear enough, if it is expressed in specific, measurable terms, the group has a chance to stay together. If, however, the goal is vague, or if the group decides to meet, and never defines its purpose, it will have trouble staying together. The more precise the goal, the easier it is for the group to work well.

In terms of meeting that goal, everyone plays different roles; some roles are related to accomplishing the task, and some have to do with the healthy functioning of the group. They change according to the occasion, and the needs of others, just as our roles vary in everyday life. The shortstop can play third base, the sales manager can take orders, the city editor can proof pages, and the brake specialist will help with body work.

Positions You Can Play: Roles in a Group

> Tell me: I will forget.
> Show me: I will remember.
> Involve me: I will understand.

Drill

EXERCISE: Who Are You?

Make a list of the roles you play in your daily life. You don't have to stick to jobs or positions, you can list your functions in helping your groups work. If you're a man, it might look like this:

son
brother
grandson
family comedian
dog groomer and walker
part-time drummer in a band
organizer of band equipment
driver
calm front man
student
a group leader in most class discussions
second-string volleyball player
ticket coordinator for athletic council dance
joker
boyfriend
encourager
debater
good neighbour

EXERCISE: Matching Terms and Definitions

You are already familiar with many of the roles you might assume in a group. See if you can match the terms and definitions given below. Some of the roles have to do with accomplishing the task and some to do with maintaining a healthy group.

Group Building Functions

1. Participation builder
2. Tension reliever
3. Problem solver
4. Supporter and praiser
5. Operations monitor
6. Comprehension monitor

a) asks for facts, opinions, background, feelings, ideas and information.
b) makes sure group members understand what each other says.
c) builds on previous comments.
d) tells jokes, increases fun.
e) mediates conflict and helps resolve it.
f) keeps track of topic and brings discussion back on course if necessary.
g) synthesizes or pulls together similar ideas.

Task or Goal Functions

7. Information and opinion giver

h) asks others to summarize or give feedback to make sure they

8. Information and
   opinion seeker
9. Summarizer
10. Energizer
11. Clarification
    checker
12. Elaborator
13. Direction and
    role giver
14. Gatekeeper

understand.

i) expresses liking for group members
    and acceptance of all, especially new
    people.

j) offers facts, opinions, background,
    ideas, feelings and information.

k) encourages others to keep working
    hard to achieve goal.

l) lets members know their contribu-
    tion is valued.

m) monitors tasks to be done; may ask
    for volunteers or assign responsi-
    bilities.

n) observes working of group and
    relays information to help group dis-
    cuss ways to improve.

(Answers: 1.l, 2.d, 3.e, 4.i, 5.m, 6.h, 7.j, 8.a, 9.g, 10.k, 11.b, 12.c, 13.n, 14.f.)

EXERCISE: Scripts Please

Depending on your role, how would you speak? Imagine that you are a class meeting to discuss the problem of racism. There are eight black students, almost all were born or have roots in the West Indies, yet all of the material studied in your English course is written by and about white North Americans. (If it's more appropriate, the minority group could be native Canadians or French Canadians, or Vietnamese, or Chinese.) Make up remarks suitable for each of the roles mentioned in Exercise 2, bearing in mind that in a successful group:

- each person is valued,
- the goal is achieved,
- open communication of ideas and feelings is encouraged.

Grill

Once you have finished this exercise, get in groups of five to six people to check your answers and discuss the following:

1. Are all these roles necessary in every group?
2. How many of these roles have you played? How many have you played at one time?
3. Would these roles be necessary in a family group? Consider the wedding discussion noted earlier.

Leadership: Taking Your Turn at Bat

Skill

Good leaders know that they are also group members; their position changes from moment to moment. Furthermore, the concept of a leader or manager sitting resolutely in the power chair is outmoded.

If each person in a group is to be respected, then each has a potential grasp on leadership. It is a more fluid concept, and group members need a lot of mutual support and cooperation to move in and out of the leader's role. A good example is the group of friends climbing the Chilkoot Pass on the Alaska-Yukon border. The woman who had done the finances and scheduling prior to the trip was a terrible climber: her knees shook whenever she had to climb from one boulder to the next and she slid backwards on the scree. Several leaders emerged for the climb. While one competent climber kept the group together and cheerful, another scouted the route ahead. Leadership is fluid.

Is a manager, boss, or chairperson always the leader of a group? Not necessarily. Good managers have in their repertoire of skills the ability to identify when to move in and out of the leadership role and when to use others in that capacity. By giving people a chance to assume leadership of the group, you are reinforcing their importance.

How do you start a group rolling? If your purpose or goal is set by a client or another manager, you need only accept or adjust it. Remember, all group members must agree on or "buy into" the task if your group is to succeed. If the goal is not defined, the group must do it.

Who does what? Sometimes, your jobs or skills define your specific task. However, good groups don't assume; they ask each other: "Klaus, how much of the ordering can you do? How much of the job can you handle?" You are giving Klaus time to think and express himself; he may say exactly what was expected, but it is important that individuals feel they have some control over their own lives, and can contribute to the group.

Next, you need to agree on a game plan or *agenda:* dates, order of events, etc. Which of the following statements respects the abilities and opinions of others:

> *"Roger, if Eileen has the wiring in by Friday, can your crew start the installation on the weekend?"*

> *"Eileen, what's the earliest you can hope to finish the wiring?"*
> *"Roger, if that's the case, what sort of schedule do you see in place for your work?"*

The second example allows group members to take an active part in assuming responsibility and planning their time. These examples also lead to a major area to consider when we study leadership—the way we talk to other people.

Open-Ended Questions and Open-Door Voices
What can you say to the following questions?

"Well, I guess we can finish now and ask Tal to report back on Monday, right?"

"Jenny, do you think it's right that the committee meet without notifying the rest of the tenants?"

"Thirty-five dollars a couple is a reasonable ticket price for the dance, isn't it?"

You can't say much can you? Questions like this finish the conversation or restrict it to yes/no answers. There is little room for discussion or the surfacing of new ideas. People who ask for yes/no replies assume that the matter is finished and deny themselves and the group responses that may have furnished a great deal of information.

John DeShano, president of Levi Strauss & Co. (Canada) Inc., described a program that his company is trying to implement. In order to focus on the next decade, they have put in place a set of values, familiar but hard to achieve.

- openness and honesty
- mutual respect and trust
- teamwork.

How can a company hope to initiate openness and trust? By communication and example. DeShano's staff have had group meetings in which company employees have been asked:

"How is this sales policy (form, request) consistent with our values?"

This is an open-ended question. It elicits thought and discussion. Other examples of open-ended questions are:

"What problems can you see getting in the way of our completion date?"

"What sort of things would make you happy at the wedding reception, Avis?"

"How can we make sure the groom's family doesn't feel left out?"

"When you're living in a tent for six weeks, what sorts of things really bug you or please you?"

"When you went through the travel brochures, what places or activities caught your eye?"

"How should we go about getting feedback on the caterers we've shortlisted to supply the cafeteria?"

What Do Words Mean? Connotation and Denotation
We're not always aware of how what we say sounds to other people. Look at the following examples and decide what causes misunderstanding, the tone or the words.

> "Genuine speech is the expression of a genuine personality. Because it takes pains to make itself intelligible, it assumes that the hearer is a genuine personality too—in other words, wherever it is spoken it creates a community."
> (Northrop Frye)

"You're dead."

"That's the most ignorant thing you're ever done."

"The jocks in the audience will understand this term."

"The ladies might have a problem with this."

"We're going to have a high old time."

"Oh great."

Now most of you can recall the expressions "you're dead." or "great" being used both negatively and positively—the difference was in the tone.

"We won a free trip to Hawaii!"

"Great!"

"My little brother's coming with us."

"Oh great."

It makes sense for a home for runaways to call itself Second Base; ballplayers understand that once you're on second you can make it home safely.

The other comments cause confusion because of the words themselves. Denotation is the direct, explicit meaning of a word; connotation refers to the word and its suggested meanings—the cultural, historical overlay a word accumulates. Thus, ignorant means "lacking knowledge." Someone can tell us we are ignorant of the feeding requirements of Indian elephants and most of us will agree, but if that same person tells us we did something "ignorant" we may be hurt. Why?

Similarly, "lady" refers to a perceived class or status; it should not be used to refer to women generally, nor should it be used in a belittling way. Thus, the statement "the Victorian Age protected young ladies to a suffocating degree" is correct; however, we now use the word women to refer to adult female human beings.

"A high old time," "a nickel bag," "a booze can," "a gay atmosphere," can mean very different things. Don't avoid them; just make sure that everyone knows what you are trying to say. The community service worker and the firefighter both use the terms "safe house." What does each mean?

Polly Adler, the famous madame, quipped, "A house is not a home." What did she mean? The baseball coach, the kids playing hide and seek, and the dog-owner all yell: "Home!" What does the word mean in each case?

Break It To Them Gently: Using Your Voice to Help

In group situations, the tone of your voice is as expressive as the words you use. How many ways can you say "I suppose you have a good reason." If a group is committed to its goal and to its members, it should avoid sarcasm; people can hurt each other with a quick word or smart remark, and the open wound may fester. Unchecked, it can infect the group.

At school and at work, we've learned to bully with our voices. A loud voice, an aggressive or pushy approach is often mistaken for efficiency. Don't be fooled by such people and don't try to intimidate others. Loud voices in a group are like bidders at a country auction; the loudest and the quickest are rarely the serious buyers. Those people wait patiently, and bid only when it counts.

Let's Get Physical

What is your body saying to other people? Have you turned to one side and pushed yourself back from the table—a position of dislike or alienation? Are your arms crossed in a "prove it" attitude. Are papers and books piled all around you like a fortress to protect you from other people?

Groups often meet in rooms without tables so that their chairs are arranged in conversational clusters. Individuals lean forward and call each other by name to encourage exchange. Talkative individuals discipline themselves to give others a chance to speak, and use their natural conversational skills to draw out their shyer colleagues.

Is all this interpersonal stuff necessary? Ask yourself. If your job, your family celebration, your personal safety, your reputation, and your productivity depend on other people, is the time devoted to making the group a success worth it?

Drill

EXERCISE: Dividing Up the Money

This exercise allows you a chance to work in a group and examine the roles you play. Working in groups of five to six people, complete the first drill and then identify which roles you assumed at various times. Were you able to use open-ended questions? Was your body language appropriate?

All groups may work simultaneously or you can use the fishbowl method: one group works and one group observes. (20-30 minutes)

Your group is responsible for dividing $3000 a month among the following services and organizations. You may divide the money any way you wish as long as the allocation is a *group decision based on criteria you discuss with each other.*

1. An AIDS education project for the three local high schools. The project leaders would work in conjunction with school staff, but their approach would be informal and oriented to the students. Project workers have liaison with provincial health workers and AIDS support groups.
2. Drop-in centres before and after school for elementary school

children whose parents both work outside the home. The drop-in centres would be located in the elementary schools, open during early morning and late afternoon periods, and staffed by a combination of paid and volunteer workers. Snacks and milk provided.

3. The local food bank needs money for rent, heat, special supplies, and salary for one full-time worker. It has been used regularly since it opened one year ago and demand for its help is growing.

4. Save the Stream Citizens' Group. The local stream, a scenic attraction of the area, is badly polluted and filled with garbage. The citizen's group needs money for a special assessment to determine what chemicals are in the water and to what level.

5. Transportation services for seniors. Many senior citizens live independently and can get out to shop and do business. However, they are unable to carry their groceries home and cannot walk far or take public transportation in the winter. A local group wants to start a free taxi service for seniors in an effort to keep them in their own homes as long as possible.

6. The Rape Crisis Centre is in danger of closing. They have maintained a 24-hour-a-day counselling and referral service for three years, but they need help with rent and utilities or they will be forced to close. They have statistics to prove that they handle a significant number of calls each week.

7. Jobs for unemployed youth. The high school is trying to start a work project for people who have graduated from high school and are unemployed. They need seed money.

Grill

Discuss the following questions in your work groups and report back to the full class.

a) Who assumed the leadership role? Was it a spontaneous action or did it have to be negotiated?

b) Did various people share leadership? Why? Is it an effective way of working in groups?

c) How important is the way you talk to and with people in group situations? How do your words, tone and manner affect others?

d) Do people in business and industry (or nursing, teaching, etc.) have the time or the money to invest in making group experiences positive? What determines their ability to share leadership?

EXERCISE: Recognizing Your Changing Roles

How well did your group function as it divided up the money?

Some members focussed on getting the task accomplished and some sought to keep a good working relationship within the group. This exercise will make you more aware of your ability to increase group effectiveness, and will help your group be more cognizant of its leadership patterns.

a) Keeping in mind the work you just did to divide up the money, complete the following questionnaire.
b) Determine your score. You will find one score for those actions that help get the job done (task actions), and another score for efforts that help maintain the group's working relationships (maintenance actions).
c) **Scoring:** In the space next to each item write 5 if you *always* behave that way, 4 if you *frequently* behave that way, 3 if you *occasionally* behave that way, 2 if you *seldom* behave that way, and 1 if you *never* behave that way.

When I am a member of a group:

_____ 1. I offer facts and give my opinions, ideas, feelings, and information in order to help the group discussion.
_____ 2. I warmly encourage all members of the group to participate. I am open to their ideas. I let them know I value their contributions to the group.
_____ 3. I ask for facts, information, opinions, ideas, and feelings from the other group members in order to help the group discussion.
_____ 4. I help communication among group members by using good communication skills. I make sure that each group member understands what the others say.
_____ 5. I give direction to the group by planning how to go on with the group work and by calling attention to the tasks that need to be done. I assign responsibilities to different group members.
_____ 6. I tell jokes and suggest interesting ways of doing the work in order to reduce tension in the group and increase the fun we have working together.
_____ 7. I pull together related ideas or suggestions made by group members and restate and summarize the major points discussed by the group.
_____ 8. I observe the way the group is working and use my observations to help discuss how the group can work together better.
_____ 9. I give the group energy. I encourage group members to work hard to achieve our goals.
_____ 10. I promote the open discussion of conflicts among group members in order to resolve disagreements and increase group cohesiveness. I mediate conflicts among members when they seem unable to resolve them directly.

____ 11. I ask others to summarize what the group has been discussing in order to ensure that they understand group decisions and comprehend the material being discussed by the group.

____ 12. I express support, acceptance, and liking for other members of the group and give appropriate praise when another member has taken a constructive action in the group.

In order to obtain a total score for task actions and maintenance actions, write the score for each item in the appropriate column and then add the columns.

Task Actions

____ *1.* information and opinion giver
____ 3. information and opinion seeker
____ 5. direction and role definer
____ 7. summarizer
____ 9. energizer
____ 11. comprehension checker
Total for Task Actions

Maintenance Actions

____ *2.* encourager of participation
____ 4. communication facilitator
____ 6. tension reliever
____ 8. process observer
____ 10. interpersonal problem solver
____ 12. supporter and praiser
Total for Maintenance Actions

Description of Task-Maintenance Patterns

1-6 Task Score; 1-6 Maintenance Score

Only a minimum effort is given to getting the required work done. There is general noninvolvement with other group members. The person with this score may well be saying "To hell with it all." Or he or she may be so inactive in the group as to have no influence whatsoever on other group members.

1-6 Task Score; 18-30 Maintenance Score

High value is placed on keeping good relationships within the group. Thoughtful attention is given to the needs of other members. The person with this score helps create a comfortable, friendly atmosphere and work tempo. However, he or she may never help the group get any work accomplished.

18-30 Task Score; 1-6 Maintenance Score

Getting the job done is emphasized in a way that shows very

little concern with group maintenance. Work is seen as important, and relationships among group members are ignored. The person with this score may take an army-space drillmaster approach to leadership.

18 Task Score; 18 Maintenance Score

The task and maintenance needs of the group are balanced. The person with this score continually makes compromises between task needs and maintenance needs. Though a great compromiser, this person does not look for or find ways to creatively integrate task and maintenance activities for optimal productivity.

30 Task Score; 30 Maintenance Score

When everyone plans and makes decisions together, all the members become committed to getting the task done as they build relationships of trust and respect. A high value is placed on sound, creative decisions that result in understanding and agreement. Ideas and opinions are sought and listened to, even when they differ from one's own. The group as a whole defines the task and works to get it done. The creative combining of both task and maintenance needs is encouraged.

Grill

1. Together, discuss the pattern of group behaviour revealed by the scores. Are you satisfied? Could the pattern be improved?
2. What have you discovered about your group?

This exercise is adapted from David W. Johnson and Frank P. Johnson, *Joining Together: Group Theory and Group Skills*, 2nd ed. (Englewood Cliffs, NJ: Prentice-Hall, 1982).

Skill

In a rain storm, you have to make instant decisions; when you're running bases, you rely on the coach's call to go home or stay on third. At other times, you have more opportunity to consider your alternatives. If you're going to buy a stereo system, you might visit sound-equipment stores, check consumer magazines, look for sales, compare prices, talk to friends, and test different systems.

It is no longer possible for human beings to base their actions on "the way it has always been done." Reflection and thought are necessary for good decisions. Furthermore, it's important to realize that there are different ways of making decisions; the situation determines the method. For example, you use one kind of decision-making when you go for the handhold your climbing instructor tells you to use, and another kind when you choose one job over another.

The Game Plan: Making Decisions

You're on a camp-
ing trip with friends
and have just put up
your tent at the Tun-
nel Mountain Camp-
site, outside Banff.
Your friends are
organizing the site
and you are starting
dinner. Suddenly it
starts to pour rain—
it's so heavy, you
can hardly see.
  *What should you
do first?* Arrange the
following activities in
the *order* you would
do them. When you
have finished, find a partner and compare answers, *and the reasons* for your decisions.

RAINSTORM: WHAT SHOULD YOU DO FIRST?

- Take clothes off the line
- Get rain gear on
- Close the car
- Put away food and supplies
- Cover firewood

- Finish cooking dinner
- Close up the tent
- Put away sleeping bags
- Take off your sunglasses
- Cover Coleman stove

The same choices exist for groups; the procedure matches the situation. However, for major decisions, group discussion is essential, and consensus should be sought. Involving all group members improves the effectiveness of the decision, it reinforces the members' sense of belonging to the group, and it increases their commitment to carry out a decision that everyone agrees to. Before you do the drill to explore methods of making a decision, remember that in thinking and deciding you have **four rights.**

1. **The right to pause.** You're working on a committee looking at halfway houses in the community. The chairperson calls to tell you an emergency meeting is planned for Tuesday night. You'll be there, right?
Pause.

Give yourself time to think. Do you have other arrangements already made? If you go to the meeting, will you be ready for a big commitment you have at work later on in the week? Why don't you ask the chairperson for time to think and promise to call back in an hour?

2. **The right to ask questions.** What's on the agenda for the meeting? Is it necessary that you attend all of it? Is your attendance essential to the group? When is the next meeting scheduled? Do you have a specific contribution to make, or could you send your remarks with someone else? You may wish to attend the meeting; in that case, there's no problem. However, if your days are already full, if you are robbing yourself of family or private time
   ask questions.

3. **The right to say no.** You can be a good worker, friend, committee and group member, and still say no. You have to be able to make decisions that will help you function well in all the areas of your life. You can decline the invitation to the meeting and offer alternatives: can you send along suggestions? can you call someone else and get caught up? is there another job that you could manage? Friends, co-workers, committees will always need you. Consider each situation carefully; you do have the right to
   say no.

   It may help the caller if you offer support and encouragement. Saying no to one thing is not a rejection of the activity or the people involved.

4. **The right to say yes.** The chairperson calls again, this time to say there's a meeting in Quebec City, all expenses paid, and your name was chosen in a draw. Do you want to go? The chairperson happens to know that Roberta has never had a chance to represent the group, and she's been overworking lately but if you *really* want to go.... Some people (and I include myself) find it hard to resist hints like this. It takes some time and determination to value yourself and
   say yes.

Drill

How many ways are there to make decisions? How does the method affect the way you feel about your place on the team? The simple exercise that follows illustrates seven different ways to make decisions and the effect each has on individuals.

EXERCISE: Guess the Number of Beans in the Jar

1. A mystery donor supplies a jar full of jellybeans, Smarties, or miniature marshmallows. The exact number must be known *but* kept secret from participants.
2. Seven groups are needed for the exercise. One person in each volunteers to be the reporter.

3. Each group is assigned one of the decision-making methods listed.
4. Using the assigned method, estimate the number of beans in the jar.
5. When your group is finished, each person completes the questionnaire individually.
6. Discuss the experience as a small group and compare your reactions as revealed by the questionnaire.
7. As a class, take time to have each reporter outline the method used by his or her group and the responses of group members.
8. When the exercise is complete, open the jar and devour the contents.

Part One

Each group receives one of the following decision-making processes to follow:

a) The member with the most authority makes the decision: One member is appointed leader by the coordinator. This person should exercise control by such means as telling the group how to sit while waiting for the decision to be made and how to use their time while she is deciding. The leader then estimates how many beans are in the jar and announces her decision to the group. All members of the group then complete the questionnaire.

b) The member with the most expertise makes the decision. The coordinator appoints the member with the most training in mathematics to be the leader. The expert then considers how many beans are in the jar, makes a decision, and announces it to the group. All group members then complete the questionnaire.

c) The opinions of the individual members are averaged: Each member independently estimates the number of beans in the jar without interacting with the other group members. The recorder then asks each member for his estimate, adds the estimates, and divides the sum by the number of members. The resulting number is announced as the group's decision. All group members then complete the questionnaire.

d) The member with the most authority makes the decision following a group discussion: One member is appointed leader by the coordinator, and she calls the meeting to order. She asks the group to discuss how many beans are in the jar. When she thinks she knows how many beans are in the jar she announces her decision to the group. This is not consensus or majority vote—the leader has full responsibility and makes the decisions she thinks is best. All members of the group then complete the questionnaire.

e) A minority of group members makes the decision: The

coordinator appoints an executive committee of two members. The committee meets away from the group to decide how many beans are in the jar. They announce their decision to the group. All group members then complete the questionnaire.

f) Majority vote: Each group member estimates the number of beans in the jar, and the group then votes on which estimate is to be its decision. When the majority of members agree on an estimate, the group decision is made. All group members then complete the questionnaire.

g) Consensus: All members of the group participate in a discussion as to how many beans are in the jar. Discuss the issue until all members of the group can live with and support the group's estimate. When an estimate is agreed on, all members of the group complete the questionnaire. (See consensual decisions on page 121.)

Part Two

After the group has made its decision, all members of the group complete the following questionnaire:

1. How understood and listened to did you feel in your group?

   Not at all 1 2 3 4 5 6 7 8 9 Completely

2. How much influence do you feel you had in your group's decision-making?

   None 1 2 3 4 5 6 7 8 9 A great deal

3. How committed do you feel to the decision your group made?

   Very uncommitted 1 2 3 4 5 6 7 8 9 Very committed

4. How much responsibility do you feel for making the decision work?

   None 1 2 3 4 5 6 7 8 9 A great deal

5. How satisfied do you feel with the amount and quality of your participation in your group's decision making?

   Very dissatisfied 1 2 3 4 5 6 7 8 9 Very satisfied

6. Write one adjective that describes the atmosphere in your group during the decision making. _____

Part Three: Grill

In your groups, discuss the results of the questionnaire. In a class discussion, consider:

1. The effectiveness of the different methods used. How accurate was each group's estimate. Was there a relationship between accuracy and group involvement in the decision?

2. What are the merits of each method of decision-making? Identify situations when you would use each? Would you explain to others the reason for your methods?

EXERCISE: Methods of Decision Making

Deciding how many beans are in a jar may not be of urgent importance, but the methods explored in the bean jar exercise have application to all kinds of decisions, from deciding on tactics for protesting nuclear arms to choosing a family vacation. Each method has its merits and is appropriate in certain circumstances.

In choosing a method, the group should consider:

a) the type of decision to be made;
b) the amount of time and resources available;
c) the history of the group;
d) the nature of the task being worked on;
e) the kind of climate the group wishes to establish;
f) the type of setting in which the group is working.

Which of these decision-making methods would you choose for your group?

1. Rely on the person in charge of the group because she should have the power to make the decision she believes is best, no matter what the rest of the group members think. The designated leader has the responsibility; she should also have the power to make the decisions.
2. Postpone making a decision and wait it out. Time takes care of everything; with a little luck a decision will never have to be made if the group waits long enough.
3. Let the expert make the decision. Give the person with the most expertise in the group the authority to make whatever decision he thinks best.
4. Find out what each member thinks, and then choose the most popular alternative. With this method the group does not even have to meet; members are polled individually.
5. Flip a coin, roll the dice, or pick a number out of a hat.
6. Rely on the person in charge of the group to make the decision, but only after the group has thoroughly discussed the issue with that person.
7. Put the decision in the hands of a knowledgeable and qualified committee that will look at the issues, decide what the group should do, and tell the group members its decision.
8. Take a vote and let the majority rule. The issues should be presented to the group, discussed, and then a vote held with the majority deciding.
9. Ask the group next door what it is going to do and then do just the opposite.
10. Obtain a basic agreement among everyone in the group as to what the decision should be. The issues should be thoroughly discussed, each member participating, until all agree on what the group should do.

Your answers to the questionnaire in the bean-jar exercise should give you some insights into the value of these methods. In your evaluation of them, consider these questions:

a) Decision by Authority Without Group Discussion
How is the leader chosen?
Do group members feel involved in the decision?
Do they understand the decision?
Are they willing and able to implement it?

b) Decision by Expert
How is the expert chosen?
Are group members involved in the decision?
Are they able to implement it?

c) Averaging of Individual Opinions
Do group members feel involved in the decision?
Do the opinions of the most knowledgeable people receive proper consideration?
Do the least knowledgeable opinions receive undue consideration?

d) Decision by Authority After Discussion
Will the leader's decision be more accurate after she has heard discussion?
Do members of the group feel involved in the discussion?
Does the leader's power to decide affect the nature of the discussion?

e) Decision by Minority Committee
Can the minority handle smaller or more specialized decisions more efficiently than the whole group?
Does the group feel oppressed by committee decisions?
Does the group support the decision?

f) Decision by Majority Vote
Is there any protection for minority views? Does the decision split the group?
Is the majority decision the best one?
Do members feel the decision is fair? Which members?

g) Decision by Consensus
Does achieving consensus take too much time?
Does every member feel he has contributed?
Is everyone committed to the decision?

Consensus Decisions: Feeling Together

Reaching a decision by consensus takes time and requires a skilful leader or leaders who can ensure that every member is heard. A decision arrived at by this method has the advantages of using the resources of all members, ensuring the commitment of each person to the decision. This in turn increases the future effectiveness of the group. It is likely to produce creative and high quality decisions. Follow these guidelines when using the consensus method.

1. Avoid arguing blindly for your own opinions. Present your position as clearly and logically as possible, but listen to other members' reactions and consider them carefully before you press your point.
2. Avoid changing your mind *only* to reach agreement and avoid conflict. Support only solutions with which you are at least somewhat able to agree. Yield only to positions that have objective and logically sound foundations.
3. Avoid conflict-reducing procedures such as majority voting, tossing a coin, averaging, and bargaining.
4. Seek out differences of opinion. They are natural and expected. Try to involve everyone in the decision process. Disagreements can improve the group's decision because they present a wide range of information and opinions, thereby creating a better chance for the group to hit upon more adequate solutions.
5. Do not assume that someone must win and someone must lose when discussion reaches a stalemate. Instead, look for the next most acceptable alternative for all members.
6. Discuss underlying assumptions, listen carefully to one another, and encourage the participation of *all* members.

Grill

1. How can the way you speak to group members assist in the consensus method?
2. In Iceland, there is a political party that works entirely by consensus. It has taken them much time and effort to develop, but gradually this all-woman party is making a national impact, and its example is felt worldwide. Could a Canadian political party work by consensus?

This exercise is adapted from *JOINING TOGETHER, Group Theory and Group Skills,* by David W. Johnson and Frank. P. Johnson, published by Prentice-Hall Inc.

EXERCISE: The 14 Worst Human Fears

In a survey of 3000 people included in the Book of Lists, a popular compendium of trivia, the participants were asked, ''What are you most afraid of?'' The results may surprise you.

1. Listed below are the 14 greatest fears. Your job is to rank the fears in the same order as that given in the list. Some answers are tied for the third and fourth places. Prepare your first list working by yourself.
2. Working in groups of 5-6 people, prepare a group list. You must prepare your answer by consensus, and each person must sign the sheet indicating that she or he agrees with the ranking and can explain the group's rationale for the order.

Biggest Fears
   Elevators
   Darkness
   Loneliness
   Insects and bugs
   Death
   Dogs
   Sickness
   Financial Problems
   Flying
   Heights
   Speaking before a group
   Escalators
   Deep water
   Riding/driving in a car

Answers

Biggest Fear	% Naming
1. Speaking before a group	41
2. Heights	32
3. Insects and bugs	22
3. Financial problems	22
3. Deep water	22
6. Sickness	19
6. Death	19
8. Flying	18
9. Loneliness	14
10. Dogs	11
11. Driving/riding in a car	9
12. Darkness	8
13. Elevators	8
14. Escalators	5

Grill

As a class discuss the following:

1. How hard did people work to make sure each person was heard?
2. What remarks were most and least helpful in getting the group to arrive at a consensus?
3. How satisfied was the group with the consensus method?
4. How accurate were your personal and group lists? Is an answer reached by consensus any more accurate? If not, what's the sense of using it?

The title tells it all. In order to resolve conflict you must acknowledge that it does exist and take the time to work it out. Controversy and conflict occur in every group; if you work together you can develop skills to deal with them openly and effectively.

Time Out! Resolving Conflict

Skill

Call Your Moves

As the centre fielder in a baseball game races for a fly ball, he calls "Mine!" If he doesn't, the chances are that the left fielder, also running with her head up, eye on the ball, will crash into her teammate. Baseball players tell each other to "call it," tell each other what they are doing, *as they play*.

Have you ever done something that seemed right, just to have another group member say to you, "I thought that was my job," or "I was counting on doing that display; it's something I've always wanted to try." Why don't group members call their moves?

If the baseball players have a spectacular collision, they apologize briefly on the field, and talk it out next time they're up to bat. Exchanges such as "I should have called it," "the sun was in my eyes and I couldn't tell if you had it," "call it next time," take place. These players clear the air because in a few minutes they will be back in the field and will need to rely on each other completely if the team is to have a good game. How many groups do this? Are members willing to put problems on the table quickly so that they can be outlined, necessary apologies made, responsibilities clearly defined, and the next move planned with confidence in each other. If the opposite occurs, if group members smother their resentment, other people may not even know there is a problem. The person with the grievance may be unwilling to participate completely and may even quit playing his or her best.

A good team shares leadership and resolves its differences through discussion.

If there is a common goal, everyone should be committed to it and willing to discuss conflict openly. Teams and groups need to *call their moves* and *talk out* their differences.

Identify, Outline, Explain, Resolve

How do you talk out your differences? Let's look at the family group. Wedding plans are halted; the caterer for the reception hasn't been chosen because no one in the bride's family is speaking to any one else. This crisis is common; wedding plans often cause stress and hurt feelings because no one applies the principles of group communication. There is little questioning, no negotiation, no job allocation, poor decision-making, no consensus-taking, and worst of all, no one is made to feel valued or special.

The present conflict exists because the bride's parents insist on a complete roast beef dinner. However, the groom's parents are vegetarians. (The bride and groom originally didn't care: they're fast-food addicts.) The bride's parents, who are paying for the reception, state that the majority of guests expect such a meal. Understandably, the groom's parents are hurt by this lack of consideration.

The bride-to-be, Avis, is not speaking to her parents; her brother and sisters cannot get Avis and the parents to talk about the situation, and the engaged couple have started to quarrel. Finally, there is a meeting of Avis, her entire family, and her future husband, Mark.

1. **Identify.** The first step is to identify the problem; that is the obligation of everyone in the group. To identify, you have to speak clearly and honestly.

   > *Avis's sister: We want Avis's wedding to be a happy time for everyone and I think we should clear the air about the difficulties we're having now.*
   >
   > *Mom and Dad, I know you've done a lot of work, and we haven't helped you much, but everyone feels wretched. I guess you feel we don't appreciate how much this means to you.*
   >
   > *Avis thinks you seem more concerned with the reception than with the hopes she and Mark have for the day.*
   >
   > *How important is the food to you?*

This is the first, the most essential, and *the most difficult* step. Family members, group leaders, committee heads, and managers think they can ignore the conflict and "get on with the job." It doesn't work. What actually occurs is that the job slows down, people spend more time dealing with the conflict than with the work at hand, and group members may sabotage each other or drift away to escape the situation.

2. **Outline.** Someone, not necessarily the leader, has to outline the situation without taking sides. (Try for open-ended questions.)

> *"Mark, how easy is it to talk to us as a family?"*
>
> *"Dad, what reasons are there for you not to look at Mark whenever he tries to explain how his parents feel about being vegetarians?"*
>
> *"Avis, what can we do now to stop arguing and make the event a happy one?"*
>
> *"Mom, what can we do to help you more?"*

"Neither misery nor folly seems to me any part of the inevitable lot of man. And I am convinced that intelligence, patience, and eloquence can, sooner or later, lead the human race out of its self-imposed tortures provided it does not exterminate itself in the meantime."
(Bertrand Russell)

3. **Explain.** Mark, Avis, or the parents may decide to tell their sides of the story. Avis's mom may think that nobody's helped: Mark's parents didn't call earlier to make plans; she made all the arrangements for another sister's wedding and was just trying to please; she and her husband have looked forward to this event for a long time.

4. **Resolve.** Individual and group needs have to be met or everyone in this situation will have permanent indigestion! There are several problems: everyone, especially the parents, feels undervalued; jobs need to be shared; more attention has to be given to talking to each other and sharing ideas than making external arrangements. This family has a lot of work to do. They need to define and list the various problems, generate possible solutions, evaluate them, make decisions and *try for consensus*. Once they carry out their plans, they should evaluate the process, so the next wedding will be happier. At what point should they involve the groom's family?

Why Bother Touching All the Bases?

This is a time-consuming and difficult process. External conflicts—the unreliable florist, the fussy client, the budget cutback, the electrical brownout—are easier to deal with than internal conflict. However, you must work through the process or individuals may resort to sniping and sabotage, and the group may collapse. Conflict is normal. It happens. *Talk it out.*

Drill

EXERCISE: Resolving Conflict

Divide into four groups and choose one of the scenarios below to act out. You must think of your role, your approach to the situation, and your language. Your words reflect your attitude and your personality. The characters outlined in the various scenes would naturally hold a variety of opinions—as a group make sure that variety is present.

You may work through the situation separately, and then present it to the class, or showcase them one at a time. You may decide on your role, and your attitude either by consulting with your group or choosing a piece of paper on which your character and stand are outlined. Your aim is to *resolve conflict*.

Scenario 1: White-Water Rafting

You are the coordinator of a youth programme for 14 to 18-year-olds in a middle-class neighbourhood. Your group is going to Vancouver as part of an exchange programme, and the participants have raised money to go white-water rafting on the Fraser River. Now there's a problem.

Several parents are concerned about the dangers of river rafting and have planned a meeting to cancel that activity, maybe the whole trip. One of them has contacted you to express concern and two more have phoned your supervisor. You are now at that meeting.

Scenario 2: Industrial Waste

You have worked for Sludge Chemical Co. for 15 years and have recently been appointed manager of emissions control. Your job is to oversee the dumping of industrial waste into the Rideau River to make sure that the chemical content is within government guidelines. You have discovered that the chemical wastes have been "unsafe" for some months and have come to a meeting of senior management to persuade them to reduce the dangerous emissions. This would mean shutting down the plant, which employs 230 people, for three weeks, and incurring heavy financial losses.

The basic conflict is whether Sludge Chemical has an ethical responsibility to stay within recommended but non-mandatory guidelines or whether its primary responsibility is making money.

Scenario 3: Hospital Services

A hospital committee, consisting of representatives of the board of directors, nursing staff, administrators, doctors, and patient advocates, is meeting. As members of that board, you must decide how much of your allocated budget and available space should be given to a counselling service for people involved in surrogate motherhood arrangements.

Scenario 4: Is a Medical Condition a Drawback?

Your college/university outing club is planning a backpacking trip to hike part of the Cabot Trail in Cape Breton. One of the members is an epileptic. You are having an executive meeting to discuss whether or not she should go. She is not present. Who decides?

Grill

1. Did people sound as if they wanted to resolve conflict or get their own way?
2. Which words or phrases helped the situation and which did not?

GREAT CANADIAN QUIZ II

Chew on a Maple Leaf for inspiration and test your knowledge of Canadian places, dates, and characters.

1. What Canadian hero started out on a "Marathon of Hope"?
2. What are the three levels of Government in Canada?
3. Other than the Green Party and the Rhinos, what are our major national political parties?
4. What year was slavery outlawed in Canada?
5. What is a furry Arctic owl doll called?
6. Who was the first woman from the Western Hemisphere to successfully climb Mt. Everest?
7. Who is the singing and stomping musician who wrote "Bud the Spud"?
8. Which national park was the first to be established?
9. Name two legendary creatures that haunt various parts of the country.
10. What schooner is pictured on the dime?
11. Who was the first woman to be appointed to the post of Lieutenant-Governor?
12. Which national pastime was a demonstration sport at the 1988 Olympic Winter Games?

   To test yourself further, consult:

John Robert Colombo, *Colombo's Canadiana Quiz Book* (Western Producer Prairie Books, 1983).

John Fisher, *The Complete Cross-Canada Quiz and Game Book* (McClelland and Stewart, 1978).

Sandra Martin, *Quizzing Canada* (Dundurn Press, 1987).

Answers: Great Canadian Quiz II

1. Terry Fox
2. Federal, provincial, local
3. Conservatives, Liberals, NDP, Social Credit
4. 1834
5. Ookpik
6. Sharon Wood, mountaineer and guide, in 1986
7. Stompin' Tom Connors
8. Banff
9. Sasquatch, Ogopogo
10. The Bluenose
11. Pauline McGibbon of Ontario, in 1974
12. Curling

Negotiating is an open process in which you are prepared to put something forward in return for what you get; it is rewarding for both sides. Bargaining is more one-sided; you are clear about your needs, and determined to achieve them. *Neither* technique involves arguing, yelling, or intimidation. *Both* rely on the way you speak as well as what you say.

Negotiating

Two international food fairs are being held this year for the hospitality industry. As the catering manager for a large hotel chain, you are expected to go to one; your boss will attend the other. One food fair is being held in San Francisco; the other in Fredericton. Unfortunately, you both wish to go to San Francisco—time for negotiation.

For this process to be effective, you both have to offer something in return for what you get. Since both parties are giving something, both are sure of winning. If you go into the meeting determined that you *are* going to San Francisco, it is not negotiating; you have to be more open about the result. In this case, your supervisor is also willing to negotiate, and you look at various possibilities. Can you both go? No, one of you must be in the office. Would you be willing to go to the national food fair this year, and the international one next year? If one of you goes to San Francisco for the food fair, the other could have first chance at the big tourism convention being held in Italy next year. In this case, your supervisor agrees to go to Fredericton; next year she'll be in Naples and you'll visit St. John's, Newfoundland.

This is negotiating; you both have a shared concern for the business, and personal interests to satisfy. If you negotiate, the work gets done, and you both win.

Bargaining

Many times, you *need* to get something done; often the other parties involved are not cooperative. This technique can be used to deal with any of the people you encounter in arranging the business of daily life: your family, your bank manager, your employer or employees, your teachers or the teachers of your children, the municipal roads board, etc. You can be successful without resorting to bullying, arguing, or demanding.

Imagine this situation. You have signed up to give your major persuasive speech next Friday. Your instructor has been clear in his discussion of responsibility; you must give the speech on the date you choose. It is a firm commitment and there are no cancellations. That very afternoon the personnel manager of a company you have always wanted to work for telephones to offer you a job interview for a summer position. Guess when the only available appointment is? You know what your public speaking

Open Negotiations and Determined Bargaining: There's Room for Both

teacher's reaction will be—no sympathy. What can you do? Request an appointment, and with an air of polite assurance, enter his office and use the following techniques:

- fogging;
- positive strokes;
- shared responsibility.

Fogging
Prepare and *practise* a phrase that expresses what you want or need and *keep repeating it:*

> *"I need to make an alternate date for my final speech."*
> Your teacher may say things like,
> *"I think the conditions were very clear,"*
> *"It wouldn't be fair to the others."*
> *"But I told you."*
> *"It's impossible!"*
> Each time, nod agreeably (because what he says is true) and say
> *"Yes, I agree but...I need to make an alternate date for my final speech."* Allow him a chance to work through all the stages of frustration involved, and at the same time, state your case.
> *"No, I don't want to fail. It's just that...I need to make an alternate date for my final speech."*

Fogging fills the room and the listener's mind with your request. It's especially useful for people who

- give up when someone says "no, of course not; *absolutely not!*";
- get nervous when others raise their voices;
- crumble when someone attacks them verbally;
- remember all their good lines *after* they get home.

Positive Strokes
Agree with the other person. Your teacher says,

> *"This is terrible!"*
> Immediately you reply,
> *"I agree with you; you are exactly right."*

Now how can anyone argue with you, when you *agree* with him? If you can honestly do it, say positive things about the other person.

> *"Your course was worthwhile, and I don't want to jeopardize my mark."*

Shared Responsibility
Request feedback from the other person and offer positive suggestions of your own.

> *"I have some possible solutions and want to know if you think they're worthwhile."*

Here's the surprise: few people expect you to ask for their opinions or assistance. In most situations, people go in with demands; here, you offer suggestions and ask for cooperation in resolving the problem fairly.

Warning! Do not give ultimatums or walk out in anger. Avoid insulting others, making "or else" statements you're not prepared to carry out, or slamming the door on the problem.

Here's another scenario. You share the housework with another human being—a partner, a parent, or a sister. In this case your sister has not done any cleaning in the past four weeks and the dust balls are bigger than your cat. You've had it.

Do not insult your sister. Instead, prepare your fogging statement:

> *"I want you to do the housework this week. It's your turn."*

She may lash out with personal insult (*"What do you know— you're only 5'2"*) or oft-repeated excuses (*"But I work hard all day"*). Do not retaliate or walk out. Instead, fog:

> *"I know your job is exhausting but...I want you to do the housework this week. It's your turn."*

When she moans that she hates housework, use the second technique and *agree with her.*

> *"You are so right; housework is wretched but...."*

If she attempts to escape with the excuse that she's busy all week, go immediately to shared responsibility:

> *"I agree it's a problem. How do we solve it? What do you suggest?"*

Remember, you aren't going to give up or forget. You are going to persist.

What Happens When Someone Uses the Technique on You?

When I went to my bank to get a consumer loan, the rates quoted were far too high; the bank next door offered a much better deal. Preparing my fogging statement, I went to the manager of my own branch:

> *"I want a loan rate that proves to me that I am a valued customer."*

To my surprise, the manager came back with positive strokes and shared responsibility,

> *"I agree there's a problem. How can we solve it."*

Fogging was the answer. It gave me time to remember the various alternatives I had considered before the meeting. I came out of the manager's office with a loan rate 3½% lower than the original offer.

When Do You Negotiate and When Do You Bargain?
Negotiation is a cleaner, clearer experience. It is possible when
people are willing to seek solutions in an atmosphere of cooperation and mutual respect. But there are many times when you
have legitimate requests that others will not consider: the principal of your child's school refuses to arrange testing to detect
a suspected learning disability; the marina owner will not give
you access to your boat after the season is over; your doctor
is reluctant to discuss the results of blood tests. Fogging, positive strokes, and shared responsibility may help you.

Drill

Should you negotiate or bargain in each of the following situations? Decide on your technique, and carry it out.

1. You want a cat; your partner thinks that, as a couple, you
   are too busy to care for a pet.
2. You want the hotel where you work to establish smoke-free
   public rooms. The other managers think that clients might
   be annoyed.
3. You want to take your holidays the first three weeks in July;
   two other people also want their holidays then. Only one person can be absent at a time.
4. Your mother wants to buy an artificial Christmas tree; you
   want a real one.
5. You and three other friends are going to the southern United
   States for study week. Two people want to hit the beaches;
   the other two want to stay at a place with more variety.

Grill

1. How did you decide which technique to use?
2. How able were you to avoid intimidation or bullying?
3. Which is more important—words, tone, or body language?

Using Signals: Language and Attitudes

Skill

Inclusive Language

What do your words reveal about your attitudes? Do you use
language that shows respect for other people and their abilities?
Sometimes, we absorb phrases and prejudices unconsciously and
they show up in our speech, hurting some listeners and insulting others. Words that were common twenty years ago have
largely been abandoned because of their insulting, often racist
overtones: gyp, savage, squaw, yellow, etc.

By valuing each person on the basis of his or her own worth,
you will be able to avoid preconceived ideas about capabilities
and attributes. In return, people will respond to an approach
they perceive to be open and fair.

Look at the way language has changed in an attempt to avoid sexual stereotyping. Jobs no longer belong to one sex or the other: there are firefighters, councillors, cleaners, police officers, chairpersons, stunt artists, camera technicians, sales representatives, and news anchors. It is important to use phrases that show women as equal partners in society. Arlene Mantle's song, "Women Hold Up Half the Sky," explains why language is important:

> You said man and he
> But where were we?
> We were invisible, we were unheard.
> ....
> Let's make it her and she,
> And you and me
> Together we'll hold up all the sky.
> We'll all be visible, we'll all be heard.
>   (with thanks to Arlene Mantle)

Thus use:

> *Wayne Yetman and his secretary Martha Ferron are making a presentation.*

rather than

> *Mr. Yetman and his secretary Martha are making a presentation.*

Alternate the order of reference so that women are not always given second place:

> *Martha Ferron and her supervisor, Wayne Yetman, are making a presentation.*

Assume that men and women can hold positions of responsibility equally:

> *Take your complaints about service charges to your bank manager. She will deal with them.*

Alternate the use of "she" and "he", use both pronouns as in "she or he will deal with them," or make the construction plural.

> *Take your complaints about service charges to your bank managers. They will deal with them.*

Unless you are referring to children, avoid the word "girls," and degrading remarks such as "I'll get my girl (or the girls) to do that tomorrow." Use a form that expresses equal status:

> *The men and women of the engineering department* rather than
> *The men and girls of the engineering department.*

It is hard, but necessary to change speech patterns. Human beings will not achieve equality if attitudes do not alter, and language is a sure indicator of attitudes. Thus phrases such as

"professionals, their wives and children,"
"help for mothers and children,"
"publisher Jack David and his daughter Maxi,"

change to

"professionals, their spouses and children,"
"help for parents and children,"
"publisher Jack David and his daughter, Maxi David, an ornithologist."

Avoid using expressions that assume certain attributes that are found in one sex, such as

"You men will understand the financial implications."

This should be changed to

"All of you will understand the financial implications."

You should also stay clear of ethnic cliches:

"Cheap Scots,"
"Amorous Italians,"
"Inscrutable Asians."

In a multicultural society, everyone recognizes the need to learn and use the correct names for various racial groups: South Asians, Inuit, Déné, Blacks, Sikhs, Métis, etc. (Further examples may be found in the checklist on inclusive language in Chapter 8, and in *The Canadian Style: A Guide to Writing and Editing,* published by the Department of the Secretary of State of Canada.)

Disabled or Differently Abled?

Most folk festivals have signers to interpret the music for the hearing imparied. When Rick Hansen wheeled across Canada, towns and cities blossomed with ramps and facilities that would make more buildings accessible to wheelchairs. It is time to develop attitudes and speech patterns that are also open to everyone. If we are sensitive to others and to their feelings, we will consider our words. How do we talk about these things? Rick Hansen gave the answer when he discussed one of the aims of the Man in Motion tour that took him 24 895 miles around the world.

Am I "physically challenged?" Am I "special?" "Handicapped?" "Disabled?" am I an "invalid?" A "cripple?" A "gimp?"...We were trying to be a messenger, to let people know that no matter what the form of physical disability—loss of limb, blindness, cerebral palsy, paralysis—everyone has hopes and dreams....

And that brings us back to definitions, and two that might help ease the confusion:

My disability is that I cannot use my legs. My handicap is your negative perception of that disability, and thus of me.

(RICK HANSEN and JIM TAYLOR. *Rick Hansen: Man in Motion*. Douglas & McIntyre, 1987. p. 174-175.)

Drill

EXERCISE: The Great Canadian Shake

The way you greet others and present yourself sends clear messages about who you are. A firm, warm handshake is a good way to welcome people and establish yourself as an equal in the group. Recognizing the need young people and some women have to practice this basic signal, my students and I invented the **Great Canadian Shake-Off.**

The aim of the exercise is to develop a great shake as opposed to a milkshake. The inventors of this game realized that people need to do whatever is courteous and appropriate in various situations. They determined that a great shake consists of:

1. the shake itself;
2. a verbal greeting;
3. direct eye contact that establishes the handshakers as equals.

To conduct your own Shake-Off, follow these steps. The instructor is responsible for supplying a suitable prize.
1. Divide into three groups. Each group should establish criteria for a great shake. Once the groups report back to the class, a final set of standards is established. (The inventors suggest a shake that is warm in spirit, fitting, and expressive. By fitting, they mean that the hands should meet in a firm clasp, and avoid the extremes of fingertips only, the bonecrusher maul, or the pump handle. The message should fit the occasion.)
2. Within your groups conduct a preliminary round of handshakes. Everyone in the group shakes hands with everyone else until you can decide on a winner.
3. Groups send their champions to the playoffs, a round of handshaking with three neutral judges. Using the criteria established by the class, the judges pick the winner and award the prize.

Grill
1. How did receiving a Great Shake make you feel?
2. How did giving a Great Shake make you feel?
3. Discuss the messages that various forms of greeting send.

EXERCISE: New Ways of Seeing: Eliminating Bias in our Language

How do the words we use make people feel good or bad about themselves? We need to feel proud of ourselves, our abilities, our colour, our size, our racial backgrounds. In the following quiz, there are traditional answers. Should we be using them any more? Were they ever accurate?

What colour is courage?
What colour is a plague?
What colour is cowardice?
What colour is the mark you have against you?
What colour is purity?
What colour is a witch's clothing?
What colour was the Monday of the recent stock crash?
What colour is the skin of the heroines in fairy tales?
What colour is a storm cloud?
What colour is good?
What colour is evil?

Grill

Think of your own lives. On days when disaster struck, what colour was the sky? What colour was the person who hurt you? Did the colour matter? How can we speak in order to say what we mean?

Winging It: The Impromptu Speech

Impromptu speeches are a challenge. Like unexpected over-time, they demand all your skills and nerve. You can handle *any* impromptu if you remember one thing:

> *An impromptu is like any other speech; it requires a thesis, a clear design, and a strong conclusion. You just have to think faster.*

In order to complete the drills included in this chapter, you have already spoken impromptu many times, and have developed skills and confidence. Consider the following suggestions, and then experiment with the final exercise.

1. A real impromptu is a surprise. It is not a speech that you decided to forget about. *Never* plan to speak impromptu.
2. Be Prepared! Experienced speakers always spend a few minutes *in any gathering* imagining what they would say in that situation. It is easier to think of one or two pertinent remarks before the pressure is on.
3. Make use of your time. You will probably have several minutes to gather your thoughts. Don't panic! Instead, follow the procedure you would for any speech:

a) Determine the subject or topic under discussion.

b) Establish your thesis. You must pause to determine what you think.

c) Calmly consider your thesis and one or two supporting statements.

d) Work out a brief outline and remember, a good grabber, a clear introduction and a strong conclusion will help.

e) Jot down your notes, if only a few words.

f) Go over your outline until you have to speak.

g) Stick to the plan. Most people who do impromptus are so nervous, they forget to coach themselves. They ramble in an attempt to use time. Say what you want to say and save the filler for your memoirs.

h) Be brief. You're not expected to know everything, so unless you were hoping for the chance, and have a speech ready, make your main points and stop.

i) *Finish. Finish strong.* Inexperienced speakers never know if they've "said enough." If you've covered your main points, and hammered them home, your impromptu is complete. Sit down.

4. Enjoy yourself. If you did the exercises Group Speed Planning and Street Practice in Chapter 3, you're ready to think and organize quickly. Add to that your skills at analyzing an audience and building rapport (eye contact, eye contact, eye contact), and you're an expert.

5. Nervousness always gets you in the throat. *Breathe.* While you are planning, writing down your ideas, mentally rehearsing, and standing to speak, *relax and breathe!*

6. If you are often asked to "say a few words," take a lesson from David Nichol, President of Loblaw International Merchants. When he was in high school, he entered public speaking contests and had an "impromptu" that he could change to suit any occasion.

A Note on the Exercises

These exercises are designed to get you on your feet, speaking with coherence and vitality. There are various methods of organization; for several consecutive classes your instructor may ask a certain number of students to prepare impromptus for that day. You may all get the topic at the same time, or, using the envelope technique, you can try the one-minute drill. The suggestions range from lighthearted themes that everyone can manage to more complex subjects. Enjoy the challenge and use that nervous energy well.

Speech Assignment: The Impromptu

1. The Perfect Royal Gift

Royal couples are fond of Canadian tours; each time they visit our country, they are presented with truckloads of typical Canadian souvenirs. You have five minutes to prepare the following speech: **"The Perfect Souvenir for Visiting Royals."**

2. The Envelope Please

Each student writes down one or two *general* topics on separate pieces of paper. The instructor collects the topics, reads them aloud to give everyone an idea of the subjects, and discards any that are too obscure. There should be at least as many topics as students present. All pieces of paper go in an envelope and one volunteer selects a topic, without looking. He or she has one minute to prepare an impromptu which itself should only last 60 seconds (a timer may indicate the 45- and 60-second marks). As the first speaker begins, the envelope passes to the next person who draws a topic and starts to plan.

The second person can prepare until the first speaker concludes. At that point, the second person goes to the front, and the envelope passes to the next student, AND SO ON....This exercise is fun. Everyone faces the same challenge and the class is generally very supportive. You'll be surprised at how well you do. Doing this exercise several times over the space of a few weeks will help you develop skill.

3. Considered Topics

You need a list of topics concerning a subject you are studying or current issues with which you are all familiar. You may prepare the list as a class or your instructor may supply it. Choose a topic and, adhering to the time limit agreed upon (15-50 minutes depending on the class and the material), prepare an impromptu.

You may wish to use some of the following suggestions:

- are dreams real?
- should you require a permit to buy a pet?
- is bribery common in business?
- dressing for work
- buying Canadian
- cults
- pregnancy and young teens

- a current movie
- high performance cars
- music in the workplace
- travelling by yourself
- butter or margarine?
- why not to swallow your gum
- is collusion inevitable in baseball?
- missing people
- parental assistance for a child living away from home
- do people regret tattoos?
- flexible work hours
- dyeing your hair
- the best roller coasters
- drug testing—who and where?
- the best investments
- adventure holidays

DELIVERY TECHNIQUES TO REMEMBER

1. Listen to yourself: are your words and tone working for you? Do you sound the way you want to?

2. Join the team: take time before meetings and speeches to get to know your co-workers or audience. Get a feel of the group so that when you get up to speak, you have a sense of the occasion and mood.

3. Use words with awareness: are inclusive language and open-ended questions part of your repertoire? Are you consciously working to build successful groups?

INTERVIEW

Roberta Bondar

Member of the
Canadian Astronaut
Program

May 13, 1988
Toronto

Roberta Bondar is a physician, astronaut, researcher and pilot. She is now being trained as a payload specialist for NASA's IML-1 mission, the space shuttle scheduled for 1991. Bondar specializes in neurology, and was director of the Multiple Sclerosis Clinic for the Hamilton-Wentworth

Region at McMaster University in 1982. She is now a member of the scientific staff at Sunnybrook Hospital in Toronto doing research on stroke patients. Roberta Bondar's humour and energy make her a popular speaker; she goes into the core of her intellectual and emotional being and speaks to people from the heart.

Q
Is it true that you had to make a speech as part of the final selection process for the Canadian space team, when you and 19 others out of 4300 original applicants made it to the final cut?

A
Yes, they wanted us to do a talk for ten minutes on one of four topics without the use of audio-visual. It was not easy, but I never really thought of being nervous. We had one week to prepare for this thing. The topic I chose was the "Role of Science and Technology

in Society." I had very little time to prepare, and I hadn't given many public speeches, just in terms of speaking to patients' families, or giving clinical days—speaking about medicine.
  I always use slides; I like talking to people as though we're watching home movies, but this speech was to be done without any use of audio-visual equipment, and I *hate* writing speeches. I find that I can't be spontaneous because the talk is something I prepared when I was in mood A and now I'm in mood B; I've met people and decided the tone should be slightly different. So, I

guess it was supposed to be a written speech and I tried. But after two pages I stopped, and started just making notes about what I could talk about when I got to the lectern. In terms of the subject material, because I didn't have much lead time, and because I had chosen how society perceives science, I went back to the early days of the American flight program when I was in public and high school. I looked at old National Geographic magazines that my parents always got, and noted all the advertisements that had something to do with the space program, because that's how society was perceiving the space program and how we could use space technology. It was right down to Sarah Coventry jewellery and getting gems from the moon. That's how I got the material for the talk.

The selection committee were all told not to smile at any jokes we cracked; they were just dead pan. It wasn't a normal audience. By the time I was finished the first seven minutes I thought, "well, these guys don't look like they're having much fun, and I don't feel like I'm having much fun." So I started straying a bit to other things I had thought I might want to say. I deliberately did not look at the person holding the big sign that told you there was one minute to go, so he kept moving it down the table. I must say that I don't like giving talks unless I'm going to have fun doing them.

Q
In other words, spontaneity is very important to you?

A
Very much so, because when I use point form, it's like a conversation with people. When you have a written text, if you try to memorize it, and not look at the notes, you can forget a line and

you're really in trouble. That is absolutely devastating.

I had a hard time in school with memory work, spitting back words that someone else had said. I liked science because you could explain it in your own words, and this approach is better for communicating ideas, presenting them in a creative way.

I'm interested in being able to speak to other people about science. When I was in university, and went home at Christmas to the Soo, communicating my ideas to people who had no science background at all was very difficult. So at Christmastime I would really make an effort to tell them.

Q
Where did you learn how to work so well in groups?

A
We had to deal with interpersonal-skill development at McMaster University Medical School in much greater depth than at many other medical schools. We learned in tutorial groups and found ways of communicating very complicated things in very simple terms to other people. Giving talks is just an expansion of that.

My tutorial groups at medical school were intense situations with six people, very assertive individuals who all had something to say *all the time*. We all wanted to show each other that we were learning this medicine stuff and were creative. It took a long time to communicate.

But we learned to function as a group; our learning was inhibited if each member did not function to promote the learning of the others.

What is your personal style in groups?

A
I listen. It's amazing how many people tell me I'm a quiet person. I'm a listener; I observe how people are interacting. I try to figure out where they're coming from, what they're trying to get out of the group, or what points they are trying to get across. And I adjust my level of contribution to that. If it's a really aggressive group, and I know I'm not as aggressive as the rest, I know I'm going to have to pitch in and not be nervous about things.

When I first started all this, I was really inhibited because everybody else had such wonderful things to say....It takes a while to get over that and be able to contribute. When I get into a group, I want to make sure I've got those feelings out of my head, and when I speak, it's going to be something positive.

Q
How can you, Dr. Roberta Bondar, astronaut, be inhibited?

A
I never think of my position; I think of what I can contribute, what my value is. What is Roberta Bondar's value here, what can I do, what can I give to the group from my personal repertoire? In terms of communication, I'm very direct. I try not to mess around.

Q
Do you have any problems in groups?

A
When I'm nervous, I start speaking quickly and that does me in. My pronunciation goes down, and my thoughts don't come out clearly enough. I find that someone else has to take those words, say them again, and then they're accepted. But I find I have to slow down and enunciate.

Q
You use audio-visual material extremely well

A
My dad has something like 40 hours of home movies of us since we were little kids. I think that seeing those movies and slides every Saturday night gave us an appreciation of being there, of being part of those activities. And there's nothing like seeing slides of the space program to make you feel enthusiastic. I find they're a good cue for you; if you know your material, you don't forget it. It depends on what you're doing, on the kind of information you're trying to put across. If you're giving a general lecture, slides with a lot of writing can be distracting but if you're giving technical talks, it's much easier to have the information on the slide, than ruffle through your notes to see if you've memorized something properly.

Q
What is your medical specialty?

A
I'm a neurologist.

What kind of presentation would you make using slides?

A
Multiple sclerosis, which affects the brain and the spinal cord, is not an easy disease to tell people about when they don't know what a cell looks like, let alone a cell in the brain. I was asked to speak for an hour to patients and their families about some of the new treatment modalities in multiple sclerosis.

I had to get very, very basic anatomy pictures. You have to look at the audience as you speak, because if they're not looking at you, you might as well walk away, turn the slides off. So I tried to get slides simple enough so they wouldn't be threatening, and interesting enough. You have to constantly remember who your audience is.

Q
Do you use a pointer with the slides

A
Yes, I use one of those illuminated arrows. I see a lot of people taking an arrow and swinging it up so you get motion sick; I use it to point at an object, but I don't run it up and down the screen.

A long time ago, my thesis supervisor told me that when I was giving presentations, if I felt at all nervous or cold, to hold the pointer with two hands, because a tremor gets exaggerated on the screen. It's amazing how many people hold this thing when they're shaking from nervousness, and it looks so bad on the screen.

Another thing about pointers is that people don't focus them before they start, or they play with them so much because they're nervous that they go out of focus. The result is a great big blob instead of a crisp arrow.

Q
Is it easier to speak now than when you first began?

A
When you give a number of talks on the same subject—now I'm not saying that all my talks are the same: I try to make them different or I'll be bored—you get so familiar with the material that it gets easier for you. And it appears easy. The average person looking at someone who talks a lot may be overwhelmed, but it's like everything else in life—it's rote learning. You're not born with all the words in the dictionary in your head, or all the medical knowledge. It's just going over and over it.

The first time I use a new slide or new information, I may make an error. If I realize it, I'll correct myself. But unless there's an expert in the audience, they may not even remember what you said. And you've got to remember that someone listening to you only takes home a fraction of what you've said. I've done 18 years of university and I'd hate to tell you how much I've forgotten.

You don't expect your audience to remember everything, so if you do make mistakes or you do forget things, you shouldn't get sweated up about it while you're at the lectern. If you remember afterwards during question period, you can bring the material back in. So you shouldn't get so nervous; you should have a main message and have interesting slides to support it.

Q
How do you practise?

A
If I'm on a plane, I think about things and make notes. Then I try to take something local and incorporate it into the talk. If I'm at a school, I talk to the teachers or principal about what the big topics are. I try to make the crowd know I'm

interested in them, to inlcude something personal.

Q
What are the most common topics you're asked to speak on?

A
Women and science. Getting young girls interested in science. They say, "what are you going to tell the girls?" and I say, "the same thing I tell the boys." It's no different—in terms of what schooling they have to have. But as for getting women more enthusiastic, there's a different message for the boys. The message for the boys is "girls can do it." And we want the other astronauts to tell the male population that women can do it. There are more messages to be given to the males to try to make sure that the road is open for women. And for women, you just say, "if you get jumped on...we have a much lighter cross to bear than we had 50 years ago and we have to work with it."

Q
How do you deal with sexism in the industry?

A
It depends on what your background has been,

how you've been beaten or scarred by various things. I've had to deal with a lot of it, and it's surprising where it comes from. Sometimes sexism surfaces on occasions when you don't want it to surface and you get angry. And that's the danger point. If you try to deal with things from an angry state, then you put yourself in a much worse position. The main thing is to try to be cool, to come back with short one-liners to put people in their place but not in a vicious way. If you're vicious, you'll just get it back again.

Q
You've seen a lot of speakers? How do we as Canadians measure up?

A
We use fewer gimmicks than people in other countries. In the United States, people use jokes a lot more. And some people, Canadians and Americans, use pointless jokes, ridiculous stuff that is completely out of context. And jokes with inappropriate sexual

connotations are beyond the limit. I remember one lecturer talking about dermatology with all these slides of women— they weren't about dermatology at all. So the women, over 50% of the That's how we dealt with that.

Q
What fascinates you about space?

A
One of the things we're doing is making our lives better here on earth. Not just understanding the global earth and the ecology of it, and the environment (which we are doing), but also looking at how the human body can be in new environments. We're utilizing space in a creative way to do experiments that would run into a dead end in our laboratory. We don't have any answers down here but in space we're in a different medium that has very little gravity. It challenges the body physiologically and it expresses itself in a different way. Suddenly—

there's the answer we've been looking for here on earth but it's been masked by one G [one times Earth's gravity].

Q
What advice would you give to people making their first speeches?

A
Being nervous may be the most distracting thing. I've told people who wear glasses to take them off but that's not such a hot idea. You have to have a good night's sleep and know the material. The other thing you have to realize is that people are there to hear what you have to say, not win the lottery based on how many "ah"s you use.

As long as you're interested in what you're doing, your audience is interested in what you're saying.
Keep the level of enthusiasm up throughout the whole speech: there's somebody out there who is as interested in minute 15 of your speech as in minute one. I've heard a lot of speakers trail off; keep the interest level up.

Roberta Bondar

Speech: A Responsibility to the World

In July, 1988, Roberta Bondar was the Honorary Director of an International Event held by the Girl Guides of Canada-Guides du Canada at Echo Valley in the Qu'Appelle region of Saskatchewan. There were over 3500 women and girls present, representing 48 countries. Bondar gave the keynote speech for "Bridges for Tomorrow," a day-long event featuring 101 workshops designed to build links of time and space and possibilities. This is an excerpt from that speech.

I'm delighted to be here. Three years ago, when I was asked to be honorary director of this camp, I thought it was a dream come true. All my life, I've wanted to be a physician, an astronaut, and a camp director....If I had had this opportunity at your age, I'm not sure which choice I would have made. I understand you have 101 choices for today. That's absolutely amazing. This might be one of the few times you can speak to people with real expertise in various fields. You are going to be in small groups to help you approach people, talk about important things, discuss issues....It's *so* important to share information. None of us would be experts in our fields if we had not discussed things with other people. There's nothing wrong with asking.

Although today is "Bridges for Tomorrow," we have to build them with bridges from the past. In years to come, when you are standing onstage, when you are my vintage, you will remember this beautiful day in Saskatchewan; you will have knowledge and drive and energy from this experience, from something someone said.

All the workshop leaders are volunteers, sharing with you because they think it's important. I want all of you to remember that you are important. Each of you has a responsibility to the world. Each of you has to carry something away from today and make it important to you because you have to share it with others. You see, I don't have any children; you people are my bridges to tomorrow. You people are going to be the bridges to tomorrow for many, many people. You have no idea who you will be touching in your lives, even in a small way, that will affect them forever.

July 16, 1988
Echo Valley,
Saskatchewan

OUTLINE OF AN IMPROMPTU SPEECH

Name: _____

Date of Speech: _____

Purpose Statement: _____

INTRODUCTION

    Grabber:

    Thesis:

    Overview:

BODY

    Supporting Argument #1

    Supporting Argument #2

    Supporting Argument #3

CONCLUSION

    Reference to purpose (thesis):

    Summary of main steps:

    Zinger:

SELF-EVALUATION FORM

This form is to help you evaluate your own speech. It can be kept private or shared with your instructor or peers.

Type of Speech: _____

Name: _____

Title: _____

Date: _____

DELIVERY
Physical Presence

Did I make eye contact with others?

Was my posture natural and appropriate?

Was I aware of my facial expressions and hand gestures?

Were there any distracting mannerisms that I was aware of?

Did I feel good?

Could I feel an energy exchange with my audience?

VOCAL DELIVERY

Was my voice under control?

Did I sound confident?

Was I aware of breathing calmly?

How was my enunciation?

Did I manage to avoid um's and ah's?

Did I sound interested/excited/committed?

How did my voice sound to me?

DESIGN AND CONTENT

How well did the introduction and conclusion work?

Did the framework unify my speech?

Was there a natural progression from point to point?

Did my notes keep me on track? Did I use them?

Did the audience seem to understand the organization of my speech?

Was the information clear?

What was the energy level of the conclusion?

What would I change the next time?

What worked very well?

OVERALL EFFECTIVENESS

Did I connect with this audience?

Did I achieve my purpose?

What do I remember most about making the speech?

What unexpected or unforeseen things happened?

What am I most pleased about?

OTHER COMMENTS

Grade:

PEER EVALUATION FORM

Peer evaluation should be done in a constructive and supportive fashion. The speaker may choose people to do assessments or they may be assigned alphabetically. Some groups maintain the same speaker/assessor teams for the entire course; others change for each speech. The instructor may wish to see this evaluation before it goes to the speaker.

Type of Speech: _____

Speaker: _____

Title: _____

Assessor: _____

Date: _____

DELIVERY
Physical Presence

Did the speaker maintain eye contact?

Did she or he establish a rapport with the audience?

Were gestures natural and effective?

VOCAL DELIVERY

Did the speaker sound convincing/spontaneous/excited?

Was his or her voice clear and loud enough?

How did you respond to the speaker's mood?

DESIGN AND CONTENT

Did the introduction interest you?

Did the overview give you an indication of the main proofs?

Did the speech flow easily and logically from one point to another?

Was the conclusion strong and memorable?

Did the conclusion reinforce the thesis and main points?

What was the thesis of the speech?

OVERALL EFFECTIVENESS

Did you learn something new or worthwhile from the speech?

Were you moved by it?

What was the most outstanding part of the speech?

What changes do you recommend?

What parts should the speaker definitely keep?

OTHER COMMENTS

Grade:

EVALUATION FORM

Type of Speech: _____

Name: _____

Title: _____

Length of Speech: _____

Date: _____

Legend: S = SUPERIOR   E = EFFECTIVE   NW = NEEDS WORK

DELIVERY
Physical Presence
Eye Contact
Rapport with Audience
Posture
Gestures
Use of Notes
Appropriate Use of Audio-Visual
Support Material

VOCAL DELIVERY
Naturalness/Spontaneity/Enthusiasm
Clarity
Variety (Tone, Pitch, Pace)
Volume
Absence of Verbal Tics (um, ah,
okay, like)
Sense of Control and Calm

DESIGN AND CONTENT
Use of Framework for Introduction
and Conclusion
Clear Thesis and Overview
Coherence/Use of Transitions
New/Interesting Information
Strong Finish

LANGUAGE
Word Choice
Impact on Audience
Grammar

OVERALL EFFECTIVENESS
Treatment of Topic
Intelligent Awareness of Audience
Achievement of Purpose
Impact on/Connection with Audience

OTHER COMMENTS   Grade:

Puttin' On The Ritz: The Social Speech

TIPS FOR SPEAKERS

Be well prepared. Rehearse your speech out loud to yourself, or a spouse, or a colleague a few times before you deliver it. Try as much as possible to be yourself at the podium. You are usually your own worst critic so don't let every little slip throw you. Just relax and enjoy your audience.
(The Right Honourable JEANNE SAUVÉ, Governor General of Canada)

1. Get the name right. This is the primary rule of the social speech.
2. Social speeches need the same thorough preparation and practice that more formal presentations require. Your friends deserve the best.
3. Use clear patterns for the introduction and thank you, presenting and accepting an award, the tribute, the toast.
4. The microphone is a useful piece of equipment. It responds to firm, precise handling. Don't be afraid of it.
5. Breathing deeply and slowly is the secret of voice control.
6. Good speakers show an awareness of, and respect for, lifestyles other than their own.

Picture the Juno awards with the host celebrity stumbling over the names of the nominees. Later, at a gala reception, you cringe in sympathy as a woman stands to propose a toast and blanks out. It's almost as bad as the time your normally talkative uncle Calen "uummed" and "aahed" his way through a thank you speech to his employees. Why does this happen?

Social speeches are often much shorter and more informal than business or persuasive speeches. Some people assume, therefore, that less preparation is needed. This is not true. If you spend so much time on a class presentation, shouldn't you concentrate more on a speech for your friends? Speeches for special occasions, the introduction, the thank you, the presentation and acceptance, the toast, the tribute, and the entertainment all require diligence and preparation. They also need a sense of the occasion and personal warmth.

Your voice adds that warmth, that feeling of joyous spontaneity. In the section on voice and gesture you'll find exercises to help you develop a fuller range of vocal expression.

The interview with the Right Honourable Jeanne Sauvé, Governor General, shows the graciousness and diligence of a person who has had to make thousands of speeches in her career, many of which were social.

The Only Rule: Get the Name Right

Is your name in this list?

Bourner	Sardella
Tzouhas	Deviatiarov
Praught	Gottlieb
Atagi	Luong
Riel	Mattice
Belliveau	Sernoskie
Ayuyao	Rouse
Kearns	Zaida

These are student names taken from the register of a conference for student council representatives. They reflect a typical cross-section of Canadian names.

Strategies for Tracking Down Correct Pronunciation:

1. **Advance warning.** The president of a retail shoe chain, Arch Heels, asks you to introduce the speaker at the annual sales convention. Your boss hands you a sheet with a few details about the speaker, an expert on orthopedic design, and gives her version of the name. It's an easy one: Haley. What is your next step? It would be a good idea to phone

the speaker to check the background information and the name. Haley looks easy, but is it pronounced Hal-ee like the comet or Hay-lee like the author? If you mispronounce a name in front of 200 people, do they care that your boss fed you wrong information? Check the name.

2. **Surprise—you're it.** Your boss meets you at the registration desk with the news that you're the one doing the introduction. What next? Remember the outline given in this chapter, organize your thoughts, practise your breathing exercises, wait by the door for the speaker to arrive, and check the name as you say hello.

3. **Smooth work.** You're on the stage and the speaker is late arriving. As the regional sales manager outlines the year's success, the orthopedic expert enters and walks to the stage. Slipping smoothly from your chair, you move to one side of the stage, greet your guest in a courteous fashion and *check the name.*

4. **Deceptively daring.** This is the situation that makes even experienced speakers check their pulse rates. You're on the stage, the guest appears before you can make a move, and suddenly you're called upon to introduce a speaker called Haley (or Praught or Ayuyao). You have several choices: guess; do it wrong and apologize (reaping scorn from everyone who knows these strategies); embarrass yourself for life with a remark like "gosh, I've never seen a name like this;" or walk over to the guest, shake his or her hand, and very quietly say, "do you pronounce your name Hay-lee?" Guest speakers always help you out because they know how much you want to get it right.

EXERCISE: Get the Name Right

Group members put two or three names, which they can pronounce, on slips of paper and sign them. Exchange lists and take two minutes to determine the correct pronunciation of the names. Taking turns, each person stands and with enthusiasm and confidence, gives a concert welcome: "And now, let us welcome—Jay Haley!!!" (*tumultuous applause*)

Cities and Towns Also Need Research

Last week, the production crew of a local radio station mocked the new announcer who referred to Gan-ann-ook: that's Gananoque (Ga na nok way) to most of us. It's unnerving to stand up to introduce representatives to a conference and discover that the list of cities represented reads like a quiz in pronunciation. How would you manage with these: Nanaimo, Port Coquitlam, Ucluelet, Tuktoyuktuk, Kluane, Kananaskis, Okotoks,

Esterhazy, Batoche, Fort Qu'Appelle, Dauphin, Gimli, Sault Ste. Marie, Penetanguishene, Etobicoke, Kapuskasing, Stouffville, Percé, Chibougamau, Rimouski, Miramichi, Antigonish, Margaree, Malpeque, Middle Mosquodoboit, Baie Verte, Souris, Port aux Basques? If you are ever in desperate need, try calling your local reference library for assistance.

Never Throw Away an Opportunity

Most of us will never get the Order of Canada, but we will still be touched when someone takes the time to express appreciation of our work or our lives. If you're asked to make a speech, don't throw it away because you are embarrassed. Focus your efforts on the other person and make use of an opportunity that may never come again.

Imagine your grandmother has her 80th birthday, and your family says to you, "Say, you took that course; you make the speech." If you toss the chance away with an offhand remark like "great going, Nana," how can you be sure that there will ever be another time for your family to acknowledge to your grandmother and to each other how much she has meant to you? The effort you take to speak is a tribute in itself.

Be Brief, Sincere, and Spontaneous

Social speeches are short and specific; they pave the way for the main event, wrap up the proceedings, or accentuate an important occasion. If you are well prepared, you can be brief, and the occasion will retain its excitement.

The key to sincerity is finding the appropriate tone. Avoid trite or exaggerated remarks such as "this cherished heritage building," "our valued customer," "this priceless collection." Speak simply and with warmth.

How can you be spontaneous and well prepared at the same time? On social occasions, your audience expects you to know the person you're talking about, and to be enthusiastic. You should not use notes when giving the speaker's name or referring to the recipient of an award. If you need to look at your notes to remember that you are delighted that Fred's work has finally been recognized, your good wishes seem just a little forced.

Research

You get information for a social speech in the same way you do for other types: *Research.* Specific, concrete examples enable your listeners to see the value of a co-worker, or understand the amount of work done by the co-ordinator of the Heart Fund. You must dig for stories, examples, numbers, quotations.

Guidelines for Special Occasion Speeches

Ask family members, friends, and colleagues for details to illustrate your remarks. Support your speech with concrete data. If your grandmother came over as a war bride, recall her experience of getting off the train at a northern settlement.

If your classmate is receiving the George Wicken Writing Award, find out who Wicken was and why the award was established.

Research involves common sense as well. If you're presenting an award to a blind co-worker and it's appropriate that you mention the fact that she's blind, what's the most considerate thing to say? How do you find out? Ask the person. That's research.

Patterns for Social Speeches: The Added Touch

Social speeches follow the same general outline given earlier:

- seize the attention of the audience and outline your topic or thesis;
- deliver the goods;
- reinforce your point and make a strong finish.

The added touch is a very specific *signal*. The audience is given the cue to applaud, the guests are given the words of a toast, the spectators are given the motion to start.

The Introduction

Your job is to establish a link between the audience and the speaker. You should make the speaker feel welcome in that group and give the audience notice that they will benefit from the speech to follow. You can help the speaker by outlining the appropriate credentials and creating an atmosphere of anticipation. How long should the speech be? In most cases, two to three minutes.

Pattern

1. **Address the audience.** What does everyone in the room have in common? Are your students interested in employment possibilities, or club members who share an interest in hot air ballooning? Establish some common ground for the meeting.
2. **Direct attention to the speaker.** Mention his or her name early and repeat it two or three times in your introduction. Remember, the audience is hearing it for the first time and wants to know *who* the speaker is, *what* his or her credentials are, and *why* they should listen. You might want to ask the speaker what credentials to mention or decide for yourself which are appropriate. Do not overdo the praise or your guest may be embarrassed.

The surprise technique: If your guest is well-known or you wish to surprise your audience, you can use the mystery approach; give all the significant detail and then say, ''and now, may I present....''

3. **Focus on the topic.** In the example on page 72, Sheri Alexander made sure her co-workers would pay attention. She wanted them to know that tropical disease is as much a matter of concern for travel counsellors as it is for doctors and adventurers.

4. **Give the signal—in this case the name.** Use your voice to build to a climax, and incline your head to the guest or make eye contact. Then, speaking *directly into the microphone,* give the cue: ''It is with pleasure that I present Dr. Fred Azouz.''

A Special Note on Titles

When you introduce the Governor General, you'll refer to ''Her Excellency, the Right Honourable...,'' a county court judge as ''The Honourable Judge...,'' the archbishop of the Greek Orthodox Church as ''His Eminence, The Archbishop of the Greek Orthodox Church of North and South America,'' your English teacher as ''Dr. Kent,'' and the police officer in charge of community relations as ''Staff Sergeant Pulford.'' How do you find out the correct form of address? A telephone call will do it. If you're stuck, ask the person directly, or his or her executive assistant. Do *not* rely on popular opinion. If you are introducing a couple, check both their names. The library system has books that list various forms of address in current usage in Canada.

The Thank-You Speech

These are short but sincere remarks. Your preparation may involve advance research or on-the-spot attention.

Pattern

1. **Reason for thanks.** If you are thanking a speaker, your function is clear. You need to mention one or two points from the talk that you found helpful or interesting, and remark on them *without* repeating or interpreting the original address. If you are thanking a conference or group coordinator, you need to give the audience a specific idea of this person's function. Statistics are sometimes amusing: 386 air flights booked, 2300 meals planned and ordered, 465 name tags lettered.

2. **Try for a balance of brevity and sincerity.** Whether you have advance notice or must plan your thanks in two minutes, take time to make thoughtful, specific remarks. By concentrating on the concrete, you avoid rambling on in the attempt to create something significant. You can be quick and still be good.

''Time is not the same for the speaker as for the audience. To the speaker it is too, too brief for what he has to say. For the audience it is a grim foretaste of eternity.''
(Marshall McLuhan)

3. **Signal—Thank the person by name** and pronounce it correctly. Finish your speech, then turn and applaud the person concerned.

How do you thank an unpopular speaker? If someone has come to justify the government's plans to locate a chemical dump in your region, that person is not going to get a pleasant welcome. Your job is to thank the government representative for the time spent with your community group. You may not like what was said but you can appreciate the time and effort that individual gave.

Presenting an Award

To make a good speech of presentation, you need to combine your natural good will with some clear organization. Why was the local owner-operator of a cycle shop voted citizen of the year? If the announcement of the award is the thesis, what follows? Three supporting reasons, which must be supported with anecdotes, quotations from neighbours, telling examples. If you can give clear cause for the award the audience will not only understand the worth of the recipient, they will also enjoy the pace and quality of your speech.

Pattern
1. **Set the stage.** Discuss the background or history of the award and the conditions concerning its presentation.
2. **Talk about the recipient.** Use concrete examples discovered during your formal or informal research. Be sincere in your remarks. You may point out how you know the award winner but do not go on about yourself.
3. **Explain the award or gift as a symbol of the group's esteem.** Even though you all contributed 50 cents each for the present, you need not dwell on the gift itself. Be sure that everyone knows that it is an honour for you to present the award and you are paying tribute to the recipient.
4. **Give the signal.** Ask the cycle-shop owner to come forward, give her direct eye contact, and perhaps a personal word. Then, speaking directly into the mike, address a few words to her, such as, "All of us think that Regina is a happier, more free-wheeling place to live because of your contribution to our community. It is with pride, Kit Creek, that we present you with this award."
5. **Help the recipient with the gift.** It takes practice to speak into the microphone, make eye contact, shake hands, and present a gift in one smooth motion. It is even harder to accept a six-kilogram Inuit sculpture wrapped in three metres of paper and secured with an entire roll of tape. *Help with the gift.* In many cases, it is expected that the person being honoured will unwrap the gift; in that case, and depending

Rick Hansen is made a companion of the Order of Canada by Governor General Jeanne Sauvé.

on its size, a small table would help. You, the presenter, might assist by holding the gift while the recipient unwraps it. The person preparing the parcel should show mercy by wrapping shoebox style—box and lid are wrapped separately, and the lid comes off quickly. Years of watching unsuspecting and flustered people trying to support an overweight prize with ·one hand, shake with the other, and trying to remember what to say, prompts this plea for assistance at awards time.

Accepting a Gift

No one expects you to have an acceptance speech planned and rehearsed; that might seem just a little too slick. If you have been notified in advance, prepare a general acceptance but try to keep your words spontaneous. If you are completely surprised, keep in mind that the audience must hear every word you say, and take the opportunity to make a short, warm thank you.

Pattern

1. **Express appreciation in simple, direct language.** Be sincere and pause, if necessary, to think.
2. **Don't apologize for being unprepared.** You are not supposed to be prepared. Enjoy the honour, and be yourself.
3. **Thank the key people who helped you.** Most successful efforts are the result of teamwork. Share the praise but do not list every person you've ever met.
4. **Again, thank the organization presenting the award.** A citizenship award is established to recognize and promote community awareness and participation. You might mention this to the audience.
5. **Open the gift if that is expected.** A group may have gone to much trouble to find something to delight you. Join in the spirit of the occasion by unwrapping the object as gracefully as possible.
6. **Accept the gift and say thank you once more.**

The Tribute

A speech of recognition follows the same pattern as that given for presenting an award or gift. Simply omit reference to the concrete object and focus on public recognition.

In recent years, students have asked for help with a far harder and sadder type of tribute, a funeral speech. In formal terms, this is a eulogy. Traditionally, it dwells on a person's attributes and accomplishments, and is sincere and simple. If you look at the example, you will see a speech that outlines the characteristics, achievements, and charm of a very devoted teacher and scholar, George Wicken. It was delivered at his funeral by his colleague, David Kent.

A Funeral Tribute to
GEORGE ROBERT GRENFELL WICKEN

Given by Dr. David Kent
Toronto
December 1984

George Wicken was many things, variously accomplished. He was a remarkable person in so many ways. His profound sympathy for other people—that reaching out from himself to the other we all experienced in relating to him—that sympathy was at the heart of his teaching gifts.

...He was a trusted, valued person. No one who knew George was neutral about him. Everyone liked him. The presence of students here today tells us in what affection he was held by those he taught.

But reaching out is tiring when combined with such a sense of responsibility and duty as George had. In his book on the Canadian poet Wilfred Campbell, itself a major contribution to scholarship on Canadian literature, George writes of the "personal spiritual experiences in nature" that Campbell's poetry describes. His annual vacation at the family cottage must have brought George the kind of self-losing experiences which gave him peace, rest, and renovation. This communion with nature allowed George to return to the academic wear and tear each August with renewed vigour.

Sympathy, or identifying with the other, is probably related to George's love of the theatre, too. He delighted in organizing a theatre outing for students and faculty. The greatest artistic ecstasy for George was attending a Broadway musical; in it were joined language, drama, and his other love, music. We all loved to listen to his reports of a trip to New York.

George was a sociable person. He loved to tell jokes. He certainly had a sweet tooth. He took great joy in rounding up tardy faculty and heading for Hospitality Place, the college restaurant. Or, he liked to use his powers of persuasion to convince us that there could be no more convivial place for lunch than at "Feathers," the English pub on Kingston Road. One of my dearest memories is the sight of George moving from cubicle to cubicle in our department office, greeting each one of us and stopping to chat as long as we wished.

Above all, George was a teacher. He loved teaching. It was his vocation, his calling, his fulfillment. Out of that love came ideas, innovative techniques, and imaginative exercises, all of which he generously shared with his colleagues. We all remember his students eagerly searching out information about their dates of birth in the newspaper microfilms or becoming genuinely excited about doing research on the Confederation poets.

...Another remark George made in his book on Campbell is pertinent here, and a reflection of his own personality. George wrote: "Commitment to others, through loyalty and love, can give life meaning." In that sentence George is still speaking to us now, speaking of commitment, dedication, enthusiasm, love. Those are values he embodied.

...If we could have told George something a few days ago, I wonder what each of us would have said. I'd like to end with a quotation out of a letter Leigh Hunt

(Continued)

sent in 1822 to Joseph Severn, the man who was caring for the dying English poet, John Keats. I think some of us might have wished we could have said this to George, even if through an intermediary. I say it now on behalf of us all:

"Tell him (Hunt wrote to Keat's friend) that we shall all bear his memory in the most precious part of our hearts...

Tell him that the most sceptical of us has faith enough to think that all (of us) are journeying to one and the same place, and shall unite somehow... again face to face, mutually conscious, mutually delighted. Tell him he is only before us on the road, as he was in everything else, and that we are coming after him."

My students, however, have generally needed help preparing shorter, more personal statements. Obviously, it's a hard thing to do. Dave Duggan, when asked to make a speech for a friend killed in a car accident, said he wanted to do it because his friend's parents had asked him to, and he wanted "to say in public how special he was to all of us." To prepare a funeral speech, consider the following suggestions.

Pattern
1. **Honour the person.** Your speech, even if it's hard on you, is a way of paying tribute to someone you liked and will miss. It is a chance to say how much that person meant to you.
2. **Outline how you knew the person.** Were you friends at school? Did you go to the same camp? Establish your connection for family and friends who don't know you.
3. **Select specific memories that bring your friend before you.** Your job is to give yourself and others a glimpse of your friend and his or her speical qualities. Choose one or two good memories: a joke shared, a camping trip, the time you were lost in Paris and your friend decided to spend the night in the police station. It's all right to smile as you remember the good times; it's a way of keeping that person in your life.
4. **Keep it short.** Don't strain your emotional reserves. Present your memories, say that you will miss your friend, and *finish*. That's often the hardest part. Dave ended his speech with the words, "John Robert was my best friend and I will miss him always."

   What if you cry? Crying is acceptable. More than that, it's common and can even occur in what should be happy speeches. In the case of funeral speeches, you should be prepared to feel the constricting of your throat that means tears are on the way. If you *practise*, you will know which words and phrases are likely to trigger tears, and you will be ready. Pause. Breathe. Coach yourself—"relax," "breathe," "you're okay." If you have to cry, do so; people will wait. This is a hard speech, but the students I know have been determined to do it well.

The Toast

Toasts are ceremonial tributes given on special occasions; the most common are a toast to the Queen, an impromptu toast, and a wedding toast. Making these speeches can be a pleasure if you remember to brainstorm, plan, and practise.

It is essential to include the signal and the verbal cue.

Patterns

A Toast to the Queen.   The Protocol Office of the Secretary of State provides a simple outline for a toast to the Queen. The person proposing the toast raises his or her glass and says, "Ladies and gentlemen, will you rise and raise your glasses in a toast to the Queen: the Queen—la Reine."

The toast usually occurs after dessert and before coffee.

An Informal Toast. Often, when you're present at a celebration or dinner, someone will say, "Let's have a toast," and look straight at you.

1. **Be Prepared.** If you can form three-part plans as you stand in line for a concert, you are used to being ready. During the soup course of a celebration dinner, you will think of one or two thoughtful and complimentary things to say. Good speakers spend much of their time thinking. They also think of the cook; make your remarks brief, or speak *after* dinner; never let a fine meal cool.
2. **Relax.** Take the opportunity to express appreciation or congratulations; focus on the person you are speaking about. Your friends look forward to your words, so enjoy yourself.
3. **Breathe.** This is an informal setting but you still need a well-modulated, resonant voice. Breathe.
4. **Make one or two sincere remarks.** If your friend has just received her pilot's licence, wish her adventure and freedom. Compliment the sense of adventure and attention to detail that led to her success. You might use stories from her training to illustrate the challenges she faced.
5. **Give the signal.** Raise your glass and address your friend directly: "Congratulations on your pilot's licence, Valerie. We wish you good weather and smooth landings: [*the cue*] To Valerie."

The Wedding Toast.   *Warning:* This is the most abused speech of all. Too many people think that if they mumble five minutes of semi-humorous anecdotes they'll have a toast. To compound their nervousness and lack of preparation, they listen to friends who advise them to have a drink to "loosen up." Too often, they lose their grip on any sense of organization or good taste they might have possessed.

The toasts are the highlight of a wedding celebration and as a speaker it is your job to plan carefully, rehearse thoroughly, and *party later*.

1. **Making a plan.** You need a three-part plan: introduction, body, and conclusion. The usual theme of a toast is the happiness of the bride and groom and you may choose to wish them happiness in their family life, their travel adventures, and their new business partnership, a log-cabin building venture. You may choose instead to outline how they complement each other in their emotional responses, their strengths, and their skills. He's a champion rider, and she composes music.

    Remember, at a wedding reception, you are facing competition from servers clearing dishes, and a hum of excitement. You need a very strong plan so that the guests can follow your remarks easily.

2. **Framing your speech.** What sort of grabber can you devise that will make a strong framework for your speech? Could you use the words of a song that the couple considers special? What about a day they celebrate? If you start with such a reference, your conclusion is already set. Refer again to the song, the special day, the way they met, and your speech will have unity.

    One father proposed a toast by noting that the wedding day was also the anniversary of the birth of Martin Luther King, Jr. He went on to wish his daughter and son-in-law the qualities that King embodied: courage, vision, and love.

    Design a wedding toast the same way you would any speech and make sure that the thesis is especially strong so that everyone will hear and understand you.

3. **Research.** If you are a friend of the couple, you will have a good source of anecdotes. If not, you have to research. Ask them for ideas, telephone family members, ask business colleagues or friends. If you are a friend of either the bride or groom, be sure to collect stories about the other person as well. A good toast should be well balanced.

4. **Consider the wishes of the bride and groom.** Talk to them about their toast, ask what they wish or do not wish included. If one or both of them have children, how will you refer to them? In a toast I recently heard, the speaker included the wishes of the children for their mother and new father. What about parents who have remarried? In the example that follows, a bride wanted her friend to toast *all* her parents. The speaker thoughtfully referred to the four people by their first names instead of outlining who was married to whom. If you're going to use personal anecdotes, make sure that you do so in friendship. Not every groom wants people to know he's afraid of lightning.

5. **Share the toast with others.** If three of you are close friends of the couple, share the speech. One of you can give the introduction and conclusion, and provide opportunities for the others to contribute.
6. **Write down the punchlines to jokes.** If there is one time you will be sure to forget a punchline, it is in front of your best friends. If you tell jokes, make sure they are funny and do not insult anyone present.
7. **Practise.** Your friends deserve the best. Make notes, practise, revise your speech, make new notes. People tend to get flustered on emotional occasions, so it's a good idea to take along an extra set of notes. I once lost mine in the excitement of getting to the church on time.

A TOAST TO THE PARENTS OF THE BRIDE
by Kimberly Mitchell

Change is inevitable and with change comes growth. Over the past thirteen years I've watched Lisa go from a "I'll try anything once" child to a serious, thoughtful woman. I don't think Lisa could have grown this much if it hadn't been for her family, especially her parents. They nurtured her as a child, watched her flourish with their love and care, and even helped her when she didn't know she needed help. Occasionally she was helped when she least wanted it. Like the time her father knew she had it for the boy behind the meat counter, and he decided to do his rendition of Quasimodo behind the shopping cart—just to get his attention. But, most of all they have given her their support. No matter what she has done, no matter what life has thrown her way, they have always been behind her, and she, in turn, has always been behind them.

Lisa really is one lucky person—she has an extended parent plan. She has four different people guiding her, four people sharing their love for her, and four different sets of ideas which have enabled Lisa to broaden her outlook on life. I'd like to make a toast to Lisa's parents and all the ways that they have helped her—to Marie-Ange, Raymond, Dawn and Patrick, Lisa's parents.

8. **Refer to the bride and groom by name.** Give them each equal billing and refer to each in his or her own right. Avoid references like "We wish Howell and his wife much happiness." They'll both be happier if you talk about, "Howell and Liane." Make eye contact with the bride and groom and let them know you are honoured to play this part in the ceremonies.
9. **Give the signal.** When you have given your friends the best gift possible, a perfect toast, give the verbal cues that everyone needs:

   Please join with me in a toast to the bride and groom.
   [*raise your glass*]:
   To the bride and groom—Liane and Howell.

10. **Enjoy yourself.** Like runners, you learn to eat and rest
    after your job is done.

SAMPLE OUTLINE OF A TOAST
TO THE BRIDE AND GROOM

Hamid Pouladvand was asked to give the toast to the bride and groom at the marriage of his friends Farouk and Debbie. The following outline of his speech illustrates how to design a good wedding toast. He researched Debbie's background by talking to her friends.

A Toast to the Bride and Groom

Intro	— greetings to the head table, families and friends
	— favourite song of the bride is "Amazing Grace."
Grabber	— one line is "I once was lost but now I'm found,
	— was blind but now I see."
	— the bride and groom also have visions of what their love can bring for them separately and together as a couple.
Thesis	— we wish them a vision of happiness
	* in their careers
Overview	* in the family they wish
	* in shared adventures
Body	— careers: Debbie — child care and youth worker
	caring, strong, perceptive person
	story of Brett and Duc
	Farouk —technician in a printing firm
	responsible, artistic
	the time we escaped our country by truck and swimming
	— family: family means Love, Fun, Freedom
	(Debbie's time with her grandparents
	Farouk's troubles with school)
	building a new family with many parts
	— shared adventures: love of travel, of auctions, of commitment to each other and personal freedom to grow
Conclusion	We wish them happiness and joy.
	We hope that the love they share will help them build a future of possibility and caring, and that the hard times they have had will make them kinder people.
	I THINK OF AMAZING GRACE AS THE LOVE DEBBIE AND FAROUK HAVE FOR EACH OTHER.
	They are not lost—they have found themselves and each other.
	They are not blind—they see love and a future together.
	We wish them a life of health and joy.
Cue	Ladies and gentlemen, I ask you to rise and join me in a toast to the bride and groom. —TO DEBBIE AND FAROUK, THE BRIDE AND GROOM

The After-Dinner Speech

After you have been initiated into the world of public speaking, someone will call and ask you to provide "the entertainment" at a luncheon meeting or banquet. Generally, you are expected to speak rather than tap dance.

An after-dinner speech provides the intellectual dessert to the meal. It may be informative or persuasive, but its distinguishing feature is your awareness of the audience, and your desire to please or stimulate them. Your audience analysis will help you choose a topic that is appropriate without being heavy. Wildlife biologists working for the National Park System do not need more data on rabies control. However, they may relate to your analysis of the most rabid species of all: the tourist. English teachers, a fussy group, do not need a plea for the protection of the semi-indefinite dangling pluperfect. They are more likely to enjoy a talk like Margaret Visser's "Butter vs. Margarine: An Epic Tale in Five Acts."

"Fighting Back: Techniques for Consumers and Community Organizers," "How to Laugh at the News," "Age and Work: the Positive Side," "What Hope Is There for Runaways?" "Working for Yourself," "Folk Legends, Cures, and Superstitions," and "Women and Music: A Changing Note," all are titles of after-dinner speeches I have heard lately that were well received. Their titles indicate both mood and content.

Generally, speakers enjoy the after-dinner slot. Dave Broadfoot, humourist and star of the Royal Canadian Air Farce, says, "I love it. You're on a good sound system and people are waiting to hear what you have to say" (*Toronto Star*, July 4, 1987).

Pattern

Many topics you are familiar with will make good after-dinner speeches if you follow these guidelines.

1. **Prepare first—eat later.** As the other guests dig into their kiwi cheesecake, you will be calmly getting your thoughts assembled, checking that your notes are handy, and starting your relaxation and breathing exercises. At the same time, you will be talking to the people at your table and finding out more about the audience. Tune in to the mood of the event.
2. **Use an upbeat or offbeat approach.** Find a fresh approach that is appropriate to the group and the occasion.
3. **After-dinner does not mean out-to-lunch.** The intellectual skills of the audience should be respected. Humour is welcome if it works for you and the topic, but a string of unrelated jokes generally falls flat.
4. **Have a challenging but not baffling topic.** The audience looks forward to your remarks but analogies and anecdotes are more suited to this occasion than complicated proofs. If

"**Stand up, speak up, then shut up. The human mind can absorb only what the human seat can endure.**"
(Hugh Shantz,—B.C. Legislature, 1959-1963)

you have a clear intro, body, and conclusion, your listeners will be able to follow you easily.

5. **Fit in with the occasion and enjoy yourself.** Commenting on the occasion, interacting with audience members, and referring to other speakers' remarks are all appropriate. Be friendly and reward the group's taste in speakers (*you*) by giving your best.

Slalom racers do not step into their skis and start a race without checking the course, the conditions, and their bindings *very carefully*. Beginning speakers are often undone because they assume that "somebody else" has made all the necessary preparations. Read this list now (and refer to the series of checklists in Chapter 8). You may not believe that any of these things really occur—until they happen to you.

a) As soon as you arrive, and before the eager hosts volunteer to introduce you to everyone, go to the washroom to calm down, comb your hair, check your clothes, and get ready for a time that is usually charged with anticipation. Halfway through your speech is too late to wonder if your buttons are done up.

b) Ask your host if you can check the microphone. They always tell you "everything's set." It may have been ready two

Speakers' Secret: Never Take Anything for Granted

hours ago when the technician went home. Can you be sure that the video camera hasn't sapped power from the sound system?

It is other people's job to check equipment, but it's your speech. Check it yourself.

c) Now is the time to be sure the slide projector you asked for is the correct kind, that the bulb works, and that the cord reaches the outlet. If anything is wrong, you have time to call for help. Furthermore, you always carry an extension cord in your trunk. (It is a speaker's rule that no matter where the slide projector is placed, the cord never reaches the electrical outlet.)

d) If the necessary equipment is in an audio-visual room, is the door unlocked, and is the technician available?

e) If you are using a film, thread it immediately and test the projector.

f) Close to the moment of proposing a toast, make sure there is something to toast with. If the glasses are empty, ask someone in charge to speak to the head server. Take nothing for granted.

Am I exaggerating? No, I am not. I have seen all of the above. Each speaker has to check things out for himself or herself, and do whatever is necessary to make the speech a success. I once flew to Ottawa to participate in a conference. When I went to check the high-school auditorium where 700 people would soon gather for the keynote speech, I found that the lighting system was being replaced and there were no stage lights! All speakers would be shadowy forms. With 45 minutes to go, I phoned a friend and she went out in the snow to take down the spotlight from her birch tree, part of her holiday decorations. She arrived with the spotlight, oven mitts to hold it with, two extension cords, and garbage bags to catch the water dripping from the still snowy frame. The speakers did a fine job *and* they were visible.

Using the Microphone

As North Americans we're used to movie images of people horseback riding, canoeing, and using microphones. These activities look so simple, we assume that anyone can do it with ease. It's a shock when the horse runs away, or the canoe zigzags endlessly. People approaching a microphone for the first time often look foolish as they crouch low or stand on tiptoe to speak. The mike seems too close, pushing into their faces, so they take a step back and become inaudible.

In order to get used to using a microphone, bring one into the classroom and get used to the following features:

• Microphones are either on floor stands or lectern clamps. In both cases, the necks are flexible.

- Floor stands have a centre join that will loosen to allow you to adjust the height a foot or more. Grasp the stand with one hand, and with determination, unscrew the centre join. Adjust the stand, and tighten.
- Handle the microphone firmly; tilt the head smoothly.
- Once the mike is adjusted, lean into it. It may be hard to get used to this object between you and your notes, but you can do it.
- The sensitivity of the equipment varies. Some mikes are omnidirectional and will pick up your voice from all sides and the top. With others, you must speak directly into the head, at close range. You've seen singers who seem ready to kiss the microphone; they do that to get maximum amplification. You can whisper into good equipment and be heard perfectly if you do it right.
- **Do not tap, or blow and puff, into the head of the mike.** To check for power, say clearly "check 1-2-3-4." This allows the technician to test for volume and feedback.

Practise handling a microphone firmly.

EXERCISE: Microphone Competence

Looking confident, walk to the microphone. Pause, adjust the floor stand, and raise or lower it. Then, adjust the head with a firm smooth action. Speaking directly into the mike, make a brief comment on

a) the ideal weekend;
b) why reggae is so popular;
c) why newscasters always smile so much on television;
d) the need for a law to ban the keeping of exotic pets such as cheetahs and ocelots.

Speak long enough so that you can explore the range and power of the equipment. You will also need to get used to *leaning into the mike,* instead of retreating from it.

This exercise is more challenging if, before you resume your seat, you angle the head, and adjust the stand to an awkward height for the next speaker. Some day, they'll thank you.

Handle the microphone firmly and smoothly. If you appear unhurried and capable, your credibility with the audience is increased.

EXERCISE: Practice Introductions Using the Microphone

Divide the group into partners.

Using information obtained from a newspaper *or* using entirely fictional details, make up a two-minute introduction for each other. Your job is to spend equal amounts of time preparing and practising the introduction.

For the actual delivery, the person doing the assignment should start from a seated position, walk to the lectern, adjust the mike if necessary, introduce the speaker, and greet him or her appropriately. The ''speaker'' should thank the host and start into his or her speech.

Once this is done, reverse roles.

Remember:

- **Design an intro similar to the example in this chapter;**
- **Generate audience interest;**
- **Make eye contact with the guest and greet him or her gracefully.**

''Everybody's Talkin' at Me, Just Can't Hear a Word They're Saying'': Voice and Gesture Exercises

Before undertaking a major social speech, you should develop some skills in controlling your voice and gestures. Speakers need clear, resonant, voices, and significant gestures.

This section deals with specific voice exercises and goes on to investigate how important the words themselves are to the impact of your speech.

What are these exercises supposed to do? They will help to develop

1. **resonance:** the richness, or mellowness of the tone;
2. **volume:** controlled and suitable loudness;
3. **pitch:** the highness or lowness of your voice;
4. **pace:** the speed at which you speak;
5. **enunciation:** the correct formation of sounds and words;
6. **inflection:** the use of your voice to create mood and meaning.

You are not aiming for a constant pace or pitch; you are trying to control your voice; it is a very powerful instrument. By using a variety of pitch, pace, and inflection you will be able to maintain audience interest and determine the sonic shape of your speech.

Breathing Exercises
Where does the air come from?
Have you ever seen a person yell until the tendons in his throat bulged and his temples pounded? The distended tendons, red face, and protruding eyes were all caused by lack of air. *Air* is what makes our voices work, and anyone who breathes only in the back of the throat ends up foolish and gasping as the air

runs out. Try this: assume an angry frame of mind and a threatening posture. Take one big breath and then, berate and threaten an imaginary foe. Do this without breathing again. Did you feel yourself losing control as your air ran out?

Try it again, but this time breathe from deep inside your chest, from your diaphragm. It's a muscle, like a wide elastic belt located just above your waist. You should feel it move if you encircle your middle with your hands. When you breathe, try to get the diaphragm to move.

Now, yell again, breathing from the diaphragm and see if there's an improvement. (Do not prolong this exercise; it's too hard on your voice.)

Rhythmic Deep Breathing

This exercise is used by speakers, actors, and students of yoga to relax and control their air supply.

Sit cross-legged (or sit comfortably in a chair) and keep your back straight. Imagine a thread suspended from the ceiling and attached to the top of your head. That should bring your head perpendicular to the floor. Your back is straight and you pull yourself up in your chest. (Imagine your sternum or breast bone is pointing the way.)

Now, shut your eyes and breathe as the instructor gives the count: *In-two-three-four, Out-two-three-four, In-two-three-four, Out-two-three-four.* Concentrate on nothing but your breathing and the instructor's voice. The exercise should continue for three to five minutes and, as you breathe, your muscles and your mind are getting ready. Many people accompany this exercise with imagining themselves on a beach or other tranquil spot and concentrate on their breathing and the details of their surroundings.

Every good public speaker does this exercise (with eyes open) just before speaking. *Never* speak without relaxing your larynx and setting a breathing rhythm. You can do the exercise in the classroom, at a conference or banquet table, or in your boss's office.

Blowing Out the Candle

There is a candle in front of you. Take one breath and expel it slowly, very slowly and evenly, in order to make the candle flame flicker but not go out. See how long you can maintain an even stream of gentle air.

Neck Rolls

It's hard to breathe if you are too tense to move. Slowly rotate your head and neck to the right; hold it there. Then roll it slowly to centre, pause, to the left, and pause again. Back to centre and repeat. Then gently tilt the neck down, pause, to centre, pause, and up. Pause, and repeat. (Do not rotate your neck and head in a circle; use this exercise instead.)

Million-Dollar Stretch
Stand comfortably with your feet spread. Stretch one arm out in front of you at shoulder height and *reach* for the million dollars someone is holding just beyond your fingertips. Reach as far as you can without bending your body. Do the same exercise to the side, and then switch hands.

Vocalization (or Grunting)
Sometimes your voice clogs and you need to exercise it. Take a breath, make a series of grunts, the kind they use in martial arts just before they clobber you. You can make several series of grunts, each at a different pitch.

Inflection and Pacing

"Where Canadians got the monotone that you're listening to now, I don't know—probably from the Canada Goose." Northrop Frye jokingly criticized his own voice on a CBC radio programme, but his comments are valid. Too often we use the same note for everything we say, and yet it is our voice that gives real meaning to our words. Do you want to express curiosity, determination, outrage? Your voice does it. To develop a vocal range, an exercise that involves a bit of exaggeration is useful.

EXERCISE: Reading to the Wall

Everyone in the group assumes her or his own place *facing* the wall. Try to leave an arm's length between each of you. Then, on a given signal, read the following passage on hypothermia *at the same time, and at full volume.*

Read the passage four times, all simultaneously, but adopt a different persona each time, trying to make your voice express the character. As a judge, you will raise the grave implications of the subject; as a television evangelist you will assure your audience (the wall) that they will go to hell, etc.

Reading #1: television evangelist
Reading #2: the nag (male or female)
Reading #3: the drunk
Reading #4: the airhead—fast as you can, no pausing

(You can also choose to be someone who is spaced out, putting pauses where none should be or a person who prefaces all remarks with "like...you know eh?")

COLD CAN KILL

Still—and this warning must in good conscience be made—cold can kill. Every skier who ventures far from beaten paths must understand the chemistry of cold, as well as the fatigue, exhaustion, and psychology that go with it.

...It is far easier to spot the symptoms of hypothermia in others than in oneself. Whenever you are traveling in a party exposed to brutal wind, damp cold, rain, or wet snow, make it a policy for each skier to watch the others for such symptoms as uncontrollable, slurred or unnatural speech, fumbling hands, lapses of memory, stumbling or lurching, and drowsiness.

...The most important step is to get any hypothermia victim out of wind and rain—indoors, if possible. There strip off all his wet clothes. If it is a mild case, give the skier warm, nonalcoholic drinks. Cocoa is great if it is handy. Or sugar water. Get the person into dry clothes and a warm sleeping bag.

...If a person should lapse into semiconsciousness or worse, try to keep him awake while you supply warm drinks. Leave him stripped and put him into a warm sleeping bag along with another person, also stripped, who is in good health. If a double sleeping bag happens to be handy, put the victim between two stripped skiers, for the skin-to-skin contact is effective.

(ERVIN A. BAUER. *The Cross-Country Skier's Bible*. New York: Doubleday, 1977. p. 93-94)

Newspaper Headlines
Each person brings in a newspaper headline and reads it three different times, each with a different mood or meaning. You can try for various effects from the quizzical to the comical.

Be firm.
In English our voices go down at the conclusion of a statement, and up at the end of a question. Don't they? Some people have a tendency to make statements sound like questions, and they sound very unsure of themselves and the situation. Their discussions sound like this: "Well, I think that first aid is really important? They should have it in all high school health classes? Definitely, I'd be more confident if I knew I could cope with a medical emergency? Translate this series of uncertainties into assertions. "Digital clocks are far easier to understand than the old fashioned kind? Everyone can say '8:15', even small children? However, I wonder if kids understand the concept of time any better, just because they can say the words? When I was younger, and had trouble telling the difference between a quarter *to* eight, and a quarter *after*, I was often late? Today, six-year-olds can say the words but they're still confused? Perhaps being late is an adult hang-up?''

Tongue Twisters Tamed: Exercises in Articulation
"Walking" and "talking" are hard words to pronounce. Familiar as they are to us, they often come out "walkin'," and "talkin'." To get used to enunciating your words correctly, look

in the mirror and exaggerate your face and lips as you do vowel sounds: a—ee—i—o—u, and oo (as in "moon"). Watch the movement of your lips, teeth, and tongue. They, along with your palate, make the sounds; we need to practise articulation that is clear, but not affected.

Say the following words slowly and clearly, giving full sound value to them:

marsh-mallow	crank-case
reek	lolly-gag
tin-tin-nab-u-la-tion	tart
fuzz	Tor-on-to
moon	Iqal-u-it
ratchet	ex-post-u-late
per-am-bu-late	poop

In speaking, it is necessary to *slow down* when you are trying to pronounce a word of several syllables. "Practically" is a good example; in a rush to get it finished, people transform the word to "practickly." Slow down and give each syllable its due: "prac-tic-al-ly." The same goes for words like "megalomaniac," "dis-associate," "antediluvian," "recognize," and "Arctic." You must also watch that you do not insert syllables that do not belong: film, *rather than* fillum; athlete, *rather than* athalete.
Tongue Twisters.   Here are some common and uncommon tongue twisters to practise:

> *Betty Botter bought some butter,*
> *But, she said, the butter's bitter;*
> *If I put it in my batter*
> *It will make my batter bitter,*
> *But a bit of better butter,*
> *That would make my batter better.*

> *How much caramel*
>   *can a canny cannibal*
> *cram into a camel,*
>   *if a canny cannibal*
>   *can cram caramel*
> *into a camel?*

> *I can think of thin things*
> *six thin things, can you?*
> *Yes, I can think of six thin things,*
> *and of six thick things too.*

> *Thirty thousand Thracians threatened Thessaly.*

> *Forty fat farmers found a field of fresh fodder.*

> *All I want is a proper cup of coffee,*
> *Made in a proper copper coffee pot;*
> *Tin coffee pots or*
> *Iron coffee pots,*

they're no use to me;
If I can't have a
Proper cup of coffee
In a proper copper coffee pot,
I'll have a cup of tea.

>   *Flee from fog to fight flu fast.*

Ms. Ruth's red roof thatch.

>   *I'm a fig plucker,*
>   *I'm a fig plucker's son,*
>   *I pluck figs till the fig pluckers come.*

Let us go gather lettuce
Whether the weather will let us or not.

>   *Ours is a sovereign nation*
>   *Bows to no foreign will*
>   *But whenever they cough in Washington*
>   *They spit on Parliament Hill.*
>   (JOE WALLACE, *Joe Wallace Poems*, Toronto: Progress
>   Books, 1981, p.7.)

Theophilus Thistledown, the successful thistle sifter,
In sifting a sieve of unsifted thistles,
Thrust three thousand thistles
Through the thick of his thumb.

Resonance, Pitch and Pacing: Exercises

Swallowing Honey.   By making a conscious effort you can
improve the resonance of your voice. If you do the breathing
exercises and your voice still seems brittle or hollow, pause,
and imagine someone has fed you a large spoonful of liquid honey.
Roll it back in your throat and swallow slowly. Speak again, and
see if the golden richness has reached your vocal cords. If you
experiment, you should be able to alter the mellowness of your
voice several times.

The Stage Whisper.   Have a partner go to the back of the
room. Then, making eye contact, whisper a secret so that your
partner hears and understands the message.

The Rich Relative.   This time your partner is your rich uncle
or aunt. Convince your munificent relative to give you the gift
you want or need. Your reasons must be so convincing and the
gift so wonderful that no one could resist.

Get Thee Hence: A Note on Gesture

If you have seen old movies, you know the melodramatic use

Do you know what this man wants? Gestures and facial expressions enliven your speech.

of gesture favoured by so-called orators and thespians. Clasping their hands in anguish, covering their eyes in shame, averting their gaze in resolution were common. Gesture should be a *natural* use of your body to

illustrate,
clarify,
emphasize.

If you need to show your audience how to position your hands for the Heimlich manoeuvre, how big a drop the stock market took, or how positive you are that your advertising concept will work, use gestures. The only guidelines are to

make them simple,
make them big,
make them count.

Are Canadians uptight? Nancy White, a singer-songwriter heard often on the CBC, describes our national reserve like this:

I've often wondered what it was that made us the Oxford in the shoestore of nations....How come we're not sexy like the French? Why are we embarrassed at parades? Why do we laugh on the inside instead of out loud....[It's] The Operation. I've had it. You've had it.

White outlines the effect of The Operation in a song called "Welded at the Hip." This is an excerpt:

That Canadian's a dear, she's kind and sincere,
But she's welded at the hip.

Chorus: Welded at the hip
So the rhythm gives us the slip,
We'd like to do more on the old dance floor
But we're welded at the hip.

...We can jump start cars, we arrive on time,
Our canoes will never tip,
But we look a little ill when we're in Brazil,
'Cause we're welded at the hip.

In the following exercises, use gestures that seem natural. Avoid the extremes of constant, nervous, jabs and flutters, or the frozen posture of terror.

Opposite Sides. A and B take positions on opposite sides of the room. They have two to three minutes to engage in discussions in which they each have definite views. Concentrate on voice and gesture. Suggestions for discussion follow; augment them with your own.

• A wants to go out for the evening; B wants to stay home.
• A thinks there are flying saucers; B does not.

- A thinks Yellowknife is an ideal place to live; B prefers Acapulco.
- A and B are two crooks planning a robbery. A wants to break in at night; B thinks a daytime plan is easier.
- A thinks B should unplug the boiling kettle; B is sure it's A's turn.
- A thinks television is primarily entertainment; B thinks its function is education.
- A thinks the Beatles were the finest musicians of the 20th century; B knows it was Bob Dylan.
- A thinks cooked vegetables should be served crunchy; B likes them mushy.
- A thinks spring break should be eliminated; B thinks it's essential.
- A thinks you should buy only new cars; B thinks that used cars give better value.
- A and B are going on holiday. A wants a quiet place to read; B lives to dance.

Charades.   This standard party game is ideal for developing significant gestures. Play it in teams using the standard categories of song, book, or movie titles.

Reading Aloud: Poetry, Plays and Children's Stories.
Performing real material gives you the best practice and the most fun when it comes to voice and gesture development. When you read plays or tell children's stories, you use your whole being to convey the drama and the mood—the experience is in your performance. The following titles and excerpts are only suggestions. There are many more for you to find and work with; the skills you refine by reading this material aloud should spill over into your speeches.

Children's Stories to Read. These stories emphasize character, mood, and dialogue. They are available in most libraries and have been performed for college audiences with great success. Prepare for 15 minutes and then perform.

Free to Be...You and Me, a Ms. Foundation Project. "The Southpaw," "Ladies First," and "Boy Meets Girl" are hilarious.

The Paper Bag Princess, by Robert Munsch. All Munsch's stories are full of sound and character.

Plays to Perform in Class. A play by Ken Gass, *Hurray for Johnny Canuck.* This is an uproarious spoof of World War II super-hero comic strips, starring the all-Canadian, Johnny Canuck, Corporal Dixon and his dog Laddie, and the brave Derek Bras D'Or. The characters, the sound effects, and humour make this a good play to use for a dramatic reading with only a little advance preparation.

Saint Joan, by George Bernard Shaw. Joan of Arc, a French peasant girl, was burned for heresy, witchcraft, and sorcery in 1431. Shaw's play shows her courage and youth. At one point, Joan agrees to recant and signs a paper that she believes will bring freedom. Instead, it promises a life of imprisonment. Joan tears up her confession and attacks her oppressors. The following passage can be read loudly and defiantly, quietly and bravely, or sadly and with resignation. Understand what is being said and find your own style.

> You promised me my life; but you lied. You think that life is nothing but not being stone dead. It is not the bread and water I fear: I can live on bread: when have I asked for more? It has no sorrow for me, and water no affliction. But to shut me from the light of the sky and the sight of the fields and flowers; to chain my feet so that I can never again ride with the soldiers nor climb the hills; to make me breathe foul damp darkness, and keep from me everything that brings me back to the love of God when your wickedness and foolishness tempt me to hate Him: all this is worse than the furnace in the Bible that was heated seven times.
>
> I could do without my warhorse; I could drag about in a skirt; I could let the banners and the trumpets and the knights and soldiers pass me and leave me behind as they leave the other women, if only I could hear the wind in the trees, the larks in the sunshine, the young lambs crying through the healthy frost, and the blessed church bells that send my angel voices floating to me on the wind. But without these things I cannot live; and by your wanting to take them away from me, or from any human creature, I know that your counsel is of the devil, and that mine is of God.
> (Bernard Shaw, *Saint Joan, Scene VI*)

Narrative Poetry. The following poems by E. Pauline Johnson, the half English, half-Mohawk poet and performer, Robert Service, poet, traveller, and bank clerk, and James Reaney, playwright and poet, are meant to be read aloud. You might work in groups, each reading a section. Experiment and concentrate on making your audience see and hear the scenes.

> E. Pauline Johnson: ''As Red Men Die''
> Robert Service: ''The Cremation of Sam McGee''
> James Reaney: ''Lake Superior,'' ''Lake Michigan,'' and ''Lake St. Clair'' from *The Great Lakes Suite.*
> Sound Poetry from b.p. nichol and bill bissett is good to experiment with.

Group Sound Poetry—''Salad Days''. Each person selects a vegetable or fruit, and repeats the name over and over, with the conductor indicating pitch, volume, emotion, pace, etc.

Barnyard Melody. The class is divided into three groups: cows, pigs, and sheep. The cows sing ''moo moo,'' pigs croon ''oink,

oink,'' and the sheep bleat ''baa-baa.'' Using the tune usually known as ''Good King Wenceslas,'' the conductor points to each group. When a group is pointed at, it sings its animal sound to the melody, and must stop when the conductor moves to the next. This is a hilarious exercise, and on paper the first two lines might look like this:

BA BA MOO MOO   BA   BA OINK, OINK OINK BA MOO BA   MOO

As well as developing vocal skills, you need to examine the way you look at the world and the words you employ to express your perceptions. The next sections on Changing Life Styles, and Wretched Phrases focus on how what you say reveals what you think.

Words, Words, Words

Opening Your Mind as Well as Your Mouth: Changing Life Styles

Is a boy living with his father considered a family? How do you differentiate between the mother who gave you birth and the mother who raised you? If you are arranging the menu for a national convention, is roast pork a good choice? How do you introduce Danielle March, the wife of your client, Keith March?

These questions are asked to give one message: our lives and social patterns are changing. You should be aware of life-styles other than your own and respect those who live them. Families don't depend on certain numbers or players; birth mothers and mothers are both important in our lives; religious and dietary preferences should be considered at large gatherings, and Danielle and Keith March (alphabetical listing) are at the head table. When you speak in public, a hasty, unthinking remark can hurt or alienate members of your audience. You have a moral responsibility to avoid spreading narrow-mindedness and prejudice, even unintentionally.

How can you become more aware of the way others live? THINK. Thoughtfulness, kindness and *common sense* are what you need.

EXERCISE: Broadening Your Horizons

In groups, discuss one of the following scenarios. At the end of the time allotted, one member of each group should outline the situation to the rest of the class and present the group's response. (This is still public speaking: stand—breathe—make eye contact.)

Scenario #1
Anna and Robert Sanchez objected strongly to the person who said they came from a "broken home." Why?

Scenario #2
Liz Markovich, mother of Simon and Jeanette, spent a long time replying to Renata, an engineer, who remarked, "Oh, so you don't work."

Scenario #3
Your class decides to have a high school reunion for graduates and teachers. You want everyone to attend and bring the people they live with. How do you word the invitation so that all those invited will know their friends and partners are welcome?

Scenario #4
The chairperson of the fund-raising campaign for a youth centre in a large city has used the phrases "surname" and "christian" name four times in the last half hour. You are uncomfortable; what can you do?

Scenario #5
The cabinet minister responsible for housing is on the radio discussing improved licensing standards for people who sell real estate. He, and the representative of the real estate board, also a man, have used the phrase "salesman" fourteen times in a few minutes. They use no synonyms. Is their credibility damaged?

Scenario #6
Dr. Marcia Powers-Dunlop and David Dunlop received a party invitation addressed to Dr. and Mrs. D. Powers-Dunlop. No such people exist. How should the invitation be worded?

Scenario #7
You work in a community recreation centre and need to talk to the mother or father of Mark Beesley. Before you call the home, what information should you get from Mark? To whom will you ask to speak?

Scenario #8
Lin Wah left the meeting in a hurry. During the coffee break, one of the advisory committee asked him how he was adjusting to Canada. Lin Wah was born in North Battleford, Saskatchewan.

Scenario #9
My grandfather was in a rage because the host at a recent movie fund-raiser had asked all the "people in their golden years" to wave their hands. There is more than a euphemism causing trouble. Why was he angry at being singled out by that or any other name?

Scenario #10

My neighbour, Keith Wood, stays at home to care for his son, Jake. His wife, Hope St. Jean, goes to work. Imagine the comments he gets from his child's teachers, his friends, and his family. What attitudes inspire the remarks?

The Difference Between Accepted *Canajun* and Wretched Phrases

In speaking, we make a distinction between words that are colloquial or familiar, and those that are overused or clichéd. As Canadians we have specific regional expressions; two good examples come from the Pacific and Atlantic coasts. In Vancouver, a musician says she is "raging around" to get ready for her show; in Dartmouth, a friend complains that his neighbour is driving him "foolish." We also have original Canadian words such as "zamboni," an ice-surface machine, and "tikinagan," an infant's cradle carried on the back. Our pronunciation of such words as lieutenant (leftenant), and khaki (kharki) renders our speech distinctive.

In his book, *Canajun, Eh?* (Don Mills: General Publishing, 1973), Mark Orkin pokes fun at our peculiar way of saying the days of the week: "Sundy...Mundy, Chewsdy, Wensdy, (Weddens Day on the CBC), Thursdy, Fridy, Sadder Day (or Sarrdy)." He also demonstrates the versatility of "eh," the verbal trademark of Canada. According to Orkin, it can "express a question, a statement, surprise, contempt, bewilderment, a dare, and disbelief." Although most speakers try to limit the use of this all-purpose interjection, it's hard to get rid of, eh?

But what prompts us to use redundant expressions? Have we become so used to repeating ourselves that we can't help saying "that shirt is fuchsia in colour" or "the crew was surrounded on all sides by the fire." We know the shirt isn't fuchsia in smell, and it's hard to be surrounded on some sides only, but our speech is replete with redundancies. What's wrong with the following expressions? What should you say instead?

circulate around
true fact
8 a.m. in the morning
proceed ahead
irregardless
repeat again
disappear from view
genuine leather
at this point in time

Do you know expressions that, although not redundant, have

become so trivialized by overuse that they are almost meaningless? Here is a list of phrases considered by one group of students to be annoyingly overused. How many more can you add?

>the long and short of it
>I know where you're coming from
>I personally think
>really very unique
>have a nice day
>political promises
>interfacing with others
>in point of fact
>world class
>the bottom line
>state of the art

When we consistently overuse words our speech becomes bland. That is the danger of using clichés, words that once had significance but now mean little. It is more difficult to search for expressions that accurately convey our meaning but the increase in clarity and impact is worth the effort. The following passage shows how clichés make our speech trite and how concepts as well as vocabulary can be clichéd.

>*Michelle was an ideal young woman. She was quick as a wink, neat as a pin, and pretty as a picture. She had only one bad habit: she used her credit cards faster than you can blink an eye.*
>
>*One day she entered an electronics store. Cool as a cucumber, she purchased a VCR and gave her credit card to the clerk, who was as cute as a button. When he phoned for confirmation, he turned pale as a ghost and flipped his wig. "Your card is refused!" he gasped.*
>
>*Michelle called the credit office and talked a mile a minute but their hearts were hard as stone. The VCR remained in the store and Michelle took off like a shot, crying her eyes out. "Have a nice day," the clerk called after her.*

Me, Myself, and I

The confusion among I, me, and myself is of epidemic proportions.

Use *I* as a subject, as you would *he*.

>*I am going to have a sauna.*
>*He is going to have a sauna.*

If the subject is compound, it makes no difference.

>*Annie and I are going to have a sauna.*
>*Annie and he are going to have a sauna.*
>*Annie and he and I are going to the sauna together.*

Use *me* as an object, as you would *him*.

Wayne Gretzky sent me his old hockey stick.
Wayne Gretzky sent him his old hockey stick.

If the object is compound it makes no difference.

Wayne Gretzky sent Annie and me tickets to the game.
Wayne Gretzky sent free tickets to Annie and him.
Wayne Gretzky sent tickets to Annie and him and me.

Some people persist in saying:

Gretzky sent tickets to Annie and I (instead of *me).*

This is like drinking tea with your little finger crooked; it seems terribly correct but it's WRONG.

The most wretched phrase occurs when people try to disguise their confusion about ''I'' and ''me'' by substituting ''myself'' for everything:

Cher sent an exercise video to my sister and myself.
My friend and myself are going to Yarmouth next week.

You would never say ''Myself is going to Yarmouth.'' So why say ''My friend and myself are going''? You can only use a reflexive (myself, yourself, himself, ourselves, etc.) to clarify or emphasize a subject or object already mentioned:

I made it myself.
He did it himself.

This matters. Your audience does not expect faultless grammar, but they expect you to know the basics. You might have doubts about your bank manager if she can't do simple math; why should your audience believe you if you can't get basic grammar right? If you study any grammar text you'll be able to find the sections that apply to speaking especially. Luckily, spelling *doesn't* count (except on visual back-up). Study the sections you know you need help with, and ask your instructor for feedback if you are unsure about your grammatical strength.

Speech Assignment: Social Occasions

The following situations can be written on cards and placed in an envelope. Each speaker draws one of the assignments. If the speech is a reply to another person's remarks (as indicated), you should consult with each other to get details clear. Alternatively, you may choose your topic.

Your assignment is graded for two things:
a) the speech itself: research, design, and delivery;
b) your feeling for the situation, and the degree of sensitivity and

courtesy you bring to
the occasion.
Dressing for the occasion
may inspire your delivery;
some groups have held
their classes in college
restaurants or hospitality
labs to create a social
atmosphere.

Scenarios
*Supply details appropri-
ate to your field of study.*
1. Vote of thanks to the
chairperson of the
United Way cam-
paign of your com-
pany. He or she
made the goal of
$500 000.
2. Introduce a guest
speaker, an expert on
tropical diseases.
Your audience may
not be generally
aware of how the
topic affects their
industry.
3. A toast to the
founder of your com-
pany. The founder is
now deceased, but
his family is at the
banquet.
4. Presentation of a gift
to someone in your
agency or business
who has done the
most to improve busi-
ness in the last year.
5. Reply to the above
speech.
6. Thank the representa-
tive of a major airline
who has spoken to
your group. (You
choose an appropri-
ate topic.)

7. A toast to your
grandmother on her
80th birthday at a
large party in her
honour.
8. Thank your local
Member of Parlia-
ment for coming to
hear the complaints
of your group. The
government position
is not popular.
9. Present a gift to your
course coordinator in
appreciation of his or
her efforts during
your time of study.
10. You have been to a
grade-eight class to
speak on a career in
your field. They pres-
ent you with a gift.
Thank them.
11. Introduce the head of
the French trade
delegation who is
going to speak to
your group on a
topic you devise.
12. Thank the head of the
French trade delega-
tion and present her
or him with a Cana-
dian souvenir.
13. The provincial pre-
mier is a guest at a
convention. Thank
him or her for the
government's work in
promoting your field.
14. At the annual
national conference
you are to make a
speech and presenta-
tion to a colleague
who has recently
received the Order of
Canada. He was

honoured for his outstanding contribution to the cultural life of Jews in Canada. You are to congratulate him on behalf of your group, and wish him well on his upcoming trip to Israel. (You have no way of knowing the religious and political backgrounds of the many people at the gathering.)

15. You are proposing a toast to the parents of the bride. You are her friend. Toast her original parents who are both present, although they are divorced and in the company of different spouses. The bride also wants her step-father, with whom she has lived for eight years, mentioned. The two couples are seated at separate tables and are pleasant to each other.

16. Reply—you are the mother.

17. Reply—you are the father.

18. You are a member of a sports team that has been together for eight years. You have all become close friends. The coach of the team is moving to New Brunswick and you have been chosen to present the gift to her or him at the farewell dinner. Your team members want you to combine humour and sincerity.

19. You are making a presentation to a member of your staff who is blind. She is an excellent worker, and you want to mention her disability but not overemphasize it.

DELIVERY TECHNIQUES TO REMEMBER

1. Practise your approach. Make your walk to the front of your room part of your presentation. It should help set the mood.

2. Get your voice to perform. Use tone, pace, volume, and pitch to create variety, emotion, enthusiasm.

3. Work your audience. Build audience rapport and involvement. Use their responses, verbal and nonverbal, to enhance your speech.

INTERVIEW

Her Excellency
The Right Honourable

Jeanne Sauvé

Governor General of
Canada

March 30, 1988

Madame Jeanne Sauvé is well known for her work as a broadcaster and journalist, as a Member of Parliament and cabinet minister, the Speaker of the House of Commons, and our present Governor General. Her investiture on May 14, 1984 marked the first appointment of a woman to this office. Her insight, intelligence, and grace make her a distinguished speaker, and as Governor General she has given hundreds of addresses here in Canada, and internationally.

Q
How do you prepare for a speech?

A
I usually sit down with my speechwriters several weeks in advance of the engagement and outline the subject and direction I would like to take in a certain speech. After they have prepared the first draft, I work on it myself for a few days to make sure that what I wanted to say is accurately reflected, and then meet with them again.

Q
What qualities in a speaker touch you?

A
I think sincerity is always important in a speaker. The person has to believe in what they're saying. And of course, they must be well prepared. A sense of humour is always a good asset under any circumstances, especially if it is a long speech.

Q
You are introduced and thanked hundreds of times a year. What makes a good intro?

A
If an introduction is well prepared and people have taken the time to get the facts and pronunciations right, it usually comes off well. It also helps to keep it reasonably short. People really don't want to hear your entire biography before you stand up. It's always useful to point out anything in a speaker's past that would draw a direct link to the group being addressed. For example, if I were going to talk to a group of Girl Guides, the person doing the introduction might want to highlight the fact that I was a Guide as a girl. It sort of establishes a common ground between the speaker and the audience.

Q
Do you get nervous?

A
I think there are very few public speakers, regardless of how experienced they are, who don't feel a little nervous before giving a speech, but I'm reasonably comfortable speaking in public.

Q
Is it difficult to address large groups? Was it hard to open the 1988 Calgary Winter Olympics—in front of 53 000 people in the stadium, and millions of television viewers?

A
It's always a little more intimidating speaking to a large group, because you have to be a bit more formal, but really the practice is the same whether you are speaking to 20 or 200. Yes, it was a bit overwhelming to open the 1988 Winter Olympics. My major concern was with the sound system, and whether or not my voice would be heard well enough in that huge stadium. There was also a time lag between the time I spoke, and the time the sound actually came out, which made it a little difficult.

Q
Do you use notes?

A
If I'm speaking at an informal occasion I usually like to have notes prepared. I don't always use them at the podium but I find it's useful to read them over a few times before I start to remind myself of all the points I want to cover. On formal occasions, I will usually read directly from my notes, and I think if it's done in a relaxed manner, it can be just as effective.

Q
When did you start to do a lot of public speaking?

A
It started in elementary school when teachers asked students to speak to the class. I suppose I really began public speaking back before I was a broadcaster. I used to travel a great deal on behalf of *Jeunesse Etudiante Catholique* in my twenties and thirties, and that usually entailed a lot of speeches. Of course, as a politician, I was called upon often to speak, and have never really slowed down since. In this current office, I can give as many as three or four addresses in a day during my travels.

Q
You seem to be so familiar with each organization you address. How do you prepare?

A
After so many years in public life, you get exposed to a lot of groups and organizations, and you become familiar with what they are all about. If I feel I'm not totally sure of what a group stands for, or their specific objectives or background, I'll have one of my advisors prepare briefing notes.

Q
As Canadians, are we good speakers?

A
Yes, I think Canadians have had some brilliant orators. We've certainly had some outstanding political speakers and there are a number of Canadians in other professions on the speaking circuit who are very effective in presenting their message. We have a very well-educated population with many outstanding national and international personalities. There's no reason why we shouldn't be good public speakers —and in two languages!

Q
Is there a speaker you especially admire?

A
The best was Don Jamieson [a Newfoundland politician, 1921-1986].

Q
How many speeches do you give a year?

A
I give literally hundreds of speeches a year, about ten or fifteen of which would be major addresses of twenty to thirty minutes. The groups range in size from ten or twenty people to thousands. The average is probably two to three hundred.

Q
Is there a speech of yours that you consider a favourite?

A
I suppose the welcoming address to the Pope seems to have drawn the greatest response. People wrote for years after, asking for copies of the text.

Q
What unexpected things have happened to you as a speaker?

A
Things happen to speakers all the time. I once gave a convocation address that was about twenty pages long. I was rolling merrily along to about page eighteen and when I finished reading it, and turned it over, much to my horror, the final pages were missing. It took a few minutes of fussing around on the podium before someone finally discovered them in my portfolio. The audience is surprisingly understanding when things go wrong; after all, we're all human.

Q
What advice do you have for novice speakers?

A
Be well prepared. Rehearse your speech out loud to yourself, or a spouse, or colleague a few times before you deliver it. Try as much as possible to be yourself at the podium. You are usually your own worst critic so don't let every little slip throw you. Just relax and enjoy your audience.

Her Excellency, The Right Honourable

Jeanne Sauvé
Governor General of Canada

Speech: Address on the arrival of His Holiness Pope John Paul II in Quebec City

In the following speech Her Excellency welcomed Pope John Paul II on behalf of all Canadians. Her remarks honour him as one of the world's religious leaders while keeping her secular position clear.

Most Holy Father:
On behalf of all Canadians, may I bid you a very warm welcome and assure you of our profound respect and best wishes for the success of your pastoral visit.

We welcome you as a pilgrim of compassion and peace. You seek to touch the innermost hearts of all men and women who care about the spiritual future of humanity.

The world is in disarray. Children seek fathers; and adults, leaders. Perhaps what is most lacking is the audacity of the prophet. We receive you as a prophet, for—more than any other contemporary leader—you have been successful in identifying the causes of our universal anxiety. You proclaim that we need fear no longer, that we must act boldly, that God is not dead and that the harm we inflict on each other comes from our inability to retain the primacy of the soul and to capture the spiritual essence of existence.

Here, native people and descendants of the founding nations await you; so too do men and women who have come here from all over the world seeking freedom. They will understand your call to the heart on behalf of others, and especially on behalf of those denied even the right to hope. They will understand you because they have discovered that the first fruit of peace is freedom—the freedom that we can show the world as proof that we have learned to live together here in genuine sharing and brotherhood.

If young people, on whose commitment you so often call, can find in your words reasons for belief, for life, we could ask for nothing better. They are much in our thoughts because they have more cause for concern than we. Perhaps they wonder whether, wearied by our moral confusion and burdened by our busy lives, we have too long neglected to identify the values we profess, and to instruct them in the true meaning of freedom. This is the light they seek.

What reassures us and has the power to move the young is the boldness, the selflessness and the tranquil assurance of your message which—even when pastoral concern leads you to strong proclamation of God's Word—reveals your love for us.

Most Holy Father, it would not be appropriate for me to interpret your call to men and women of all faiths and convictions only in terms of my own. However, I can ask all my compatriots to reflect on your words. Their message is both vital and universal.

When the tumult surrounding this unprecedented visit has died away, we will be able to delve further into the mystery of an encounter which, we will come to realise, was not like any other. It will leave in our very soul a permanent mark—a mark such as Jacob received after wrestling with the Angel—which will prompt us, at your instigation, to join the unflagging ranks of those who pray, and those who work for peace!

Your Holiness, Canada salutes you and thanks you. Canadians will be with you throughout your tour and, at each stop, you will have evidence of their gratitude and affection.

Sept 9, 1984
Quebec City

Speech: Special presentation of the Order of Canada to Mr. Rick Hansen

On March 29, 1988, Her Excellency honoured the vision and courage of Rick Hansen.

Mr. Hansen, Distinguished Guests, Ladies and Gentlemen:
There are few Canadians who have touched the minds and hearts of their compatriots as profoundly as has the recipient of this morning's Order of Canada. It is therefore with a reflection of the pride and gratitude of an entire nation that I have invested you, Mr. Hansen, as a Companion of this distinguished Order and thank you for the tremendous inspiration and enlightenment which you have provided us through your remarkable journey around the world. Your personal commitment and vision, and your tremendous sense of tolerance and humanity have enhanced us all, providing us an opportunity to reveal to

ourselves and the world all that is best in us as a people and as a nation.

We have been moved by your tremendous courage, and by your determination to prove through your own example what can be accomplished by one man alone. I think particularly of the effect that you have had on the children of the world, how your journey has altered their perceptions and offered them a hero whose triumph is not founded on the glories of war, but on a mission of tolerance and of peace. The good will engendered through your Man in Motion tour will be reflected a hundredfold in the actions of those you have inspired. We are proud as a nation to call you a native son, and to recognize all that you have accomplished through this, an investiture of the highest Order of the land.

Mr. Hansen, there are few people in this world who can reflect upon their life at such a young age as yours and be secure in the knowledge that they have made the world a better place, but such is the incredible magnitude of your accomplishment. We look forward to that which you shall accomplish in the future, of the continued benefits to be realized through your leadership and initiative, and we congratulate you most sincerely on the honour bestowed upon you this day.

March 29, 1988
Ottawa

OUTLINE OF A SOCIAL SPEECH

Name: _____

Date of Speech: _____

Purpose Statement: _____

INTRODUCTION
    Grabber:

    Thesis:

    Overview:

BODY
    Supporting Argument #1

    Supporting Argument #2

    Supporting Argument #3

CONCLUSION
    Reference to purpose (thesis):

    Summary of main steps:

    Zinger:

SELF-EVALUATION FORM

This form is to help you evaluate your own speech. It can be kept private or shared with your instructor or peers.

Type of Speech: _____

Name: _____

Title: _____

Date: _____

DELIVERY
Physical Presence

Did I make eye contact with others?

Was my posture natural and appropriate?

Was I aware of my facial expressions and hand gestures?

Were there any distracting mannerisms that I was aware of?

Did I feel good?

Could I feel an energy exchange with my audience?

VOCAL DELIVERY

Was my voice under control?

Did I sound confident?

Was I aware of breathing calmly?

How was my enunciation?

Did I manage to avoid um's and ah's?

Did I sound interested/excited/committed?

How did my voice sound to me?

DESIGN AND CONTENT

How well did the introduction and conclusion work?

Did the framework unify my speech?

Was there a natural progression from point to point?

Did my notes keep me on track? Did I use them?

Did the audience seem to understand the organization of my speech?

Was the information clear?

What was the energy level of the conclusion?

What would I change the next time?

What worked very well?

OVERALL EFFECTIVENESS

Did I connect with this audience?

Did I achieve my purpose?

What do I remember most about making the speech?

What unexpected or unforeseen things happened?

What am I most pleased about?

OTHER COMMENTS

Grade:

PEER EVALUATION FORM

Peer evaluation should be done in a constructive and supportive fashion. The speaker may choose people to do assessments or they may be assigned alphabetically. Some groups maintain the same speaker/assessor teams for the entire course; others change for each speech. The instructor may wish to see this evaluation before it goes to the speaker.

Type of Speech: _____

Speaker: _____

Title: _____

Assessor: _____

Date: _____

DELIVERY
Physical Presence

Did the speaker maintain eye contact?

Did she or he establish a rapport with the audience?

Were gestures natural and effective?

VOCAL DELIVERY

Did the speaker sound convincing/spontaneous/excited?

Was his or her voice clear and loud enough?

How did you respond to the speaker's mood?

DESIGN AND CONTENT

Did the introduction interest you?

Did the overview give you an indication of the main proofs?

Did the speech flow easily and logically from one point to another?

Was the conclusion strong and memorable?

Did the conclusion reinforce the thesis and main points?

What was the thesis of the speech?

OVERALL EFFECTIVENESS

Did you learn something new or worthwhile from the speech?

Were you moved by it?

What was the most outstanding part of the speech?

What changes do you recommend?

What parts should the speaker definitely keep?

OTHER COMMENTS

Grade:

EVALUATION FORM

Type of Speech: _____

Name: _____

Title: _____

Length of Speech: _____

Date: _____

Legend: S = SUPERIOR   E = EFFECTIVE   NW = NEEDS WORK

DELIVERY
Physical Presence
> Eye Contact
> Rapport with Audience
> Posture
> Gestures
> Use of Notes
> Appropriate Use of Audio-Visual Support Material

VOCAL DELIVERY
> Naturalness/Spontaneity/Enthusiasm
> Clarity
> Variety (Tone, Pitch, Pace)
> Volume
> Absence of Verbal Tics (um, ah, okay, like)
> Sense of Control and Calm

DESIGN AND CONTENT
> Use of Framework for Introduction and Conclusion
> Clear Thesis and Overview
> Coherence/Use of Transitions
> New/Interesting Information
> Strong Finish

LANGUAGE
> Word Choice
> Impact on Audience
> Grammar

OVERALL EFFECTIVENESS
> Treatment of Topic
> Intelligent Awareness of Audience
> Achievement of Purpose
> Impact on/Connection with Audience

OTHER COMMENTS

Grade:

If I Only Had the Words: Meetings, Debates, and Presentations

TIPS FOR SPEAKERS

1. Skid School lessons also work for speakers under pressure:
   - don't panic
   - take your foot off the brake and steer
   - steer in the direction you want to go.
2. Meetings are often arranged before they start; do the necessary preparation, and check in with others.
3. Your voice can influence an edgy or hostile group. Do you sound reasonable?
4. Language should communicate information. Use jargon only with insiders, and don't use bafflegab at all.
5. Prepare questions that might be directed to you during an interview or presentation. Can you reply using a clear plan?

What happens when someone asks you to speak at a meeting or unexpectedly puts you on the spot? How do you react to pressure? "I don't—I forget nine tenths of the English language" was one person's response. That's the reason for this chapter. It outlines how to participate intelligently in business and community gatherings. The exercises will help you become adept at thinking and speaking on your feet. You will improve your reaction time, and develop the skills needed to present, debate, respond, sell—whatever you need to handle the occasion well. Thirteen situations are presented; each one involves specific communication skills and each involves speaking extemporaneously.

At the end of the chapter is a speech by David Nichol, President of Loblaw International Merchants. Nichol has won worldwide recognition for his marketing of "President's Choice" products, and his success owes much to his flair for talking to people and winning their trust. The interview gives a hint of his enthusiasm and drive.

First, acquaint yourself with some general guidelines. They apply to meetings, interviews, and community presentations. Once you have practised the techniques of thinking on your feet, choose the specific situations you most want to learn about. The more you experiment, the better you'll get.

Skid-School Lessons

Have you ever panicked when your car started to skid? Quick responses can save your life. Skid schools, driving programmes that teach you how to handle treacherous situations, force you to perform well under stress. The rules are simple, and they also apply to speakers facing slippery conditions. The primary rule is *avoid the skid*. Predict the situation and take precautions to avoid going out of control. However, if you do start to slip, follow these three rules taught at skid-school courses:

1. Don't panic.
2. Take your foot off the brake and steer.
3. Steer in the direction you want to go.

Translated into speaking terms, they read:

1. Don't panic: Breathe—get oxygen to your brain.
                Pause —assess the situation.
2. Get your brain in action. *Think* of what you want to say. *Breathe*.
3. Have a thesis, one main idea, and *steer* toward it.

For those people who do a few spins before they acquire the knack, the best thing about Skid School is the large expanse of uncluttered lawn. The classroom is your protection. Don't worry if you freeze the first time; follow the rules.

Audience Awareness

What do we mean by the word audience? They are the government representatives you are meeting with about zoning regulations, the town council you have to convince about a group home, the service club for whom you are arranging a tour, the employees coming in for the annual convention, the hiring committee interviewing you. Audience analysis is essential *every time*.

Good speeches falter when they are inappropriate for a specific group. Take the time to learn about your audience. Then assess what strategy will work, what expertise or experience you have to offer to the discussion. Dean Alan Hockin, of the Faculty of Administrative Studies at York University, says that to be leaders in business, graduates must communicate well within their organizations, with consumers and advocacy groups, and with government agencies, frequently at a very high level. Imagine yourself outlining a merger to the groups Hockin mentioned. How would the same information be handled in each case? What differences are there in the way you handle a financial statement at a directors' meeting, and at an annual general meeting of shareholders?

Although details may change, there are similar challenges in every field. How does a community worker explain a change in policy to staff members, clients, local politicians? Is there a difference in the way you outline a new drug therapy to the parents of your clients and a reporter?

Pace

"Pick up the pace!" "Watch your pacing!" "Pace yourself!" Actors and athletes use this phrase all the time to refer to the tempo of their activity. You can use it too if you remember this simple acronym; it describes four techniques that work. Most of them are good common sense—the very thing you need when pressure builds:

P Preparation and Practice
- Prepare for the unexpected by imagining various scenarios and your reactions.
- Be aware of pertinent issues.
- Read background material *in advance*.
- Get to meetings and conferences early enough to mingle. Go to receptions and ask, "what do you think are the big issues facing us next year." You can allude to these in your remarks and really get the attention of your listeners.
- Practise organizing in a hurry, developing clear thesis statements and three-part plans.
- Practise making your point using a conversational tone.

A Attention
- Pay attention to the mood of the meeting.
- Pay attention to the remarks and needs of others.

C Connection
- Build rapport. Eye contact, body language, verbal remarks, conversations during the break, all help you to *connect*.

E Evaluate
- Evaluate your own contributions. Did you do as well as you had hoped? What were the good points of your presentation? What can you improve? Did you feel in control? Did you enjoy yourself?
- What can you improve next time?
- How did others do? Were there techniques you admired and can adapt to your own style?
- Were you prepared? Did you understand enough of the background politics to grasp the situation?
- What will you do differently next time? What will be the same?

EXERCISE: One-Minute Impromptus

"What will replace croissants as the trendy thing to eat?" When people throw odd questions at us, we often try to stumble through. We ramble and go off topic. This exercise reinforces the lessons you learned for the impromptu:

a) stop and think;
b) get a main idea;

c) put it across;

d) give an example;

e) finish!

Remember to challenge yourselves. Develop a list of fresh topics by working from a local newspaper. You can decide if everyone will use the same topic or choose from the list. Each speaker should have one minute to prepare.

Handling Unexpected Questions on the Spot

Questions that you didn't anticipate or are slightly offbeat may upset you. If you forecast questions, you have a good chance to develop and rehearse your responses, but if you're caught off guard, the following technique works.

1. **Pause.** Don't panic at a silence. A pause is good for your image. You appear thoughtful rather than glib, and show respect for the question. Get comfortable with a pause.

2. **Clarify.** Ask questions to clarify the matter. This gives you more time to think. It also ensures that you are on the same track as your questioner. If I ask, "when is civil disobedience acceptable?", you may ask me to clarify what I mean: nonviolent actions? in time of peace or war? public or private objections?

   If it is clear that you are totally ignorant, *don't bluff.* You'll sound as if you are. Admit you're not sure, (you needn't apologize) and promise to get back with an answer within a specific time.

3. **One point plus amplification.** Make a clear statement, with some examples or explanation. In effect, this is a thesis and one or two supporting points. (Three *would* be excellent, and in accordance with previous directions, but this is under pressure.) *Do not babble. One point is sufficient.*

4. **Involve the other person.** Stockpile phrases that you can use to elicit a response from the other person. This helps you to discover if your answer was appropriate, and gives you breathing space. It helps turn a potential grilling into an exchange of ideas. "Does this hold true in your situation?", "will this suggestion work?", "does this match your experience?" are standards that work well.

> **"Look wise, say nothing, and grunt."**
> **(Sir William Osler)**

EXERCISE: Handling Unexpected Questions
on the Spot

In this exercise, it is important that the class be supportive.

a) Together, class members generate a list of questions. These are placed on a table.

b) The group chooses partners. One person goes to the table, and selects a question that his or her partner will find challenging, yet manageable, and asks the question.

   Alternative method: The instructor selects a student, then points randomly at a question.

c) The speaker answers from his or her desk. Arranging the desks so that class members can see each other may help the group focus their attention.

d) Practise the technique. Answers can be one or two minutes long, sufficient to experiment with the process. Remember that this is a learning experience; the instructor may take time to coach the speaker through the four steps: pause, clarify, make one point plus amplification, involve others.

Students generated these questions:

- What should be done about people who push on buses and subways?
- How can individuals support black South Africa's fight for freedom?
- Should the government give more funding to college and university students?
- What do you think of daytime drama (the soaps)?
- Should there be more choice in your college program?

- Should sex be taught in elementary schools (grades 1-8)?
- Is there an improvement in the number of nonsmoking areas?
- What's wrong with capital punishment?
- Who would you choose as a Canadian hero and why?
- How far should free speech go?

- Should students work a minimum number of years between high school and college or university?
- How do you feel about impromptus?
- What do you think about people who help themselves to bulk food while shopping?
- What was your favourite disaster?
- Are summit meetings worthwhile?

- How much does the Royal Family mean to you?
- Should surrogate mothers be forced, if necessary, to give up their babies?
- Should escort services be allowed to advertise in the yellow pages?
- Is Christmas too commercialized?
- Is Sunday shopping a benefit or a detriment to society?

- Do celebrity concerts influence world events (e.g., Live Aid, or the benefit to mark Nelson Mandela's 70th birthday)?

- What part of Canada is the most intriguing place to visit?
- Do you like the latest developments on *The Young and Restless*?
- Is drug abuse common in professional sports?
- What do you think of condom commercials on public and private TV stations?

- If a major disaster occurred, and you had approximately one hour to live, how would you spend your time?
- Should the minimum driving age be raised?
- If you had to cross rough water, would you prefer to use a sailboat or a canoe?
- Knowing what you know now, if you were to live your life over, what would you do differently?
- Should a woman have a baby if she wants children but does not want to get married?

- Do high performance cars have a place on our highways?
- Do you dress for comfort or for success?
- How do they get the gooey caramel into the Caramilk bars?
- Should you lie in job interviews?
- Should young offenders accused of major crimes be charged under the Young Offender's Act or in adult court?

- Is there a place on television for garbage interview shows such as Geraldo Rivera's?
- Cheat sheets or students' salvation: what's your opinion of "Coles Notes"?
- Is big-name wrestling a sport or a soap opera? Why is it so popular?
- Should we have no-fault insurance?
- What one course would you die for?

- What one course would you die in?
- Should funeral services advertise in the media?
- What's a good way to answer the following question in a job interview: "Are you planning to stay with this company or is this position just a stepping stone?"
- Should police require a search warrant to enter a building or should the law be changed to allow them to enter on suspicion?
- Does an accent make a difference in your chances for success?

- Would you rather be called "bland" or "pushy"?
- Is Elvis alive?
- If you found bags of money on a highway, would you try to return them?

Do you feel more confident about thinking on your feet? Have you acquired skills to help you present ideas clearly on short notice? You are ready to apply these lessons to the following situations.

Meetings

The mark of a good meeting is whether anything comes out of it. And that's usually a function of being organized in terms of knowing what you want to accomplish, and having a plan to get there.
(DAVID NICHOL)

Good meetings are like sailing. If you take good material, assemble it carefully, get an experienced person at the helm, chart your course, enlist crew members who know their job, use the wind to your advantage, and react well, it's smooth sailing. But if your preparations are sloppy and the crew uncooperative, you will be either becalmed or exhausted from zigzagging your way nowhere.

In order to discuss the components of good meetings, we are going to look at two examples. The first is a national meeting of Levi Strauss & Co. (Canada) Inc. Called the Special Integration Sales Meeting, it was held in 1987 to integrate the sales and marketing functions of Levi Strauss and GWG, both owned by the same parent company since the early 1960s.

The second example is a community meeting coordinated by the Ad Hoc Committee to Stop Sexual Assaults in Guildwood Community, part of Metro Toronto. Citizens, concerned about the number of rapes by strangers in their area, met several times to arrange a public meeting.

How did both groups start?

Aims and Objectives

Why are you meeting? What goal have you set? Too often, people hear the word meeting and start to spout jargon: quorum, rules of order, closure, point of order, minutes, seconders, limiting debate. These steps in the *process* should not obscure the *purpose*. When you plan the meeting, establish a philosophical base; it's your purpose or goal. You will also have objectives; these are tasks or actions.

If you cannot identify goals, the meeting may be unnecessary. *Never* call a meeting that is not required. Everyone's time is valuable; it is insulting to spend 35 minutes in transit when there is nothing to discuss. Small details can be handled by mail or conference calls.

John De Shano, President of Levi Strauss & Co. (Canada) Inc., stresses that, in order to work well, the company espouses three values: openness and honesty, mutual respect and trust, and teamwork. The purpose of a Special Integration Sales Meeting of Levi and GWG sales representatives was to build a team founded on those goals, and to exchange a vast amount of information. As De Shano says, ''there was a lot of history to get rid of." The meeting sought to build one team composed of equals; thus, internal competition would be eliminated, and retail service increased.

The task was related to the goal—information exchange. De Shano jokingly called the meeting, "everything you always wanted to know about the other brand but nobody would ever tell you before."

Diverse community groups often require more time to establish a common purpose. The Guildwood group identified four goals:

1. to allow women to move freely at all times of the day and night;
2. to turn anger into future action;
3. to express sympathy to the victims and families;
4. to inform and educate people about sexual assault on the street, and how to maximize their own safety and that of others.

Their specific objectives were to have each person:

1. take away a practical idea to increase his or her own safety, and that of others;
2. commit herself or himself to one action related to personal or community safety.

Once your aims and objectives have been clearly identified, the next steps follow logically.

Setting the Agenda

When setting the agenda—the items of business to be considered—it is customary to call for input. Once the tentative agenda is set, you may wish to circulate it (by telephone, fax, or mail) for approval, and then make any necessary adjustments. It is important to distribute the agenda well before the meeting. Some items need brief descriptions, reasons for consideration, or supporting material. If you append background material, be sure to note the pertinent agenda item. Allow yourself enough time to get translations done, and remember to supply them whenever necessity or courtesy dictates.

At the beginning of the meeting, it is customary to restate the objectives of the meeting. You may ask if the agenda as presented is satisfactory; at this point others may add items.

Doing Your Homework

"I could hardly keep up. Everyone except me knew what was going on." This common cry of the novice means that he or she thought going to a meeting meant remembering the date and location. For meetings to accomplish anything, the participants must be ready. Have you read all the previous minutes?

Have you thought about what you've read? If you have a suggestion in regard to one of the agenda items, have you done preliminary research and prepared a brief summary, with copies to be distributed if necessary? Have you noted pertinent questions? Too often, I have sat at meetings where the business discussed seemed to be a surprise to some people. Do your homework. You can't speak if you haven't thought.

If you are new to a group, if there are factions you need to deal with, if you want support for your ideas, spend time on the telephone. People need time to consider suggestions, and an informal call can prepare the groundwork for a productive meeting. Often, this preparation determines the outcome of the meeting; it is naive to neglect it.

Setting the Scene

Picture yourself at your first big meeting. You leave home early, shovel out the driveway, drive 25 minutes through rush-hour traffic, find a parking space, and crowd into an elevator. When you emerge on the ninth floor, what do you need? A friendly welcome, the smell of fresh coffee, introductions, and directions to the room. Good visuals, flowers, or a thematic display also create positive feelings.

Meetings start well before the chairperson calls for order. An atmosphere of courtesy and efficiency goes a long way to starting things well. When you coordinate events, pay attention to details. There are entire marketing books that tell you how to *win* the client. They outline such "techniques" as gourmet snacks and table linen in the national colours of foreign clients. These are just good hospitality. Remember Maslow (refer to the chart in Chapter 3), and take care of people's needs; make them feel important as soon as they walk in the door. The feeling of good will thus created will extend to the meeting itself.

Parliamentary Procedure

Who chairs the meeting? The person who called the meeting (in business the boss) often does, but there are other possibilities. If you recall the discussion of leadership in Chapter 4, any person can act as leader or chairperson. The position can be rotated, or a skilful leader can be asked to guide the procedure. This allows the head of the organization to participate and speak more freely.

Parliamentary procedure and common rules of conduct are given in great detail in *Robert's Rules of Order,* the most widely used guide of this type in Canada. However, the following brief outline may help you to follow or conduct your first meeting. With luck, it will start and finish on time, deal with matters intelligently and decisively, show respect for the rights and needs of all members, and accomplish something positive.

Sample Agenda

a) Opening
   — call to order, welcome, introductions by chairperson
   — check on quorum (a majority of members eligible to vote [50% plus 1] unless otherwise stated in bylaws). This is necessary for voting, making motions, etc.
   — presentation of agenda
b) Approval of minutes
   — approved as read, corrected, or written (is it a wise use of time to read minutes that were circulated?)
c) Reports of elected officers
   — corresponding secretary's report
   — financial statement given by treasurer
   — president's report if required
d) Reports of standing committees
   — standing committees report in logical order or in the order they are listed in the bylaws
   — motions arising from the reports of officers or standing committees are taken up immediately
e) Business arising from the minutes
   — any question arising from the minutes or shown as carried over from the last meeting
f) New business
   — correspondence that requires action
   — disbursements of funds
   — additional new business: members may introduce further items or can move to address any matter before the group
g) Program
   — program items in order: each should be introduced and outlined by one person. The chair will then open the discussion.
   — Motions may be made by the person introducing the item or by any member. Amendments are made and the vote taken. This should be an efficient procedure:
      all in favour;
      all contrary minded (a reasonable alternative to ''all opposed'');
      all abstentions;
      the motion is carried (defeated, tied).
h) Further business
   — chair asks if there is further business before adjournment
   — date of next meeting is usually set
i) Adjournment
   — this is done by motion and vote or general consent.

Putting Ideas to the Meeting

1. **Obtain the floor.** Address the chairperson by his or her official title and wait to be recognized.

A group presentation on marketing strategies for industrial equipment.

2. **Make a motion.** Begin by saying, "I move that...." Make your statement clear and concise. Write it out ahead of time if it is involved. To be sure it is recorded correctly, pass a written copy to the recording secretary; e.g., "I move that the college consider observing Groundhog Day (February 2) with a one day holiday."
3. **Seconding a motion.** An idea must be seconded before the floor is open to discussion.

Speaking in the Meeting

You will quickly learn the correct procedures for speaking in a meeting. Such things as addressing the chair, making succinct motions, and asking for clarification come with experience. However, it requires good communication skills to listen to what is being said, *and* what isn't, to present your own ideas clearly with thesis (your suggestion) and overview, followed by brief supporting statements. Remember that although you are sitting, you are making a speech. Your presentation must be well-thought out, and rehearsed if necessary. Meetings are groups in action and good members know and perform the functions outlined in Chapter 4.

Communication Patterns

Personality and purpose determine the communication patterns of meetings. Look at the diagrams below and discuss what is happening in each situation. How will the communication pattern affect the members of the group and the results of the meeting? How effective is each in the short term and in the long term? How do seating arrangements set the tone for the group, and influence discussion?

Communications Patterns

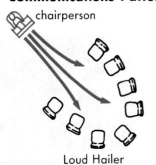

Loud Hailer

Old Pals

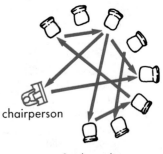

Spiderweb

Business involves people; whether the product is processed steel or health care, people and ideas are most important. And business leaders are unanimous: good communication skills are

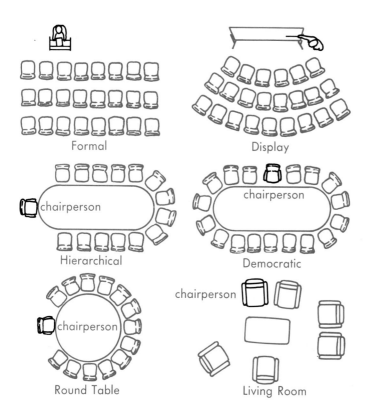

Formal

Display

Hierarchical

Democratic

Round Table

Living Room

essential. David Nichol says that people convince him about a concept by

> *Having their arguments well marshalled, being able to communicate on an emotional level.*

Don't Read to Me!

There is nothing more futile or alienating than watching someone read a report. There are human beings in front of you—talk to them. As John De Shano says:

> *Don't read to people! Don't stand up in front of four people or four hundred and read to them. It's insulting. Hand it to them. Let them read it. Then ask if they have any questions. Talk to them.*
>
> *Have notes: don't get lost, but whatever you do, don't read to them. It's a personal insult for people to read to me. I know how to read. Tell me how you feel about it. Talk to me.*

You may gather from De Shano's outburst that people often read in meetings. They do. Perhaps they think it adds authority to their reports. It doesn't. It's boring. Save reading for those occasions when you have to agree on the exact meaning of a sentence: then use your reading and reasoning skills appropriately.

Keeping on Track

It's easy to start off on topic and end up on a totally unrelated subject. We can plot a discussion of health costs like this:

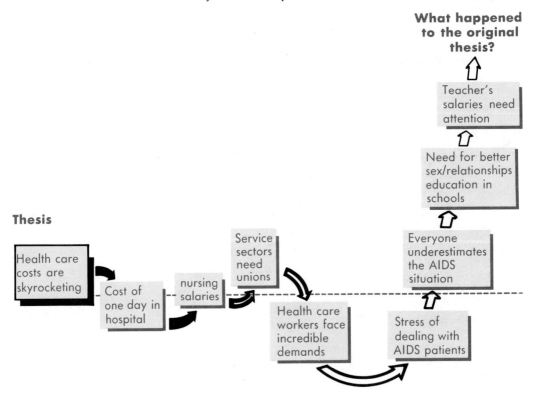

When do you bring people back to the matter at hand, and when should they be given time to explore? If you set goals for the meeting, you can assess if they are being met by the discussion. Avoid being too quick to rule people off topic; sometimes you may be so task-oriented that you are unable to perceive the potential value of the discussion. However, if neither the needs of the group nor the purpose of the meeting is being satisfied, you (as chair or as member) can steer the group back to the topic of discussion. Use a courteous reminder such as, "that brings up possibilities I'd like to ask you about later. Could we finish with this item now."

Remember, we all get off topic; our own diversions only *seem* inspired.

Covering a Lot of Material

Some chairpersons, when faced with many reports or papers, establish that they will focus on three or four points from each. They can call for areas of concentration or establish them arbitrarily. Similarly, the meeting can divide into groups, spend some time on particular papers, and then highlight the significant parts to the committee as a whole.

Groups who, because of distance, meet infrequently often use these methods to make handling of routine material more efficient. Obviously, critical or contentious issues have to be handled differently.

Convincing Others

Follow the rules for all good speeches.

- Analyze your audience.
- Research carefully.
- Establish your thesis and overview in a three-part plan.
- Marshal your supporting arguments.
- Use ethical, emotional, and logical appeals.
- Use eye contact and body language to communicate.
- Avoid rambling and unnecessary apologies or self-deprecation.
- Deal with the suspicions or criticisms of others *before* they do, and put things on your own terms.
- Make your point and *stop talking*. The hardest part of making impromptus is knowing when to stop.
- Use good group communication skills and get into the right frame of mind. Some people are sought-after for committees because they make meetings productive events.

EXERCISE: Mock Meetings

a) Divide the class into groups; you may organize yourselves around vocational interests.
b) Form an imaginary company or organization, assign yourselves appropriate roles, and decide upon a reason for meeting.
c) Draw up an agenda and include any supporting materials.
d) Wearing nametags to identify your role, participate in a mock meeting, showing good speaking and group skills. The chairperson will use a reasonable form of parliamentary procedure.
e) Groups can work simultaneously or present their meeting for the class. Evaluation should be done by each group for its own performance.

EXERCISE: Communication Patterns

a) Each group of five or six people is given a ball of wool and a topic of general interest (bulk-food stores, liquor at sports events, bodybuilding, vegetarianism, how to get rich, etc.)

b) The discussion should last three to four minutes during which the participants pass the wool from one person to another in the order in which they speak (Jane talks; when Thanh follows her, he gets the ball of wool; as soon as Kim starts, the wool passes to her, etc.).

c) At the end of three minutes, observe the pattern created. Do some people have more strands of wool than others? Does the number of strands relate to their function or to an imbalance in speaking patterns?

The Eating Meeting

You have invented a new safety helmet for cyclists. The owner of a chain of cycle shops is in town for a conference, and invites you to lunch with her and her marketing director. This is more than a meal; this is an eating meeting. Here are some pointers gathered from people who "do lunch," and from students who have served them.

- Be punctual.
- Try to relax.
- Get rid of your coat and boots.
- Introduce yourself and shake hands (see p. 135 for the Great Canadian Shake).
- Show concern for others—a little social interaction.
- Eat moderately and drink little or not at all.
- Be organized—have your notes in your jacket or at hand in your briefcase: no fumbling.
- Be sure to have a pen.
- Have written or mental notes about your questions or concerns and consult the notes to make sure all are covered.
- Consulting notes shows you have shown the others the courtesy of preparing. This is no time to pretend indifference.
- Try to anticipate questions and have answers ready.

Now a word on table manners. Your manners are as much a part of your image as your clothing and grooming. If you need a refresher course, have your grandmother check you out. It's unnerving to realize suddenly that you don't know which is the bread and butter knife. You will always get by watching the most experienced member of the group, but eating meetings are popular, and you will be more at ease if you acquire appropriate manners.

Remember, too, that your server is important. Do not clank your glass with your cutlery, and *never* call anyone except your mother "DEAR."

GREAT CANADIAN QUIZ III

Real Canucks will know the following expressions. Select the correct answer or definition for each of the following.

1. The Latin version of our national motto
   a. *semper ubi sub ubi*
   b. *a mari usque ad mare*
   c. *injuria non excusat injuriam*
   Translate it into one of our two official languages.
2. *Castor canadensis*
   a. a laxative popular in pioneer times
   b. a recent line of fishing gear made in Red Deer, Alberta
   c. the beaver, symbol of Canada
3. Sugaring off
   a. a new treatment for diabetes
   b. a process used in maple syrup making
   c. motto of a Calgary diet clinic
4. Arctic char
   a. a variety of salmon found in northern waters
   b. a Baffin Island domestic
   c. a green leafy vegetable, popular in Yellowknife
5. Tidal bore
   a. a deep cleansing laundry detergent
   b. any Maritime politician
   c. the high tide that enters the Bay of Fundy
6. The Group of Seven
   a. a financial conglomerate that controls western oil
   b. an internationally famous lacrosse team from Montreal
   c. a group of modern painters, founded in 1920
7. Sourdough
   a. the devalued Canadian dollar
   b. a fermented bread dough used in rough baking
   c. a bad-tempered cook
8. Potlatch
   a. a West Coast Indian celebration
   b. a dime-bag
   c. Canadian for the lid of a saucepan
9. Fiddlehead
   a. the name of a literary magazine published in New Brunswick
   b. an edible fern
   c. a Yehudi Menuhin groupie
10. Avro Arrow
   a. a high performance car manufactured in Tofino, B.C.
   b. a light crunchy chocolate bar
   c. an advanced supersonic interceptor jet aircraft

(Continued)

11. Chinook
    a. a warm wind in Western Canada
    b. an Eskimo toast
    c. an undesirable person
12. Ceilidh (*kay-lee*)
    a. a traditional Gaelic gathering for song and story
    b. a type of grasshopper
    c. a large stick used to frighten off aggressors

To test yourself further consult:
John Robert Colombo, *Colombo's Canadiana Quiz Book* (Western Producer Prairie Books, 1983).
John Fisher, *The Complete Cross-Canada Quiz and Game Book* (McClelland and Stewart, 1978).
Sandra Martin, *Quizzing Canada* (Dundurn Press, 1987).

Answers: Great Canadian Quiz III

1. b, "from sea to sea," "d'un océan à l'autre"
2. c
3. b
4. a
5. c
6. c
7. b
8. a
9. b
10. c, programme cancelled in 1959
11. a
12. a

Jargon and Bafflegab

Draw left while we do an upstream ferry; then do a crossdraw to pull us into the eddy.
(Canoeing jargon)

Insert the program disk into the drive, select Floppy Disk A with the mouse pointer and drag it on top of the Floppy Disk B icon.
(Computer jargon)

Jargon is the language of insiders which is used almost as a short form to discuss common interests. Every industry uses it; movie theatres don't have commercials, they have "corporate trailers." When is jargon appropriate? If your objective is to present your ideas clearly and convincingly, *everyone* has to understand. Describing your company's computer software to school trustees as, "this multi-tasking software offered by ComputerWhiz, which allows both an XTRA-based zowie and a 930-based whatzit to execute concurrently," is inappropriate, nothing less than self-aggrandizement.

Professor Richard Coe of Simon Fraser University writes:

Properly used, jargon allows precise, efficient communication among specialists. But use becomes abuse when those specialists (or any-one else) directs jargon at people likely to be confused or intimi-dated rather than enlightened by the technical terms. Whether jargon...is an effective use or a pernicious abuse of language depends on context and audience.

As a speaker, you should listen to yourself and others to make your words accurate, lively, and descriptive. If you find jargon interfering with real communication, get rid of it.

Bafflegab is worse; it is the piling up of words, especially long, impressive ones, to avoid actually saying anything. Bafflegab includes such devices as euphemism, the prissy substitution of less specific language for direct words. Thus, you are not fired, you are "dehired," "released," or "nonretained." A fence becomes a "nonecological boundary" in the words of the National Capital Commission, and Expo '86 terminology included "guest relations facilities" (toilets), and "security hosts" (site police). Richard Coe calls this abuse doublespeak:

> People use doublespeak to sell you something you don't really want, to intimidate, to impress—and to evade responsibility. One way or another, to cheat in such a way they can't be held responsible.
> ...Because the very act of using language implies an intention to communicate information, doublespeak (which either communicates misinformation or no information) is an abuse of language.

If you listen closely, you'll notice that the phrase "at this point in time" is a warning light that bafflegab is being used. A public official, put on the spot for an explantion, attempts to bluff his or her way through with a line such as

> *Although it is important to interface with the media in a significant mode, it is imperative that I interact with my peers at this point in time prior to releasing meaningful information on this overload situation.*
> Translation: I'm not talking now.

Examples of bafflegab are found everywhere. Fred Doucet, a senior adviser to Prime Minister Brian Mulroney, denied that the Mulroneys had a nanny. Rather they employed a staff member who "interfaces with the children in a habitual way." Airline officials tell their customers, "we're in a flight overload situation." *Translation:* the airline has sold more tickets than the plane has seats.

Avoid bafflegab; it is a pompous, deceitful way of talking. If you have nothing to say, admit it.

> **"All his speeches would read both ways, so that he could interpret them as he liked: so whichever way things eventuated, he was always right."**
> **(T.C. Haliburton)**

EXERCISES: Bafflegab and Jargon Decoded

1. Decode the following; the first five are proverbs, the last is a book title.
   a) "Individuals resident in crystal edifices should refrain from the promiscuous catapulting of geological specimens."

b) "The ingestion of the edible product of the Pyrus malus vegetation at least once during the earth's cyclical rotational movement upon its axis will restrain the taker of the Hippocratic oath who is the medicinal prescriber."

c) "Antithetical elements always seem to evidence an enticement effect upon one another."

d) "The trek and expedition that consists of a multitude of distance units always commences with the act of completing the initial foot movement that will propel one forward."

e) "The lack of that which is urgently required or desirable is the gestating principle of all experimental processes and fabrications."

f) *The Covert Intelligence Gatherer Who Sought Shelter From the Intemperate Atmospheric Environment.*

Answers:

a) "People who live in glass houses shouldn't throw stones."
b) "An apple a day keeps the doctor away."
c) "Opposites attract."
d) "The longest journey starts with the first step."
e) "Necessity is the mother of invention."
f) *The Spy Who Came in from the Cold*

2. What are LRTAPs (lartaps)? If you worked for the Water Quality Branch of Environment Canada in Yellowknife, you would know about a study done to show the possible effects of Long Range Transport of Atmospheric Pollutants.

How often do you use series of initials in your speech? How many of the following do you know?

CBC	NHL	RCA	TLC	MD	MS	CNE/PNE
CPR	CNR	TTC	MSE	JFK	NBA	NAACP
ANC	HIV	MVP	VIP	RRSP	RSVP	TGIF
FBI	RCMP	CIA	UFO	VCR	NATO	EEC
GNP	MBA	BMW	HBC	PMO	MP	MPP/MLA
CEO	BLT	NDP	NFL	PMS	PC	CRTC

3. COTE Public Doublespeak Award
The Canadian Council of Teachers of English presents an annual Doublespeak Award, "an ironic tribute to those who mislead the Canadian public by abusing the English language." Set up your own panel to judge the most hideous example of doublespeak in your own college or university, or submit examples of public doublespeak, in English, committed by a Canadian, or in Canada, or about Canada to:

Professor Richard Coe, Chair,
CCTE Commission on Public Doublespeak,
English Department,
Simon Fraser University,
Burnaby, BC   V5A 1S6

Presentation

When you speak to a group in order to outline a policy, product, or program, you must be ready to transmit a great deal of information. Your success is measured by how well your audience understands you, or by how interested they are in your product. Presentations, because of the amount of material covered, are often very tedious. *You* will be successful because you know that a presentation is like any other speech. You need to:

a) Research your audience and material;
b) Organize;
c) Rehearse;
d) Relax.

David Nichol says that when he talks to his employees and management teams he tries

> *to talk with emotion, to get excited, and to get others excited. ...Most people are afraid to let emotion into it. So they hang onto that script, they read it—I mean they shouldn't have chairs; they should have beds for the audience.*

The best thing for you to do is pinpoint what your audience is interested in, and what your central focus should be. Whatever you are presenting, these pointers will help. The word audience refers to whomever you have to address: employees, clients, visiting representatives of outside institutions.

Build up a Feeling of Trust

Ron Skuba is a product manager for General Electric Medical Systems. He specializes in computerized tomographym magnetic resonance that creates images of the body. He may work two to three years for *one* sale; the machines range in price from $500 000 to $2.7 million. He is convinced that people buy from a person rather than a company, that his credibility and integrity help to make the sale. He visits his clients several times each year to explain how the machines work, their clinical value, and economic advantages. In order to make a sale, he has to help his clients persuade the administrators who control the budget.

Donald Meisner, President of Nordic Sales, a company that retails communications equipment such as copiers and fax machines, believes that honest, timely discussion is essential. He uses electronic devices to keep customers informed, to give them background for meetings, and to follow up afterwards. Meisner's favourite saying, ''You no longer commute to work; you communicate to work,'' is worth noting. Keep the telephone companies and the postal service busy: use them before and after your presentations.

Use a Variety of Material

If your presentation is detailed and perhaps a bit dry, vary the media you are using. Overheads are good unless you use 35 of them in a row. Switch from overheads to flipcharts, to slides, in order to inject variety. This takes practice, and you should set up all the machinery beforehand, and do a complete run-through.

Working With a Partner

Two education experts had to give an overview of how the changing school curriculum affected the amount of time spent on language studies in the secondary system. Most of their findings relied on dozens of tables of statistics. Working as a team, they took turns guiding the audience through a lot of material. One speaker tended to be precise and analytical; the other was more of a raconteur, giving stories of the students affected. They worked well together.

Determine the Needs of Your Audience

Whale-watching is increasing in popularity. If you are a scientist presenting a study to your colleagues, all with similar backgrounds and wanting to learn much in a brief time, you can pack your talk with as much detail, jargon, and statistics as you wish. That's what your audience wants.

If you are talking about the scientific purposes of whale-watching to a general group, however, your presentation should focus on two or three specific ideas. That way your audience will understand and be motivated to support your work.

What happens if you are allotted ten minutes to outline a very complex employee incentive program? Is it better to rush through the entire program or concentrate on a few highlights and invite questions? If you are tempted to cram everything in, ask yourself, "Why am I speaking? What is appropriate for this group, for this gathering, for this time slot?"

Diverting Attention from Trembling Hands

Have you ever seen an apparently competent speaker betray her nervousness when she placed a transparency on the overhead? When we are forced to watch a person obviously overcome by anxiety, it is hard to concentrate. You can avoid this by having the first transparency in place before you start; that way you just have to flip on the machine. You can also have a helper who changes the material when you wish. If you *know* your hands shake, use the magician's best trick—divert your audience's attention.

Use Audio-Visual Support Wisely

Audio-visual material is used to *accentuate* the speeches, to bring the meeting up. Schedule it to build interest. In other words, you don't need it before lunch: everybody's already lively. You may need it mid-afternoon when everyone is sleepy. Of course, people like to inject flashiness into their meetings, to use videos for memorable openings and closings. This is fine as long as the program keeps on rising, and the focus is on the speakers.

Job Interview

How well do you communicate at the interview? Whether you are applying for a new position, working your way up the corporate ladder, or representing your company in its campaign for new clients, you need to speak well. Let us assume you have done your résumé, researched this particular company, dressed well, and made it to the location promptly. What next? *Breathing exercises:* they'll help you relax and get your voice ready to perform with assurance. When you are shown into the office, approach your interviewer, introduce yourself, and shake hands. You make an immediate impression with

- **eye contact**
- **the tone of your voice (courteous, firm, relaxed)**
- **your handshake (warm, firm, and fitting)**

It is important *to behave as you wish to be treated.* If you want to be perceived as a person of worth and talent, have confidence in yourself. Your inexperience can always be remedied. Decide what you want and act appropriately.

There are two scenarios to note. The first is the *one-minute wait.* When you enter the interviewer's office, he or she is on the phone, (it's always Los Angeles or Boston, never Charlottetown or Kapuskasing). You are waved to a seat and wonder what to do. Do *not* pick lint from your clothes or adjust your trouser legs. If you feel nervous, pull out a pen and make a note, review the plans you made on how to fix your car—look efficient and busy, fidget administratively. When the interviewer gets off the phone, go back to the intro-and-handshake routine.

The second, and very common, scenario is the *weak-female routine.* Women are waved to chairs by gallant men who say, "here, take a seat." Rarely do people collapse from the long walk across the office. If you want to be perceived as competent, ignore the gesture, and introduce yourself with a pleasant handshake.

During the interview, you may be asked some unexpected questions; for instance, "Do you enjoy socializing with co-workers outside the office?" or "How do you define a team?" This takes discernment on your part. Is the question appropriate? If it is, take time to answer it honestly and thoroughly. You have no idea what has gone on before your arrival and perhaps no indication of the real challenge of the job. If two departments are merging, there may be a need for someone who is good at promoting cooperation and teamwork. This may not be on the job description but may be very much in the mind of the interviewer. If you check the section, ''Handling Unexpected Questions on the Spot,'' the steps are simple to remember: pause, clarify, make one point plus amplification, ask for feedback.

Media Interview

In their efforts to be immediate, radio stations want to talk to people directly connected with a news story. Thus, the scientist at a nuclear power plant can no longer assume that management will handle all interviews; direct answers have more credibility. Similarly, hotel and restaurant workers are contacted about the impact of international summits on their industry, and union stewards go on the air to discuss negotiations between management and labour.

Although the following pointers will help you in dealing with all media, they relate particularly to radio interviews.

Preparation

- When someone calls to ask for an interview, make sure they are setting a date in the future, not recording your remarks immediately. Insist on a chance to prepare.
- Pause: is is appropriate for you to do the interview? Do you know the details? Are you the logical choice? If it is not appropriate, say no or suggest someone else.
- Ask the researcher who calls you about the format of the interview. How long will it be? What usually happens? Will you be speaking live via telephone or in the studio?
- Cover your behind. If a sensitive issue is involved, make sure you have called your employer, or in the case of associations, your colleagues, to outline your point of view. You may not have essential information, and it's humiliating to be corrected in a subsequent interview.
- If you are not familiar with the show on which you will appear, start listening. You usually have at least one day. If not, call a friend who listens to the station. Research the usual format of questions—confrontational, ''what is your opinion?'' ''is it true?'' etc.

On Air

- **Be sure of your one main point and three supporting arguments.** Try the one-sentence shower test described in Chapter 2. The interviewer takes care of the intro and conclusion.

- **It is easier for the interviewer and the audience if you number your reasons.** ''Well Joe, I think my dog Annie should be the next mayor. She's got the three essential qualifications: she's smart, she photographs well, and she loves catered receptions.'' Then elaborate.
- **Use notes—a few key words or phrases.** This is no time to wing it. This is pressure.
- **Speak clearly.** This is a radio audience. Breathe in order to get your voice into a mellow range, and hold on. Don't get so excited that you tighten up and race to the end. Radio can be very hard if you're in a studio for the first time; it's a hectic place with people signalling and moving all at once.
- **Make eye contact with your interviewer.** Use the same speaking techniques you would with a larger group—remember, they are out there. If your interviewer is looking at the traffic reporter or the control room, imagine someone at home listening to you and talk to that person.
- **Keep the interview on track.** Consider this advice carefully. You know a lot about your subject; that's why you were asked on the show. To the station, you are just one of many interviews: they are not experts. So, when the interviewer asks something that is not relevant or seems to be filling time, say, ''Yes, that's a possibility, but there are other considerations.'' Don't wait for the interviewer to give you space; you have only three to five minutes, and they speed by.
- **Practise at home.** Get your friends or partner to throw all sorts of questions at you to see how well you handle them, and how well *you work in your main point.*
- **Rehearse your first line.** The first line is crucial. You always sound better after you've warmed up. If you are contacted over the phone, someone will call, ask you to hold, and suddenly the next voice is the interviewer's and it's live. While you are standing by the phone, breathe, and rehearse your opening line *out loud, exactly as you want to say it.*
- **Sound like yourself.** Don't be overly formal. Use everyday examples.
- **DON'T:**
  - knock the media on air;
  - say ''no comment'';
  - be tempted to speak about things beyond your area of knowledge;
  - lie;
  - let other people put words in your mouth. Say ''no,

that isn't an accurate picture. Let me tell you what really happened'';
— hog the limelight: give others credit if you are part of a group.

An interview is a speech: *organize, rehearse, relax.*

Panel Presentations

When you are asked to take part in a panel, it is important to determine your role. Is your job to

- give background on the topic?
- rev up the audience for subsequent speakers?
- present one particular aspect?
- put the topic in a perspective that is acceptable to the audience?
- ease tension?
- present a different or opposing point of view?

In other words, if I'm part of a panel discussion of AIDS being sponsored by the local Parent-Teacher Association, my function may be to explain why it is appropriate to have a policy regarding the treatment of people who contract the disease. As a teacher, I would point out that it serves the best interests of the students, the community, and the staff. Other panelists provide factual information on AIDS, deal with the fear of the community, and present the students' point of view.

Determine your function by discussing the program with the coordinator, telephoning the other participants to discuss their viewpoints, and using your common sense. As June Callwood says in the interview in Chapter 7:

> *I prepare by giving a lot of hard thought to the audience, what experience they've got, and where they're at....I think about what kind of expertise I'm addressing and where it is that I've got anything that's useful or helpful.*

No matter how many assurances you are given about the sound system, check it personally. The last time I was on a panel, we discovered that the television crew had plugged in to the main power source, and the "perfect" sound system was in trouble.

A good panelist arrives early enough to meet the organizers and other participants, and get the mood of the audience. During the discussion, *be attentive* to the speakers and to audience reaction.

Debates

Debating is an invigorating test of your organizational and speaking skills. Debates are not free-for-alls; they have a distinct format that ensures a fair hearing for each side. In the exercises below, you work as part of a debating team. It is wise to appoint a coordinator, someone who ensures that the group divides the research reasonably, touches on the most significant points, and keeps to their schedule, both in preparation, and in debate.

As a debater, it is important that you marshal your arguments to include logical, emotional, and ethical appeals. Your success also depends on your ability to predict and deal with key issues your opponent may raise. When deciding on the order in which team members will speak, assess the strengths of each person. Can the first speaker set the scene and engage the sympathy of the audience? Are there others on the team more suited to a precise discussion of statistics, or a forceful negation of the opposing side's main points? Arrange the speaking order to include a strong introduction, a logical presentation of arguments, and a memorable conclusion.

Usually, the team speaking in favour of the motion will be allowed a certain time to refute the remarks of their opponents. Make sure that the person chosen to handle the refutation can do the job clearly and briefly. She or he will need to have good self-control: debates are often charged with high emotions. The following exercises provide opportunities for you to combine your ideas and your delivery for maximum effect.

EXERCISE: Formal Team Debate

Organize the class in teams, two teams to a topic. One team will speak for the resolution, and one against it. Designate one person to chair the proceedings. That same person may judge the debate, or you may wish to appoint a panel. The debate is judged on the basis of the arguments presented and the effectiveness with which they are advanced.

These guidelines are to be followed:

a) Establish a set time for preparation, equal for everyone. You may wish to combine time in class and opportunity for outside research.
b) Each person on a team must speak once.
c) No person can speak longer than 90 seconds at one time.
d) The team speaking for the resolution may have 90 seconds rebuttal time.
e) Each speaker addresses the chair. The team speaking for the resolution starts the debate, and the first speaker formally presents the resolution.
f) Judging: the chair or the panel announces a winner based on form and content. The class may then wish to have an open vote on the resolution itself.

Suggested Topics

1. Resolved that euthanasia should be a medical option available to those who are in great distress.
2. Resolved that the state of marriage is a prerequisite condition for a sexual relationship.
3. Resolved that censorship has no place in a democratic society.
4. Resolved that drug testing of employees in any industry is a violation of human rights.
5. Resolved that all discrimination against people with AIDS and high-risk groups be made illegal.

EXERCISE: Open Debate

This format allows more class participation. Each motion has a proposer and a seconder, and an opponent and a seconder. The order of speakers is: proposer, opponent, seconder to the proposer, seconder to the opponent. The debate is then open to the floor. The chair maintains order, enforces the 90-second time limit, and ensures fair treatment for both sides.

In this type of debate, an outside judge or panel is useful.

Suggested Topics

1. Resolved that the business of journalism is to sell papers by whatever means necessary.
2. Resolved that the criminal justice system is biased against poor, non-white, defendants.
3. Resolved that better education would be possible if grades were eliminated.
4. Resolved that television stations be required to have at least 50% Canadian content in their programming.
5. Resolved that service technicians (auto mechanics, electronic and small-engine repair persons, etc.) have a right to charge as much as the market will bear.

FIXED LINK CROSSING DEBATE: CHARLOTTETOWN, P.E.I. JANUARY 14, 1988

Should Prince Edward Island have a fixed link (bridge or tunnel) to New Brunswick? Will such a link irrevocably alter the nature of island life? Twelve debates were commissioned by Premier Joe Ghiz and held throughout the island in preparation for a referendum held on January 18, 1988. One such debate took place in the Prince Edward Hotel on January 14, 1988; it featured formal remarks by selected debaters followed by remarks from the floor. The following excerpts reflect the strong tradition

(Continued)

of story-telling found throughout the Maritimes. Both debaters tell stories although their presentations differ greatly in tone and approach.

The first speaker is Jennifer Christopher , an eighteen year old high school student from Three Oaks High School in Summerside. She was chosen to represent the "no" side on the platform. Her approach is sincere and direct; her youthfulness and inexperience are presented positively. Her indirect reference to age garnered considerable laughter.

> Because I've been speaking out in this debate, some people have spoken to me and my parents saying, "What does she know? She's just a high school student. It's true that I have not read all the reports and I don't understand all the technical talk, but I am concerned about the future of the island. Also I know that this decision is going to affect me longer than it will affect most of you.
>
> One of the things that really bothers me is that there is so much talk about convenience and waiting for the ferry. I don't think that we should look at it this way when our environment is involved, and our very way of life is involved, and when people's jobs are involved. We shouldn't just be looking at convenience. I like what one woman said in the paper: "I don't want to compromise my island, my environment, for my convenience."

The second speaker is Harry MacLaughlan, a very well-known sixty-one year old Charlottetown businessman who represented the "yes" side. His dry humour pokes fun at those who fear progress and hold "the old days" in false reverence.

> I was born and raised at the farm in Stanhope, Prince Edward Island and I have never moved very far away. I have seen what has happened in the agriculture from milking cows on a milking stool—and pulling one tit and sometimes two at a time—to watching the milking machine; to the stable cleaner; to the manure spreader; to the electric light; to the potato harvester—first we used to pick potatoes and put them in a basket and put them in the cart and then take them and dump them and push them into the cellar and crawl around there on your belly. Ladies and gentlemen, I say it is high time we got on with the show, and not be fooling around.
>
> [Or what about] the runways at the Charlottetown airport when we're running around here having meetings saying we don't want them. We don't want the building that's going up there. We don't want this. We don't want that. The children wouldn't sleep at night. The traffic will be going in. The planes will be roaring. We don't want the runways. All we want is just to go in the house and stay there and wait for the mailman to come and get our [government] cheque.

What was the result of the referendum? The vote on January 18 showed 59% in favour of the fixed link, 41% opposed.

A local issue may someday prompt you to speak: it may be a school problem, a business improvement scheme, a homeowners' coalition trying to get contractors to finish the job, the need for traffic lights, an interval house, or better ambulance services. When you want to know the inside details of organization, maintaining morale, and dealing with antagonistic opponents, consult this interview. The advice given is clear and comes from experience.

Community Meetings: Everything You Want to Know Before You Speak

Cynthia Patterson is the coordinator of Rural Dignity, a citizens' group opposing the closure of rural post offices. She is 32 years old, born on the Gaspé Peninsula, and committed to a rural way of life. Since January 1987, she has been criss-crossing Canada by train, bus, truck, ferry, and plane. In approximately 15 months she has spoken at 60-75 community meetings and given hundreds of radio, newspaper, and television interviews.

When I spoke to her on April 26, 1988, she was in the middle of a ten-week national speaking and organizing tour.

What is the platform of Rural Dignity?

We oppose Canada Post's corporate plan to close, amalgamate, or privatize all of Canada's 5221 rural post offices over the next ten years. They propose to do this by "attrition" or "accelerated attrition." After we win this one, we want to concentrate on other rural issues, because we believe that villages have the potential to offer a very rich and integrated way of life.

How do you handle radio interviews?

Radio interviewers in particular are interested in their province or city exclusively. They don't want a national perspective. My remarks are as particular and specific as possible—in terms of geography and how the issue affects that place. In Winnipeg, I want to tell them how many post offices there are in Manitoba, how many employees there are, and how many POs have closed in the past two years in Manitoba. I prepare that info for every province, before I do radio interviews in that province. It's important to be as specific as possible and relate it to what's happening in that place.

Use live interviews; if there's any point that's been left out of the print media, say that on a live interview, because they can't cut it out. Whenever I tell newspaper reporters that 83% of the employees being affected are women, a glazed look comes over their faces, and it's never in the articles.

When I use it on live radio interviews—it can't be cut.

Do you have to educate interviewers in the course of the interview?

Yes, quite often. I may turn the questions around. If that person is not familiar with the material, he or she can't ask the right questions, and the listeners won't get the necessary info. When that happens, I usually try to take over the interview or else it's going to be a a waste of time. I use phrases like: "let's look at this example", or "there's another point to consider," etc.

What sort of advance information do you give interviewers?

We mail out a press kit about a week in advance; ours has cows all over the envelope to get their attention. Inside there's a page on the event and the reason for it, a page on the background of the organization, and a collage of articles showing the national scope of the issue. There's also an information sheet outlining how many rural post offices there are and how many have been closed.

It's important to make follow up calls the day before a press conference. You phone all the papers, and radio and television stations to remind them of the event, time and place. You get some good coverage out of those calls.

Do you mention other people in your interviews?

Yes, and it's good to be as specific as possible. Whatever province I'm in, rather than just saying we have the support of the National Farmers' Union, I use the names of local supporters. Always be as particular as possible.

What happens when you're put on the spot in a public meeting?

The only time I feel put on the spot is when people ask me what I think they should do in their communities. I don't think we should tell people what to do. Our role is to advise and suggest—but not tell them what to do. I may turn the question back on itself and get the person to ask another question. If I can't deal with how the question is coming at me I will answer with a question, and get the inquiry to come a different way. Meanwhile, I've gained myself a bit of time to be thinking and I've also diffused it a bit.

Do people attack you when you're on the platform with Canada Post?

Only the opposition attacks me. The most difficult session I had with them was in Riding Mountain, Manitoba. The Canada Post rep there personalized all his remarks—"she says that," "she's doing this."

He also tried quite a trick—I got to the meeting early but he was there earlier, and had brought his own equipment and a closed podium with a mike. Now he was a very large man, 6′2″ and about 225 pounds. I pointed out that if I used his podium I'd be invisible to the audience. He said it didn't matter; the mike had a gooseneck and I could just bend it down—a little voice coming from nowhere. I didn't use his stuff; I stood at the table, completely visible, projected my best, and asked everyone if they could hear.

How do you manage against such formidable opposition?

You can make disabilities into advantages. Whenever Canada Post makes a presentation, they send three to five people, and to represent Rural Dignity there's only me. Now, I'm not a tall woman, and I have this squeaky voice that I have to deal with. When I stand up, I introduce myself as Cynthia Patterson and say I'm the person accused of spreading rumours and using scare tactics. The audience just cracks up.

Do you use humour?

Yes, I'm a great believer in it. It also helps to get you out of tight spots. I also use emotion. I feel passionately about the deruralization of the world, and I'm trying to do my part here in Canada. The language that I choose to use reflects my love of rural life. Canada Post uses that bureaucratic language full of long words and tons of facts and figures.

What sort of language do you use?

I use statistics precisely and I fill that out with very simple and direct language that speaks to the audience about their own town. I try hard to get into a town the night before or the morning of a presentation, and I go all around talking to people. Then at night, I speak to the audience about their own community—"I understand you lost your railway station 5 years ago and your school two years, and right now you've raised quite a large sum to restore your church." I also tell them where I come from and a bit about my village; then I'm real to them and they're real to me.

How do you finish?

I often use poetry or song lyrics to close—that seems to work for me.

You also need to direct people to take an action. Instead of just airing the issues, they go away with something specific to do: a letter writing campaign, a telephone tree in their village so they can all take turns calling the politicians. I share ideas across the country because sometimes we seem so isolated. When I'm in New Brunswick, I'll tell them what the people in Riding Mountain did, or how the people in Aylesbury, Sask. formed a human chain around their post office to keep Canada Post out.

I also swap good lines and give credit for them. Then the fact that this is a national network is made clear. Lloyd Pike is a school teacher and councillor in South River, Newfoundland. When Canada Post went in there to propose Superboxes, people said, "what about our Newfoundland winters, and our storms?" Canada Post said, "you have nothing to worry about. We have improved and upgraded our Superboxes and we have galvanized them.'' Lloyd Pike replied, ''but sir, our senior citizens are not galvanized.''

What else do you have to be aware of in public meetings?
I find myself having to defuse the crowd sometimes when they start to harass Canada Post.

I also don't want the crowd to get side-tracked.

Sometimes it's hard to remember we're fighting a corporate plan, not the people on the stage. I try never to make personal attacks for that reason.

How did you get started?
I remember reading that when you've got something to say you believe in, you won't be shy to speak out. And that's true. My first public meeting was in Foxtrap, Newfoundland. Our president couldn't make it in from New Brunswick because of a blizzard. He said matter-of-factly, ''you'll have to do the meeting.'' So I did. And I haven't stopped.

How do you keep going?
I'll tell you what gives me a great deal of courage. It's thinking of the talking women who went before me—the abolitionists, the suffragettes, the pacifists. What they have done allows me to see myself not alone, but as part of a strong tradition. When I'm sure I cannot face another strange bed or one more full travel day, I think of Emmeline Pankhurst, Charlotte Perkins Gilman, and Vera Brittain. They inspire me to go on.

Keeping Cool Under Fire

Have you ever been stunned by an unexpected attack? How do you manage in a group where tempers are running high? Remember, you have the choice either to assume the mood of the group *or* to create your own. Let's say you are participating in a national conference, and your group is still pulling things together two days before the opening. As you drive to your last meeting, you know that the group is anxious, almost frantic, as they rush to get papers photocopied, briefs written, and so on. What is your choice? How do you want things to proceed?

First, centre yourself. Think about your skills, your purpose in attending, and what you hope to accomplish. Know that you are capable. The next step is to decide on the mood you want to create. Do you want your colleagues to be brisk, competent, confident? Is it time to reflect on your original purpose and make sure you are on the right track? It may be necessary to heal personal differences that anxiety has caused. Choose your mood, and decide on the tone you need to create it. You can create moods by the way you speak.

At the meeting, voices are raised, and accusations made. How can you help? First, stay calm. Give others time to work out their frustrations. Then, once they've talked things out, ask if they still wish to proceed? Are your goals in place? List the items you must deal with and put all the simple matters first. By resolving a series of small details, you are establishing a pattern of agreement and rapport, and the task doesn't seem as large. You are then ready to deal with more thorny issues.

If your group is still upset about major matters, all you can do is keep the tone conciliatory, and remind them that they are there to get ready for the conference, and it's in their own interest to work together.

If you can focus your mind on *how* you wish to be, and *what* you want to happen, you can influence the mood of others. Your tone will do that. Do you remember all the voice exercises? Your voice is very important in establishing the tone. It is the barometer of your confidence. If you are tense or overly excited, your voice will be coming from high in your head, and you will sound anxious. If you can get that voice to come from the heart, you radiate control and confidence.

How do you respond to people who try to unnerve you with a personal attack? Many people freeze. I have often thought of a perfect comeback to a comment—six hours later. First of all, you must realize that personal attacks are unethical. In the case of a personal putdown, you should not reply. Say clearly and firmly, "I don't agree," or "that remark is inappropriate." Then, ask the group to return to the question being discussed. As a speaker, you should remember that insulting others or their ideas reflects poorly on you. As Eddie Greenspan observed:

> *You can't win by calling the opposing views stupid, or belittling them—no matter how stupid they are. As a speaking device, belittling the other side is a losing technique.*

Talking for a Living

Some people speak for a living. Their jobs require that they talk to others for most of the day. How do they manage? A tour guide, a front line person for a major credit card company, and a telemarketing sales supervisor were asked about their success.

L. Venandos: Tour Guide, Jasper Alberta

L. Venandos is a nineteen-year-old tour guide who lives and works in Jasper. Her summer job is to take groups of tourists up and down the Jasper Tramway, pointing out the various mountain ranges. When I rode with her, the presentation she gave was lively, and full of easy-to-remember observations. For instance, she pointed out that the town of Jasper was in the shape of a J for its name. She also likes to include jokes for people, and makes up her own patter; like all good guides, she tries to be interested in her own material.

Sandra Clements: Front Line Phone Person for Canada Trust, MasterCard Security

Sandra Clements has to deal with clients who are often angry or upset. She takes the calls about lost or stolen credit cards, and speaks to people who have been robbed on the street or in their homes, or who have had their cards used fraudulently. In order for the computer to provide personal identification, she must ask callers personal details: height, weight, hair colour, birthdate. I, like many other callers, was disturbed when she asked for the names of close relatives. Her soft calm voice and patient manner took the edge off my irritation.

Sandra Clements says that many people get upset but she remains calm and says,'' I'm sorry. I don't want to cause you confusion or frustration but I need this information. Please cooperate.'' She generally gets the data she needs.

B.J. Danylchuk: Telemarketing Sales Supervisor, *The Globe and Mail*

B.J. Danylchuk values the power of a person's voice. She has worked as a musician and a lawyer, and is convinced that telephone sales are the most powerful marketing tool. In her business, rapport is achieved by the voice rather than by one's physical presence, and that voice has to come from the heart, the area in your chest that produces a mellow, sincere tone. B.J. offers the following guidelines:

1. Picture the other person and talk to that person.
2. Listen to nuances of the voice to determine the appropriate approach. If the person is rushed or seems upset, ask if it's better to call back. If you hear noise or other voices, suggest another time to talk; the customer will appreciate your respect for his or her schedule.
3. Listen for paper noises. If you hear the rustling of paper and suspect they're leafing through their mail, say, ''are you looking for your contract? I have it right here.'' Help the customer focus on your call.
4. Suggest ideas to maximize their business. If you think of your clients' interests first, they'll trust you far more than the caller who is just trying to make a quick sale. This will result in far more business for you.

Speaking on the Telephone

As the telecommunication industry makes trans- and intercontinental calls a normal part of our lives, we must reconsider the way we plan and transact our telephone calls. Gillian Snook, National President of the Canadian Institute of Travel Counsellors, estimates that 95% of the business of her industry is done on the telephone. As legislation in the travel industry gets tougher, travel counsellors have to be absolutely sure of their information. They must also be able to communicate well with clients who spend tens of thousands of dollars on their travel arrangements. The ability to listen well, to empathize, to handle questions and complaints, to sell a package, is needed in all fields.

Organization and delivery are as important on the phone as they are in other speeches.

1. **Plan the call.** Why are you calling? What is your objective? Have you arranged the topics for discussion wisely (do you start with easy topics and lead up to the major point)? Is there background information you should have?
2. **Write down your plan.** If you have a list of items before you, you will sound organized and be able to conduct your business smoothly.
3. **Adopt a speaking posture.** Sit up straight, and imagine the person across from you. Make imaginary eye contact. Don't tuck the phone under your chin; it sounds like you're strangling. If you have to eat, drink, or talk to others, don't do it when you are on the phone.
4. **Take telephone calls seriously.** Give them the same consideration you accord face-to-face interviews, and treat the caller with respect. Give yourself time and privacy to make calls, and try to eliminate extraneous noise.
5. **Get the name right.** If you are placing a call to someone you do not know, do your research and get the person's correct name. Have you noticed the effect that using someone's name has on your relationship? There's a fine line between a friendly use of one's name, and a slick overuse.
6. **Finish the call.** This does not mean to hang up. It means that you clarify what has been decided, and what action will be taken. Future appointments are booked. Finish with a firm, clear statement.

Speaking Out-of-Doors, to Large Groups, and to Children

Know your environment: if you are speaking outdoors, make sure of what is behind you. If there is a trampoline or a highway for your audience to look at, their attention will wander. Good speakers make sure that the podium is situated so that the audience looks at the speaker, and *not* into the sun. As a speaker, you can deal with the glare, but if your listeners are blinded, they won't be able to see you.

Make sure there is a sound system. There are good portable systems for rent everywhere, (you may wish to carry your own). If you're speaking to over 30 people you'll need it.

Will you be speaking to children? Again, check the environment. What is your competition? Do you have a grabber that will get their interest? I once spoke to 400 children between the ages of 8 and 14, and they were extremely restless. I started with some challenges: how many could bend their arms behind their backs and up to their necks? Then I put signals in my speech: whenever I mentioned a certain name they had to stand on one foot. It was noisy whenever that happened, but everyone listened for the signal. Children like to have fun. You can supply fun and a good speech.

The biggest group I ever spoke to was 16 802 people in Maple Leaf Gardens. The energy level was great. Such opportunity is rare, so I gave considerable attention to my main idea. Big crowds require clear ideas simply expressed, and repeated several times. You need to keep your speech short—when 16 802 people fidget, they make a lot of noise.

For all these special cases, know your environment, think about what will work best, and experiment. If your speech is interesting, clear and brief, and repeats key ideas, you and your audience will have a good time.

Hotel managers, real-estate developers, airport personnel, and retail salespersons know that crowds can be volatile and sometimes unpleasant. Your ability to develop trust on the part of the group is the key to success. Whether you are at a podium or with a line-up, you must be able to establish a rapport, and make sure that others see you are making an effort to work for them.

Jack Boddam has been manager of a movie theatre for almost forty years. When he has to face impatient patrons, he reassures them, "I have 37 years of experience and I know there are plenty of seats. It looks like a lot of people to you, but trust me, there's room for everyone." He makes sure that his customers see him check the auditorium for numbers, and the line-up for those who try to butt in.

He is also honest. He announces limited seating, "Please go in, and find a seat. If it's not satisfactory, I'll refund your money automatically." By establishing an atmosphere of fairness and trust, he relieves the tension in a crowd. Once that happens, they become more reasonable individuals.

When you have to deal with a crowd, use your voice to establish trust and allay anxiety. Establish a sense of calm, fair play, and control, and the explosiveness will subside.

Know your entrances and exits. Marilyn Brooks, the fashion designer, remembers being introduced at her first big show in 1968. The host called out, "And now, here's Marilyn Brooks." She took the wrong turn, and with four models dressed as nymphets in chiffon, ended up in the boiler room. She could hear the host still calling, "Now where *is* Marilyn Brooks?"

Crowd Management

Speech Assignment: Thinking on Your Feet

Your job is to create a situation which offers challenge and a chance to develop new skills.

1. In consultation with your instructor, choose one of the many examples of meetings, presentations, or interviews detailed in the chapter and create your own situation. You should prepare an outline of what the environment is, who is involved, your purpose, your methods. You may work individually or in groups.
2. Prepare the necessary background material (hand-outs, agendas, résumés, overheads).

3. Set the stage, and present your situation, speaking appropriately for the situation.

DELIVERY TECHNIQUES TO REMEMBER

1. Use the Skid School formula to respond to unexpected questions.
2. Focus on making connection with others—use eye contact, body language, your voice to eliminate barriers.
3. Make sure you can hear your thesis and overview, even under stress.
4. Relax! Try to explore the situation rather than reacting to it hastily.

INTERVIEW

David A. Nichol

President, Loblaw International Merchants
Winner of the 1987 Ursaki "Marketer of the Year" Award

March 14, 1988
Toronto

David Nichol is a trusted personality in thousands of Canadian households. His "Insider's Report" may be one of the most widely distributed food

publications in the world. Along with Georgie Girl, his dog,

he has convinced Canadians that his "President's Choice" products are the finest available. Nichol's ability to speak sincerely to strangers has made him one of our country's most famous marketing executives. During this interview, Nichol developed his own system of public speaking: *The Gordie Howe Approach.*

Q
Why do you make speeches?

A

Because I care. You know, Gordie Howe, in all his years playing hockey, before every game, he had a ritual. Just before he went onto the ice, he used to go into the washroom and throw up. Gordie Howe, until just recently when Gretzky broke his scoring record, was the greatest hockey player that ever was, and until he stopped playing hockey, he used to lose his supper before every game.

When you speak, you have a tremendous obligation to your audience—these people are giving you their time and you have to entertain or educate them. Most people just try to fill time, fill up their twenty minutes. Instead, they should take a lesson from Gordie Howe. They should care so much, it hurts.

Q
How important is it that people in business speak well?

A

A large part of business is selling; selling means convincing people. You can't convince people except through communication; therefore, people with good communication skills, written or oral, have an enormous advantage.

Q
How do people convince you about a product or a concept?

A

If it's a product, seeing the product.
Having their arguments well marshalled.
Being able to communicate on an emotional level.

Q
Is it important to be able to speak in business on an emotional level?

A

Absolutely! Everything is emotion. You need a good balance between logic and emotion.

Q
Why do people believe you and your personal advertising techniques?

A

I care, and I care about what people think of what I say. That concern comes through.

Q
Do you enjoy talking to groups?

A

You know, I *hate* public speaking, I just absolutely detest it. Public speaking is a form of examination. You go up in front of two or two thousand people and bare your soul in terms of capabilities. And people can tell if a speaker is a phony, if they care, if they believe in the subject, if they respect the audience, and if they're a vital human being or part of the army of living dead. Now if people can figure that out about you, especially if you have an established public image, that is a very high-risk situation.

I know the emotional price I'm going to pay every time I speak. I know the emotional energy I'm going to use and I could be using it to create the best Dutch Butter Cookie in the world. And yet there are certain audiences that it's important to persuade, and so I use that energy to do it.

Q
Do you get scared?

A

People should be nervous; if you're not scared to death before you give that speech, chances are it's going to be a bomb.

Don't be afraid of the fear. Use it to your advantage.

Q
How do you use the nervousness positively and avoid making a fool of yourself?

A
Fighting it through the first time. For me, that's Blenheim High School, Heart of the Golden Acres, down near Chatham, Ontario, 2500 people, a public speaking contest—"My trip to Mammoth Cave." That is the first speech I gave—stalactites, stalagmites—in front of 2000 kids who know you're a jerk anyway. After that, they lock you in a room and give you a title for an impromptu speech and 15 minutes to prepare. Then it's back in front of 2000 kids for "It Happened on my Christmas Vacation."

And you go all around the small towns doing the speeches and you get used to it. Getting up is not so hard to do, especially if you're Irish like I am and have a touch of the old malarkey. All of that fear gets the adrenalin going and you use that adrenalin. You say to yourself, "let's just go and get 'em." You get tired and bored of being scared to death.

Q
When is a speech really exciting?

A
When you get all of that energy going and you get up and speak without notes.

Q
Do you know what you're going to say?

A
Sure, it's all written down in point form. I like the security blanket of those little cards. But when you get off to a good start, when you're enthusiastic, you can forget about the notes and let the good times roll. When the spirit hits you, when you've spent a lot of time planning and you're totally prepared, then you don't need the notes.

Too often, speakers, including me, go to the security blanket when it's not necessary.

Q
Do people pay attention to what you say?

A
We don't understand the power of TV; I gave a speech when I won the Ursaki Award, the top marketing award in Canada. A few days later, I was in Marrakesh, Morocco, in the Mamounia hotel, one of the top hotels in the world, out in the desert, the Atlas mountains in the background, a bazaar and snakecharmers, the setting sun—it looked like a scene from Casablanca—and a guy I've never seen before comes up and says "Hey Dave, that was a great speech you gave last week. I saw it on TV". He was a travel agent who is going to take people around the world on a 747 and stay in the best places in the world. People everywhere hear you.

The whole speech was propaganda, you know—it was the Mammoth Cave technique all over again.

Q
How do you speak to your employees and management teams?

A
Same way. I try to get excited, and to get others excited. Most people are afraid of dying during their speech. And most people are afraid to let emotion enter into it. So they hang onto that script, they read it—I mean, they shouldn't have chairs, they should have beds for the audience.

Q

What speech of yours do you like?

A

I am most proud of the introduction to the Ursaki Award speech when I talk about my theory of the filter in the minds of human beings. I knew what I wanted to say but it was all extemporaneous. If I could give a whole speech like that, I'd be happy.

Q

What makes a business meeting good?

A

Whether anything comes out of it. And that's usually a function of being organized in terms of knowing what you want to accomplish and having a plan to get there.

Q

Do you really choose President's Choice stuff yourself?

A

Yes, I just tasted a series of canned seafood products from Chile, mini rice-cakes, dry soup mixes from Israel to see how they compare to Knorr, President's Choice macaroni and cheese to see if it's too salty. I choose them all.

I'm about to bring out a new version of the President's Choice chocolate chip cookie. It's got the maximum number of chocolate chips you can put in a chocolate chip cookie; it's made of 100% butter. I'm going to call it "The Decadent." It's the best chocolate chip cookie in the world.

Q

Is that really your dog?

A

Yes, that is my dog.

Q

If you had all the beginning speakers of the world assembled in your office, what would you tell them? What is the most important part of speaking well?

A

Emotion—use it. Don't be afraid of it. If you're not nervous, your speech isn't going to be good.

David Nichol

Speech: The Filter Between Our Brain and Our Mouth—Accepting the Ursaki Award

Nichol's style is eclectic, weaving seemingly dissimilar references together. His speech is like a verbal "Insider's Report," and it is directed to insiders, a group of colleagues gathered to honour him. He starts by describing the moment when he confided to Jimmy Graham, a product developer, that he had been nominated for the Ursaki "Marketer of the Year" Award.

Now let me give you my theory about the filter between our brain and our mouth that enables us all to live together.

Here's how it works. Your brain may have thought when you saw me coming in, "There's the guy with the ugly dog who writes that ridiculous comic book." Now, that thought goes from your brain, through your filter and when we meet you say to me, "Dave, I just love your 'Insider's Report' and I'm crazy about that darling Georgie Girl." Now, I'm sure that you've met people in your life who were unfortunately born with no filter at all. As a result, whatever comes into their mind comes immediately out their mouth. However, for most of us, our filter fails only on rare occasions.

Well apparently, Jimmy's filter crashed at that particular moment because he looked at me over his auslese and said, "*Well, you know, Dave, you did have a 'little bit' of help.*"

Well, you're wrong, Jimmy, *I had a lot of help*.

First, Mr. Chairman, let me thank you for this very important honour, which I am pleased to accept on behalf of the thousands of people who have played a role in changing Loblaw Companies' image over the past 15 years.

I particularly want to acknowledge the role played by the store managers. When I first became president of the Loblaws stores here in Ontario, it didn't take me long to realize that *I* was totally ignorant about what had to be done.

Now, there's something to be said for ignorance. In a number of instances, because of our ignorance, we didn't know what *couldn't* be done, so we went ahead and did it! When we introduced no-name products 10 years ago, the marketing experts took one look at them and announced to the press, "They haven't got a chance. They'll be gone in a couple of months."

Ten years later in many of our stores, no-name products represent over 25% of the groceries we sell.

However, most of the time my ignorance just caused problems. I remember that I once had the great idea of having a steak sale at ridiculously low prices right in the middle of the summer. We must've wiped out every steer between here and Medicine Hat. However, the butchers were dropping

in their tracks; the customers were mad because they couldn't get all the steaks they wanted; and it cost us a fortune.

After a few mistakes of that magnitude, I figured I should talk to someone who could tell me what to do. So I got in my car and travelled around the province talking to small groups of store managers. They told me what to do. And it worked.

The other two people I would like to particularly acknowledge are Dick Currie, the President of Loblaw Companies, and Galen Weston, the chairman of Loblaws' Parent Company, George Weston Limited.

I find it difficult to imagine another environment that would have been as receptive to the number of innovations that Loblaw Companies has implemented over the past 15 years.

Can you imagine the scene when I first came to Dick with the idea of the "Insider's Report"?

"Dick, I've just come back from California where I've found the greatest new marketing idea—it's called the 'Insider's Report.' "

"Who writes it, Dave?"

"A guy called Trader Joe."

"Trader Joe? What's it like, Dave?"

"Well, it's like a comic book that's sort of a cross between *Mad* magazine and *Consumers Report*."

"A comic book? Tell me, Dave, how would we personalize it to Loblaw Companies?"

"Well, we'll fill it full of cartoons of Georgie Girl and three bears called Teddy, Terri, and T.J."

"Georgie Girl, and three bears?"

Dick quickly reviewed in his head our track record and said, "You know, that might be just crazy enough to work."

One of the most popular new management books is entitled *Innovation*, and it's written by Richard Foster, a director of McKinsey's London office. His thesis is that the business world is changing so quickly that the key to survival is creating an environment that encourages and nurtures innovation. Under the leadership of Mr. Weston and Mr. Currie, Loblaw Companies should survive very well indeed.

...I once heard a definition of the Ideal Marketing Strategy as "one that your competitor is unable or unwilling to follow." The "Insider's Report" and the President's Choice products really are the only two things that we have ever done that nobody has tried to replicate. Are they effective? Well, our Christmas "Insider's Report" will be distributed the middle of this month in eastern Canada, in Ontario and across the prairies. In the United States, we'll see issues in St. Louis and Dallas.

It will introduce 125 new products and will contain 91% of our own items and 9% national brands. How much product will it move over five weeks? Approximately $70 million dollars of food and non-food products. Why do people read it? Because it's different, because it's entertaining, and because it's meeting one of the new consumer's real needs—it is supplying them with useful information about new products.

I was watching the news the other night and Scotty Reston, probably the most respected U.S. newspaper man of his generation, who served for 30 years as the Washington bureau chief for the *New York Times*, was being interviewed at the time of his retirement. He made the point that probably no generation has gone through as much change as our own. Every institution and relationship that you use to anchor your lives to is being constantly challenged. Attitudes towards marriage, sex, parents, children, the Church, education, government—all of these traditional anchors are in the midst of tremendous turbulence. This means that individuals and businesses are at tremendous risk now. However, there's another way of looking at it.

To quote Peter F. Drucker: "A time of turbulence is also one of great opportunity for those who can understand, accept and exploit the new realities."

I thank you for your attention and on behalf of Loblaw Companies I thank you again for the Ursaki Award.

Nov. 17, 1987
Toronto

OUTLINE OF A PRESENTATION, DEBATE, OR INTERVIEW

Name: _____

Date of Speech: _____

Purpose Statement: _____

INTRODUCTION
    Grabber:

    Thesis:

    Overview:

BODY
    Supporting Argument #1

    Supporting Argument #2

    Supporting Argument #3

CONCLUSION
    Reference to purpose (thesis):

    Summary of main steps:

    Zinger:

SELF-EVALUATION FORM

This form is to help you evaluate your own speech. It can be kept private or shared with your instructor or peers.

Type of Speech: _____

Name: _____

Title: _____

Date: _____

DELIVERY
Physical Presence

Did I make eye contact with others?

Was my posture natural and appropriate?

Was I aware of my facial expressions and hand gestures?

Were there any distracting mannerisms that I was aware of?

Did I feel good?

Could I feel an energy exchange with my audience?

VOCAL DELIVERY

Was my voice under control?

Did I sound confident?

Was I aware of breathing calmly?

How was my enunciation?

Did I manage to avoid um's and ah's?

Did I sound interested/excited/committed?

How did my voice sound to me?

DESIGN AND CONTENT

How well did the introduction and conclusion work?

Did the framework unify my speech?

Was there a natural progression from point to point?

Did my notes keep me on track? Did I use them?

Did the audience seem to understand the organization of my speech?

Was the information clear?

What was the energy level of the conclusion?

What would I change the next time?

What worked very well?

OVERALL EFFECTIVENESS

Did I connect with this audience?

Did I achieve my purpose?

What do I remember most about making the speech?

What unexpected or unforeseen things happened?

What am I most pleased about?

OTHER COMMENTS

Grade:

PEER EVALUATION FORM

Peer evaluation should be done in a constructive and supportive fashion. The speaker may choose people to do assessments or they may be assigned alphabetically. Some groups maintain the same speaker/assessor teams for the entire course; others change for each speech. The instructor may wish to see this evaluation before it goes to the speaker.

Type of Speech: _____

Speaker: _____

Title: _____

Assessor: _____

Date: _____

DELIVERY

Physical Presence

Did the speaker maintain eye contact?

Did she or he establish a rapport with the audience?

Were gestures natural and effective?

VOCAL DELIVERY

Did the speaker sound convincing/spontaneous/excited?

Was his or her voice clear and loud enough?

How did you respond to the speaker's mood?

DESIGN AND CONTENT

Did the introduction interest you?

Did the overview give you an indication of the main proofs?

Did the speech flow easily and logically from one point to another?

Was the conclusion strong and memorable?

Did the conclusion reinforce the thesis and main points?

What was the thesis of the speech?

OVERALL EFFECTIVENESS

Did you learn something new or worthwhile from the speech?

Were you moved by it?

What was the most outstanding part of the speech?

What changes do you recommend?

What parts should the speaker definitely keep?

OTHER COMMENTS   Grade:

EVALUATION FORM

Type of Speech: _____

Name: _____

Title: _____

Length of Speech: _____

Date: _____

Legend: S = SUPERIOR   E = EFFECTIVE   NW = NEEDS WORK

DELIVERY
Physical Presence
Eye Contact

Rapport with Audience

Posture

Gestures

Use of Notes

Appropriate Use of Audio-Visual
Support Material

VOCAL DELIVERY
Naturalness/Spontaneity/Enthusiasm

Clarity

Variety (Tone, Pitch, Pace)

Volume

Absence of Verbal Tics (um, ah,
okay, like)

Sense of Control and Calm

DESIGN AND CONTENT
Use of Framework for Introduction
and Conclusion

Clear Thesis and Overview

Coherence/Use of Transitions

New/Interesting Information

Strong Finish

LANGUAGE
Word Choice

Impact on Audience

Grammar

OVERALL EFFECTIVENESS
Treatment of Topic

Intelligent Awareness of Audience

Achievement of Purpose

Impact on/Connection with Audience

OTHER COMMENTS   Grade:

There Comes a Time: The Persuasive Speech

TIPS FOR SPEAKERS

1. Be sure your commitment to the topic is sufficient to move your audience.
2. Your preparation, concern, and attitude will help establish your credibility.
3. Ethical, logical, and emotional proofs touch different segments of your audience. Balance your act.
4. If you encounter a hostile reaction, remember that ideas are at odds, not people. Ask for a fair hearing and work towards understanding.
5. Name-Calling, Poor Analogies, and Flag-Waving are errors in logic that ethical speakers avoid.
6. Convince your listeners; don't coerce them.
7. A good plan gives you enough structure so that you can wing it when the occasion is right.

Whatever form you use, subtle or blunt, humorous or not, it's all to persuade.
    (EDDIE GREENSPAN)

The audience yearns for you to do well; they don't want to watch you make a mess of it. They're totally on your side, and there's very positive energy going for you.
    (JUNE CALLWOOD)

All speeches involve persuasion. If you urge others to spend money on a major advertising campaign, to adopt slo-pitch for their ball league, or to add anchovies to a Caesar salad dressing, you are persuading them.

This chapter deals with types of persuasive speeches, appeals that you may use, adapting to your audience, and informal logic to help you. It then gets into **advanced technique:** how to adapt to the moment, how to ride the wave of audience reaction and enjoy it.

Why Are You Speaking?

The first rule of persuasive speaking is, *have something to say.* Avoid the temptation to talk just to hear your own voice. Think hard about the topic and hammer out a precise statement of your position. If you aren't sure of what you think or what action should be taken, you have work to do.

Most important of all, *be sure your commitment to the topic is sufficient to* move *your audience.* Remember that not everyone can speak on all topics, even good ones. Acid rain is a major threat to our environment but it may not be sufficiently immediate to give you the power to convince others. On the other hand, the need for organ donors may be a subject that you can really get a handle on.

If you have a clear, specific purpose in mind, a purpose that you believe in, your enthusiasm will give your speech credibility and strength.

Types of Persuasive Speeches
A persuasive speech urges an audience to think or act in a certain way. Generally, your purpose is to move the audience

- to adopt or change an idea;
- to confirm or reinforce a concept or belief;
- to adopt a course of action.

Speeches to Adopt or Change an Idea
Convincing your audience that airbags should be standard features in all cars, or that exotic animals should not be kept as pets, are examples of this type of speech. Obviously, some people will already share your opinions, and others will have to be

persuaded. Once the idea is accepted, action may follow, but the focus of the speech is on the logical support of your thesis.

Speeches to Reinforce a Belief
Strengthening your audience's commitment against apartheid or for the protection of our wilderness areas confirms widely held ethical and social principles. Does this type of speech always have to be so serious? Not necessarily. Convincing others that real Christmas trees are better than artificial ones, or that a rural life is superior to an urban one, are also effective themes.

Motivating Your Audience to Act
One student made a powerful speech on behalf of Amnesty International, a civil-rights group concerned with the release of political prisoners. He concluded by distributing stickers and buttons obtained from the organization, and gave each person a form for donations and an envelope. Another asked group members to take out their drivers' licences and check the section provided for consent to organ donation. She asked everyone to give the matter deep thought and sign the forms within 48 hours. In each case the speakers gave good arguments, and provided specific tasks for the audience to do. The time frame provided even firmer direction.

How Do You Persuade Others?

Use yourself as a test case to determine what kinds of information are persuasive. When the question of extraterrestial visitors arises, for example, are you more convinced by the opinion of a scientist from NASA, statistics documenting the number of UFOs reported last year, or a first-hand report of one such encounter? Most people lean toward one type of proof or another, and good speakers know that in order to touch all facets of each listener, and all segments of each audience, they must use a variety of appeals. The most common proofs are ethical, logical, and emotional.

Look at your audience as a group of people who have come to eat at your restaurant. Some anticipate a good meal because they know the chef's reputation and appreciate the atmosphere of your restaurant. Others are more concerned with selecting food that will give them the balance of nutrients they require without unnecessary additives and fat. The remaining diners are won by the meal itself: the presentation, the aroma, the *taste*.

In your speech, you require the same balance of credibility, solid information, and emotional or gut appeal.

Use Real Examples to Make Your Proofs Convincing
There is no better way to nail down each point than to give an example. References to real people, places, news events, or

job experiences familiar to your audience will help them understand your arguments. Let's look at some examples.

You belong to a group lobbying the federal government to approve the sale of a particular pain-relieving drug. To prepare for your speech before a committee you have collected many statistics and read many scientific studies. Just a little more research will give you specific stories of individuals whose present pain is intolerable, examples of the drug's success in other countries, estimates of the financial benefit to local companies, and the actual statements of doctors who wish to use the drug.

If you're discussing the benefits of pet ownership, you can quickly find examples of children, seniors, and people with medical problems, whose lives are enhanced by the love and companionship of animals. Your local humane society will supply pictures and histories of pets waiting for adoption. Intellectually, your audience will be convinced by your brilliant proofs; emotionally, they will be touched by your anecdote of Ben and Kodiak, a little boy and his adopted cat. The combination makes for a *memorable* speech.

Remember, whatever your proof, make your point, back it up with specific examples, and repeat it.

Establishing Credibility

When you set out to move others to action, to reinforce a belief, or to change an idea, you must establish your ethical base, your credibility. Your verbal and nonverbal messages affect your audience and their willingness to accept your ideas. For what reasons do people believe you? Here are some of the more important.

1. **Your competence or experience.** Your knowledge of the field and your qualifications go a long way in establishing your competence in the minds of the audience. If you want to argue that all food and beverages should bear a full list of ingredients, which would cut down on the number of allergy-related deaths, what details will convince your audience that you know the topic? A background in nutrition, medicine, or food preparation will help. Experience in the restaurant business would provide insight, as would personal experience with allergies, or membership in an organization concerned with the problem. Tell your audience of the research you have done, such as interviews with victims of allergy-related illnesses.

   If you're trying to persuade a hotel chain to increase their wheelchair accessibility, your case will be strengthened if you demonstrate first-hand knowledge of the needs of wheelchair users, *and* familiarity with the hotels themselves.

   Sometimes you have to establish a link with your audience. A young travel counsellor with *very* short hair, dyed

Rehearse your speech with a friend. By preparing well, you demonstrate respect for your audience.

a vivid red, made a presentation to a seniors' club regarding a group tour of the Rhine Valley, which would include visits to vineyards and castles.

In order to assure the group that she knew both the area and her clients' needs, she started by describing the trips she had taken with her grandmother and friends, and the physical demands of the Rhine trip. This established rapport with the group and added to their confidence in her judgment.

Make sure that the program notes and the remarks of the person introducing you include any background information (degrees or diplomas, work or volunteer experience, personal interests) that will establish your credentials.

2. **Your respect for the audience.** Speakers who arrive on time, who are well prepared, and who have practised their speeches demonstrate respect for their listeners. A speaking engagement is serious: you don't come to a business presentation with notes half-done, and admit you threw a few ideas together in the car; don't do it for a speech. Take June Callwood's advice:

> *I assume I'm speaking to highly intelligent, well-informed people....I prepare by giving a lot of hard thought to the audience, what experience they've got, and where they're at. I don't want to patronize people with information they already have....I think about what kind of expertise I'm addressing, and where it is that I've got anything that's useful or helpful.*

You may still have to explain concepts and techniques in clear, direct language, but follow Callwood's example and show respect for the intelligence and sincerity of your audience.

3. **Your intent.** The representative of an association of banking institutions recently announced the banks' intention to go into the auto-leasing business. When the interviewer asked how much money the banks would make, the spokesperson replied that it didn't really matter how much profit was involved, the banks were only interested in providing their customers with better services. Snickers were heard all the way to Moose Jaw.

Remember, your audience will wonder why you are so concerned. If you have a personal motive that is justified, state it. If you are presenting a plan that is in the best interests of your listeners, make sure they know it. The more positively others perceive your motives, the more likely they are to listen to you.

4. **Your character.** What sort of impression do your words, your warmth, and your concern make on your audience? Do you cite reasonable examples and select your words judiciously? Are you fair in your treatment of opposing sides? Do your words include your entire audience, without making disparaging assumptions based on education, income,

sex, or race? Are you interested in presenting your ideas intelligently or in belittling opposing views? Are you committed to your own suggestions?

When you talk to people, you can affect their lives. You may not think you're doing it, but your remarks can give others the courage to go on, a new idea, advice they need that very day. When you realize how important speaking is, it adds conviction and energy to your presentation.

EXERCISE: Coast-to-Coast Debates

From Prince Rupert to Cornerbrook, Canadians have favourite topics for friendly debate. Divide into small groups and decide what your thesis would be in each of the following cases. Then, outline several ways to establish your credibility for each.

a) Is it worthwhile rustproofing your car?
b) Should you lie flat when a bear attacks you or face the animal in an upright position?
c) Is there such a thing as a Canadian identity?
d) What repellent is guaranteed protection against mosquitoes?

Facts and How to Find Them

Finding facts, verifiable information to support your arguments, is not hard, but you have to have the *energy* to dig for them. First, you must formulate specific questions. After that, telephone calls, personal interviews, and library materials will provide the back-up you need. Sometimes, just one statement from the *right* source will clinch your argument.

Most researchers know the value of telephone calls. If you're doing a speech on the success of franchises and need to know how much of every consumer dollar is spent in a franchise operation, go to the library. If the data given is not recent, consult the telephone book to get the name and number of a national franchise organization. Call that organization and research the corporate structure—in other words, find out the best source of reliable information. It may be the president, vice-president in charge of membership, or the public relations director. Be sure to get both names and the title right. You then telephone that person directly, give your name, and your request, and make it clear that your interview will be brief—three to five minutes. What if it's long distance? Is the information worth the expense? You may with to make a person-to-person call to ensure that the person is there and will speak to you, and then call back directly at a cheaper rate. If your source is out, you have saved money and can leave your name and number for a return call. Telephone research is surprisingly successful; you get accurate, up-to-date information and inside leads; however, be prepared to work to get the call, ask specific questions prepared in advance, and record the details correctly.

Once you have the data, be sure that the proofs you present are reasonable. The section on informal logic that follows later in this chapter should help sharpen your sense of analysis.

What Facts Do You Need?

Consider your audience. Are you speaking to people who focus on dollars and cents? Will expert opinions convince them? Do some listeners have fears or biases that need resolving?

Once again, take the example of the student who spoke on the need for organ donations. Her long-term goal was to make her audience more aware and supportive of organ donation; her immediate objective was to get them to sign their donor cards. She had done a thorough audience analysis:

> *I knew Milene could only be reached with facts and statistics. Gabriel responds well to humour, and you* [the instructor] *would be looking to see if I had covered all the angles.*

She supplied statistics outlining the actual and potential numbers of lives saved and the reduction in health-care costs if donors are found quickly. A combination of humour, scientific fact, and expert opinion helped her address the unspoken distaste some people have for losing parts of their bodies, even after death, and the fear of premature removal. By calmly presenting the information, she convinced many class members. Her conclusion was the clincher. In it she referred to the drama of a small child who had waited for a transplant. Everyone knew the story.

Follow Your Heart: Using Emotional Appeals

Do you remember the name Lindsay Eberhart? She was a toddler whose life depended on finding a kidney donor. For months, the media headlined the need for a transplant, and her story emphasized the need for organ donors. John Aird, who was then the Lieutenant-Governor of Ontario, visited the child and encouraged her parents. When the child received new kidneys, her skin lost its sickly, greenish hue, and she became an active, vigorous three-year-old.

By using the story of Lindsay Eberhart, the student made the issue of organ donation real and immediate. Those people who could not identify with an impersonal organ bank were able to make a personal connection with a suffering child. Her need and her joy inspired and *convinced* them.

Stories of real people, with names, ages, and personal details, touch the emotional level of your audience. If you use

the story as a *framework,* you can start by presenting a situation and the dilemma it involves, work through the solution—
the main part of your speech—and conclude by finishing the
story. Good storytellers include details to make their tales as
real as possible—without violating the privacy of the individuals
concerned.

Which Emotional Appeals Work?

The best advertising campaigns feature nostalgia, animals, love
of family, a sense of adventure, and wacky humour. It takes
great skill to assess which tactics work and which turn people
off. You cannot manipulate your audience or take unfair advantage of their vulnerability (see the interview with June Callwood).
You can, however, make effective appeals to a wide variety of
emotions. These are just a few:

- Empathy with and sympathy for individuals and groups;
- Pride in a neighbourhood, school, firm, or in the audience's
  potential or achievements;
- Determination to perserve and attain a goal;
- Pleasure;
- Pride in having one's worth or work acknowledged;
- Protective instincts for children or environment;
- Anger at insult or injustice;
- Competitiveness.

You can design your speech to include an emotional appeal in
the introduction and conclusion; your listeners will pay attention quickly, and remember your comments clearly if they are
emotionally engaged.

EXERCISE: Emotional Appeal

The last speech in this book is by Rose Anne Hart. It is one
of the finest speeches I have ever heard and it uses an emotional appeal, in the form of a story, to make the main point.
Read the speech (or watch it on the video *A Class Act*) and see
how many different emotional reactions you have to it.

What Part Does Humour Play?

A computer specialist was speaking on the financial losses caused
by the pirating or unlawful copying of computer software. His
presentation was good, but inevitably his audience began to drift.
The line, ''Speaking of access, I have probably spoken to
excess,'' brought them back with smiles and renewed interest.

　　For humour to be effective, it has to be natural for you. If
you force jokes or inject them inappropriately, you will look silly.
On the other hand, humour has great advantages. It relieves
fatigue, and it can break the sombreness of a dry or heavy

presentation. Outlining the problems of Canadian publishing, one speaker summarized a lengthy presentation of statistics with the pungent observation that ''Canadians spend less money on new books by Canadian writers each year than Americans do on cat litter'' (taken from David Olive, ''Good Reviews,'' *Toronto Life,* June 1988, volume 22, number 6). The comparison was alluded to often in the ensuing discussions.

If emotions are running high, a light touch may relieve a tense atmosphere. Humour, in the form of irony, can allow you to tackle a subject far more pointedly than is otherwise possible.

Humour can be used for serious purposes, to relieve the listing of impersonal data, or to create a bond among audience members. Experiment with it, using your friends for your rehearsals, and develop an approach that is natural for you.

Balancing Your Act

Reason, emotion, or credibility alone won't win your audience. You need to balance your arguments in order to connect with the different levels of awareness in each person. David Nichol was asked if emotion was necessary in business. He erupted:

> Absolutely! ...*You need a good balance between logic and emotion.*

Speakers often feel as though they are doing a high-wire balancing act. The audience is there as a safety net and they're ready to respond to your appeal; design your act carefully and *practise.*

EXERCISE: Mini-Persuasives: Understanding the Strategy

To persuade means to induce or lead others to your way of thinking. This exercise is a trial run in formulating a clear thesis, and selecting supporting arguments that are balanced. Your proofs must also be geared specifically to your audience, taking into account the logical, emotional, and psychological approaches possible.

Decide whether the entire class will all do the *same* assignment, or choose among the four possibilities.

You have 24 hours to prepare your speech, and it should only be two minutes long. Strive for good audience rapport—CONVINCE THEM.

a) What person or group has done the most, in the last month, to make the world a better/worse place?

b) Your classmates have financial resources that they wish to invest. Persuade them to invest in a particular project which you have a personal interest in. It may be

- an invention,
- a movie idea,

- a game,
- a community group.

c) What is the best *new* thing in the business world? (Consider personnel policies, opportunities, machinery, concepts, markets, government support, etc.)

d) Give details of a court case that is being covered by the media. Outline which side appears more prepared, or more likely to win, *or* more justified in its claim.

EXERCISE: There is a Difference

There is a difference between a speech that sells a product and one that advances an idea. In one case, the focus is on getting the best deal; in the other, on adopting an idea or course of action. This exercise demonstrates the difference in approach and emphasis.

You may choose to make either Speech (a) or Speech (b). The presentations should only be one and a half to two minutes long.

Situation 1: Traffic Lights

a) Sell a traffic light, the fixture itself, to a town council about to install several new lights.

b) Convince the council that a traffic light is necessary for safety at a busy intersection in your neighbourhood.

Situation 2: Reggae

a) Sell a collection of reggae records to a young disc jockey who wants to improve his or her collection of dance music.

b) Convince your school board that music from various cultures should be included in the music appreciation course offered in local high schools.

Situation 3: Automobile Insurance

a) Sell automobile insurance to a group of college/university students.

b) Convince an investigating committee that automobile insurance rates are unfair and outrageously overpriced.

EXERCISE: The Taped Interview

This exercise allows you to experiment with your voice as you project a character you invent. The interview should be taped and last approximately three to five minutes. The emphasis is on vocal quality and the interest level generated. Students have

adopted such diverse identities as the math teacher students
love to hate; a representative of Street Haven, a youth drop-in
centre; the president of the society for the preservation and
encouragement of respect for mothers-in-law; an Oreo cookie;
an exchange student; and Garfield.

Instructions:
a) Keep your own identity or adopt another character or persona. Make sure you know exactly who you are and what
   you wish to say in your interview.
b) Prepare questions for a partner; they should lead into the
   responses you have designed.
c) Have a short rehearsal with your partner. She/he will
   introduce you and conduct the interview, using the questions
   you provide.
d) When you have finished, you may exchange roles.
e) Submit the tape to the instructor; listening to the tapes in
   class is a good lesson in character projection and voice control. The interviews may be graded by the instructor or by
   a panel of class members.

Evaluation Outline for the Taped Inverview
Character Chosen:

Voice
　　Enunciation:
　　Emphasis:
　　Clarity:
　　Tone:
　　Emotional content:
　　Projection of warmth:

Pacing
　　Use of pauses:
　　Variation of tempo:
　　Emphasis:

Overall Effect
　　Projection of character:
　　Awareness of audience:
　　Special effects:

General Comment

Grade:

Every time you speak, you have a responsibility to examine the ethical base of your remarks. When others give you time on their program, they accord you a special status. You should attempt to maintain an ethical principle, that is, a standard of beliefs and behaviour that you follow and that you expect from others. Our society has a general code of ethics; you may have your own as well. As a speaker, you hold a position of privilege and must consider what arguments are justifiable to prove your point. In an attempt to determine your own ethical standards, consider the following guidelines.

Ethical Responsibility in Persuasive Speaking

1. **Advocating dangerous or illegal behaviour is unethical.** Arguing for the legalization of marijuana is one thing; suggesting that teenagers use the drug is unacceptable. It is unethical for you to try to convince others to do something which may be harmful or unlawful.

2. **Lying or suppressing information is unethical.** Lying is universally unacceptable. During the Watergate crisis, Richard Nixon made the remark, "I misspoke myself." His attempt to doubletalk his way out of a lie made the situation worse.

   If you know of major drawbacks to your plans, you must mention them, and use the opportunity to present solutions or alternatives. This does not mean you have to include every single drawback or difficulty; common sense will help you make the distinction between a significant disadvantage and a minor problem.

3. **Name-calling is unethical.** Attacking another person or group by calling them names is unacceptable. A speaker who thinks he or she is in the company of a sympathetic crowd may attempt such inflammatory references as "welfare bums" or "slime buckets," but such attempts usually backfire.

4. **Citing "technical ignorance" or "expert authority" as an excuse is unethical.** If you are discussing reducing costs in your business and a colleague recommends using someone who can crack computer codes and sell you software programs at reduced rates, what is your response? If your money-saving friend says that this person is a "computer expert" and knows what's legal or not, does that absolve you of the responsibility of verifying the legality of the action? Does your personal lack of computer knowledge make you any less innocent of wrongdoing?

   What about a local politician who is speaking on behalf of a chemical company in danger of being shut down. The company is accused of emitting PCBs, cancer-causing agents, into the atmosphere. However, they have several "expert

252   Speaking Our Minds

opinions'' that the emissions fall into the ''safe'' level. What is safe? Can the politician base her personal support on the reports of experts?

> It does not follow...that the more facts you know or the more of the subject you have studied, the more *morally relevant facts* you know. Even in highly technical matters it is possible for the non-expert to obtain at least as good an understanding of the morally relevant facts as the expert. And, the non-expert may have a far superior understanding of the relevant moral considerations. Technical experts can be moral morons just as ethics experts can be technical morons.
>
> (CONRAD G. BRUNK, ''Professionalism and Responsibility in the Technological Society,'' in Deborah Poff and Wilfrid Waluchow, eds., *Business Ethics in Canada.* Scarborough: Prentice-Hall Canada Inc., 1987, p. 66)

Dealing With a Negative or Hostile Audience

How do you define a hostile audience? They are generally people who oppose an idea as vigorously as you support it. That's the key: ideas are in conflict, not human beings. By remembering that, you should stay clear of personal attacks and unpleasantness. Just because people do not agree with you, they may not disagree; they may be uncommitted. You can view the commitment of the audience to ideas on a sliding scale. If you believe in your proposal (and you should not be speaking if you don't), your aim is to bring the audience along the scale. A 100% change of mind may not be possible *the first time* but you can attempt a process of gradual persuasion.

There are specific steps to remember in dealing with an audience opposed to your ideas.

> "It was not ideas I was giving them exactly, but rather ferments— something which I hoped would work like yeast in their minds."
> (Nellie McClung)

1. **Get yourself ready.** What is your purpose? Do you want to add to the conflict or defuse the situation? If you go into the group in a combative state of mind, your body language will communicate your antagonism immediately. If you concentrate on a rational presentation of ideas, if you admit that your audience may have justification for their outlook, you're in a better position to convince rather than clobber them.

   Is your voice under control? In Chapter 6, we discussed the way the voice can either adopt the tone of the situation or establish a new one. Concentrate on achieving an atmosphere of courteous exchange; use words that acknowledge the intelligence of your listeners. Breathing exercises can help you achieve a sense of calm that extends to your voice; that evenness will gradually affect others.

2. **Acknowledge your audience's position.** Students who suddenly learn their fees will increase 25%, vacationers forced to move to a smaller, less convenient hotel, homeowners facing expropriation, all have a right to be upset.

Admit that their distress is justified and do not trivialize their situation by citing other, more dramatic crises.

3. **Request a fair hearing.** Agreeing with your audience that they have valid complaints is a good way to start. You may be able to find one or two other points of agreement. It is psychologically important to concur on some points: the necessity of immediate action, the distress caused to everyone, the need for clarification. This puts you all on the same side. Then you must firmly request their time for a hearing. The mark of an intelligent person is his or her ability to give a fair chance to a speaker presenting an unpopular position.

Explain that you have an ethical responsibility to present alternative ideas or plans. If you can, compliment your listeners on their fairmindedness, and remind them again that ideas, not individuals, are in conflict. After all, the search for truth or for a solution, not the passion of confrontation, should be the main object.

REQUEST A FAIR HEARING

4. **Predict objections and take care of yourself.** It's naive to assume that everyone will support such obviously good schemes as a national holiday in midwinter or medicare for pets. If you realize that some people will be unsupportive, you'll be ready for those cold looks. Don't be put off by negative eye contact or people holding signs that say "You Doorknob." Somewhere, you will find someone who will offer support, and you can follow June Callwood's lead:

> Usually, I find several faces that are sympathetic. I couldn't talk to a hostile face; I'd stop looking at that person. It would discomfit me too much. I look at fairly sympathetic faces, and I watch them carefully to see what's happening. I check them over and over again.

EXERCISE: Check it Out: Analysing a Speech Made in Favour of Trapping

Few issues are as explosive as the question of animal rights versus the trapping of furbearing animals. In January 1987, the Canadian Arctic Resources Commission held a symposium in Montreal entitled "The Use of Northern Wildlife: Animal Rights, Subsistence, and Commercialization." Thomas Coon, a chief of the Grand Council of the Cree, and a member of Indigenous Survival International, made a speech outlining the need to protect native trapping rights and way of life.

Read the speech carefully; if possible, rehearse and present parts of it. Note the appeals to reason, to exchange, to noninterference. Coon provides a background for southerners to understand the native way of life and draws parallels between native and non-native conservationists. Outline, with specific references, why this speech is a good presentation to a hostile audience.

THOMAS COON
Grand Council of the Cree
Indigenous Survival International
Val d'Or, Quebec

Sometimes, I feel that I and my culture, my tradition, my way of life are being questioned. This is why I would like to say a few words in my Cree language. Maybe you will learn some Cree words from me. I hope in two days we will be able to share many things. I am sure you can learn from me and I can learn from you. ...I sometimes have a hard time finding the correct English word to use, but I never have a hard time trying to find the correct word in the Cree Indian language. When you are northern, you learn to love the surroundings, the environment, the wildlife, and the human beings that are around you. You learn to respect all that is around you. You learn to share your harvest, and you learn to help each other, because that is the only way you will survive in the north. I will never criticize my neighbour; I don't intend to, and I hope I don't start today or in the next few days, because I am very hurt and my people are very hurt when they hear there are animal-rights groups and people down south who are threatening our way of life, our culture. They hear there are people down south who do not know, or who do not understand our way of life, who are questioning our profession as good wildlife managers, who are questioning our culture, and questioning our way of life.

The people up north do not want to be bothered to face such problems, because they always have lived traditionally, in harmony with nature. For centuries and centuries, our people have lived off the land, and they intend to for many centuries to come. We have harvested wildlife for centuries and centuries, and I am very pleased today

(Continued)

to know there is not one species that is on the endangered list that we have been harvesting for all these centuries. And this is why we don't understand why there is a question that our way of life and the way we have utilized animals for a living is no longer good.

The animal-rights activists have really bothered northern people. Surely some of the things they do are good things, but surely some of the things they do are damaging to aboriginal people's economies. We all have seen and experienced the seal issue, how it destroyed the seal market, and how it has hurt some Inuit communities. How would you feel if 60%, 80%, or 90% of your income was taken away from you? How would you feel when you have little children, a family to support? Killing a market is just like taking the food away from the family's table. Those people were poor before the ban, and today they are poorer. Must we continue, must that be repeated—the damage, the hardships to native people? I hear "anti-fur," "anti-trapping," "anti-harvest." There is no doubt in our minds up north; we are the next target. Surely, they will kill the market, because they have all the power down south and we don't up north. We are the weak, we are the poor, we will lose. But we have lost so much in the past that we must defend the little that we have left. There is no doubt that the anti-harvest campaign strikes at the heart of the aboriginal peoples' economy.

Why is our traditional way of life tied down to the fur industry? There is always the concept of trading in the traditions of native people. I mentioned earlier that you must help each other, you must respect each other. In doing that, you trade. I trade my beaver with my neighbour and, in turn, he gives me moose meat. I trade my mittens with him, and, in turn, he gives me something else. That trading has always been there, and so has trade with the other parts of the fur industry—we do that. We trade the fur pelt for an income. And when Canada stops trading, then I will stop trading. The income that we get from fur pelts enables me to go to the trap-line when I am harvesting wildlife. But once that's gone, I will not be able to practise that, and many of our people will not be able to. You have now forced me, displaced me, from the land.

The animal rights people...will not only destroy the fur market, but also our way of life, my culture. It will destroy my traditional life style. You know, sometimes we really have to put ourselves in the place of the people who are suffering in order to get the real taste of pain and hardship. The families up north are very isolated, as I explained earlier, and they need this income and this market in order to survive. When we make presentations such as these, not only do we speak of protecting the market, but of protecting our way of life, our culture, which is being threatened now by various animal-rights activities and campaigns.

I have two questions that I have never been able to answer. One is rights. What is the definition of rights, animal rights? Can we really, as human beings, think the same way as animals think? Can we put ourselves in them and say, "These are the rights that animals should have; this is the way animals feel"? Cruelty is another. I try to compare the way we take animals with slaughterhouses. I don't ask how animals are taken in slaughter-houses, and I don't want to know. Taking life is definitely a cruelty. No matter how we die as human beings, no matter how we take life, it is cruelty. No matter what way we take life it is cruelty. Killing a culture, killing a society, and killing a way of life is definitely a cruelty. My culture will die in agony.

I am pleased to know there are people down south who are concerned about the

(Continued)

environment. We have always been environmentalists; we have always been conservationists. We have always practised that; it is part of our tradition, and now it's being questioned.

As a wrap-up, I want to say, that on the anti-trapping, anti-fur, anti-harvest campaign, the native people in Canada have more to lose than any other segment of the fur industry if these campaigns are successful. I would like to share with you my definition of wildlife. We all know wildlife is a renewable resource, and, in our religious beliefs with land, we believe that wildlife is there for a purpose: for man to make a living off. To me, wildlife is a gift of the Great Creator. These are the gifts of nature. Wildlife is the fruit of the land. Thank you.

"It Ain't Necessarily So": A Brief Guide to Informal Logic

One thing that will have your audience fidgeting in their seats is a lack of sense. An understanding of logical reasoning will add strength to a foundation of research and good design. The most important step is simply to ask yourself, "Does this make sense?" Do your thesis, supporting arguments, examples, and statistics make sense to you?

Your audience will be asking, "Do I agree with this statement? Is it supported by believable facts? Is it a reasonable consequence of facts I know?" If you have done your preparation logically and well, they'll be on your side.

Logical Reasoning

There are three categories of formal logical reasoning behind most arguments: deductive, inductive, and syllogistic reasoning.

Deductive Reasoning

In deductive reasoning, a conclusion about a specific idea is arrived at after considering a number of general examples. In arguing against her city's bid to be an Olympic site, an alderwomen might quote examples from several past Olympic Games "Every city that has hosted the Olympics in the past has exceeded the budget. We will exceed our budget too, and we cannot afford to do this."

In a way, deductive reasoning is used to predict the future from past events. This works well, provided that the past events are truly comparable to the event in question. Olympic events *are* perhaps fated to go over budget. If the general facts are not true, however, or if the situation is different, the conclusion could be invalid. The city might already have sufficient facilities available so that the budget could in fact be met. The alderwoman may have ignored some examples of Olympic Games that stayed within their budgets.

Is it reasonable to argue, "There has never been a woman

prime minister. Therefore Ms. Tremblay will not succeed in her bid for election''?

Inductive Reasoning

With inductive reasoning, the thought moves in the opposite way, from specific examples to a general conclusion. The number of specific examples studied must be quite large to arrive at a valid conclusion. Statistics are often used in this type of argument. For example, census reports for two separate periods indicate a drop of 40% in the number of people reporting any religious affiliation. These figures represent statements made by millions of Canadians. From these figures you may reach the general conclusion that religion currently has little effect on Canadian life.

This type of reasoning can be dangerous if the sample used to supply the data is too small. In the media, we often hear of one or two immigrants to Canada who have been terrorists or who are criminals. From these examples, many people conclude that all immigrants are threatening and immigration should be curtailed. Is this a logical conclusion?

Syllogistic Reasoning

A syllogism produces a conclusion from two or more pieces of information. These first two ideas are called the premises. For example:

All large cities have garbage problems.
Windsor is a large city.
Therefore, Windsor has a garbage problem.

If the first two premises are true, and if they are related, then the conclusion, as above, is valid.

There is a danger with syllogistic reasoning, however, if the first premises are based only on opinion, or on incorrect or incomplete facts:

Francophones and Anglophones can't get along.
Students from Laval are Francophones; students from Ryerson are Anglophones.
Therefore, students from Laval and Ryerson can't get along.

Is this valid?

Often, one or more of the premises is implied rather than stated. For example, ''Many of Canada's top businesspersons dine at Winston's. Therefore, Winston's is an excellent restaurant.'' Unstated is the second premise that top businesspersons only dine at fine restaurants. Be sure that premises, spoken or unspoken, are valid.

These three types of reasoning form the basis of most conclusions or arguments that you will try to present, although they are not usually so clearly put as in the examples. In calling for restraint in the use of nuclear power, a speaker may say, ''Look at what happened at Chernobyl and Three Mile Island.'' The thought moves from specific examples to the general conclusion: inductive reasoning. A plea to keep alcohol out of a local sports stadium based on experiences in other stadiums makes use of deductive reasoning. Knowledge of these three forms, will help you build strong, reasonable speeches, and can be used to test your arguments.

Errors in Logic

There are pitfalls to be wary of. Be sure to avoid the following errors that weaken the force of your arguments.

Name-Calling

Attacking a person rather than an idea is not a valid reasoning technique. Traditionally, this is called an *ad hominem* (''against the person'') attack. The character of a person proposing an idea is usually irrelevant to the quality of his or her ideas, and using words like ''wimp'' or ''pinko'' does not advance your case. If you have proof that a person supporting a gambling setup is a known criminal, that is a serious allegation and a sound attack of the proposal. However, most name-calling is not relevant. Referring to people who advocate stricter drinking-and-driving controls as a bunch of temperance nuts does not lead to audience confidence. Even when you challenge a concept, your words cannot be gratuitously inflammatory; you must back up your remarks with fact and logic. A speaker who claimed that withdrawal from NATO was a ''dangerous and naive policy'' may have had some reasons for such an opinion. But simply using these words with no backup would not convince anyone who was not already of that belief.

Generalities

Speaking about something in broad general terms suggests you don't have specific facts. Comments such as ''Everyone knows that all our best doctors are going to the U.S.'' or ''All the studies show that children need two parents'' are signals that generalities are being paraded as truth. Have specific studies to back your points. Too general a statement leaves you open to contradiction.

Cardstacking

It's not fair to present your argument as if it's the only one. You don't have to argue the other side of the case, but you can't leave the impression that it doesn't exist. For example, in arguing for the retention of a wilderness area near your city, you must face the claims of developers and show how they could be met elsewhere. Then present the ecological and recreational benefits of the land. A balanced approach has more weight than one that stacks all the cards in your favour.

Can you outline balanced arguments for

- banning leg-hold traps?
- French language schools?

Jumping on the Bandwagon

"*Everyone* is doing it!" Despite what you told your mother when you were thirteen, the fact that *everyone* is shredding their pant legs and shaving one half of their heads is *not* sufficient reason to do so as well. It is deductive reasoning gone wrong: all too often everyone *isn't* doing it. The group sampled may be too small to give reliable data; the research methods may be insufficient; the circumstances in which the audience find themselves may be very different from "everyone" else. Do the following statements, heard in the cafeteria of a large university, convince you?

"Many athletes take steriods. Obviously it's necessary if they want to compete internationally."

"Everyone's investing in real estate. The profits are incredible, and you can double your money in a year."

"Joint custody of children by parents who have divorced is spreading like wildfire. It's obviously a good idea."

Reliance on tradition is another form of jumping on the bandwagon. The plaint that "we've always done it this way" is not a convincing argument. There may indeed be valid reasons for actions confirmed by tradition to be continued; the practice of one vote for each citizen is an electoral process worth preserving. Other examples may be more questionable. The declaration that "we've always been a monarchy and always will be" is not a strong proof. The pros and cons behind the tradition must be explored.

Ridiculing

There's many a true word said in jest.
(T.C. HALIBURTON, Sam Slick's Wise Saws)

Sometimes it is fun to make your opponent's ideas look ridiculous, and this can be part of a good argument. If it's your *only* tactic, however, think again. If in highlighting one facet of a position, you ignore other valid parts, your criticism of your opponent's position is weakened. An environmental group is trying to protect a marsh. An opponent jeers, "Who needs to save a bunch of bugs?" A thoughtful listener will realize there is more than bugs at stake, and dismiss such a comment. William Lyon Mackenzie King, prime minister from 1921 to 1930 and from

1935 to 1948, often consulted the spirit world, communing with his mother and his little dog, Pat. A historian who dismisses King's achievements for this reason ignores, at the peril of his argument, the actual content of King's policies.

Experts

It's good to have experts to support your ideas, to have big names on your side. However, use experts with care. Be sure they *are* experts, recognized in an appropriate field, and well known to your audience. Be sure their comments are up-to-date and appear free from bias. A gay community leader speaking in support of the ordination of gay and lesbian ministers may *appear* biased to an audience. They may think, "What else would you expect him to say?" Balance your experts to include those who do not have such a strong identification *only* with the idea you are advancing. Ask another person in favour of gay and lesbian ordination to speak, as well as a representative of the gay community. Remember also that experts often conflict; your opponent may have an equally forceful expert to counteract your point. Thus, use experts only if they will really build your case.

If you are using an endorsement, that is, supporting your case with the statements of known authorities, avoid the appearance of bias. Do you remember those advertisements for "Shiney Bright," the toothpaste that nine out of ten dentists recommend? Did you ever wonder *how* the sponsors conducted their survey?

Be sure that the endorser has some relevance to your cause and does not have an automatic obligation to support you. In the following examples, discuss the relative merits of the endorsers:

1. For your presentation on the need for wheelchair access to a new sports complex: wheelchair athlete Rick Hansen and/or Olympic skier Karen Percy;
2. For the lobby for financial compensation for Japanese Canadians uprooted during World War II, David Suzuki and/or the leaders of the federal opposition parties;
3. For your fight against the use of animals for laboratory experiments in cosmetic firms, the head of ARK II, an animal rights group and/or a fashion and beauty commentator.

Circular Reasoning

Beware of circular argument, which doesn't really prove anything, and only brings you back where you began. If A is true because B is true, but the proof of B is A, watch out. A statement such as "Canadian singers will never be internationally successful because they're too Canadian" only takes you back to your original premise that Canadian singers can't make it outside Canada. You don't prove a point by stating it twice.

"Native peoples should stay on reservations because they can't integrate in our society" is also a circular argument. The reason native peoples can't integrate is their isolation on reserves. The circle of this argument needs to be broken by a broader definition of terms, and a wider exploration of the facts on which the opinion is based. Do native peoples wish to integrate?

Irrelevant Conclusions
A conclusion should not appear from thin air. It must follow reasonably from the speaker's previous remarks. In the following example, the speaker begins by detailing the problems of implementing the Official Languages Act, and how the implementation differs from the purpose of the legislation. Abruptly, he concludes that the act is discriminatory, although he has not raised the question of discrimination at all in his argument. The conclusion does not make sense:

> *The intent of the Official Languages Act is to guarantee a person's right to be served by federal agencies in either of Canada's official languages. But the implementation of the Act often serves a different purpose. That's the trouble with the Act, it's discriminatory.*

Is the following conclusion logical?

> *The sale of cigarettes is not illegal. Therefore, a law that bans smoking in the workplace cannot be valid.*

Misuse of Anecdotal Proofs
Stories of how your aunt's divorce cost her the business she'd helped build, or how the lack of basics in your child's primary education ruined his chance at college add force to your speech. But personal stories or anecdotes should not stand alone; additional reasons are needed. Businessman Bud McDougall said his only regret at leaving school at 14 was that he hadn't left earlier. Does this prove that schooling does nothing for your career?

Confusing Opinion with Fact
Take care to distinguish between facts and opinions, and acknowledge the latter for what they are. Do not pretend that they are facts. Facts can be verified; opinions must stand the test of time to be found true or false. For example, Maritime fishing crews wear copper bracelets to protect them from arthritis and rheumatism. Is the effectiveness of these bracelets a matter of fact or opinion?

False Facts
The most logical, well-reasoned argument will crumble if it is based on false facts. Be sure your research unearths the most

recent and reliable information to support your case, and evaluate your sources carefully. (This is discussed in detail in Chapter 3.)

> Is it a fact René Lévesque wanted to destroy Confederation?
> Is it a fact that sex education in the schools leads to promiscuity?
> Is it a fact that it's illegal to pick trilliums in Ontario?
> Is it a fact that a balanced diet requires 170 grams of meat per day?
> Is it a fact that ice worms exist only in folklore?

Flag-Waving
Although Canadians are not prone to this type of fallacious reasoning, they are sometimes sucked into a larger political machine. Statements such as ''we must allow the testing of missiles with nuclear capabilities in order to protect the safety of the North American people,'' or ''an armed presence in Central America is essential to guard our way of life,'' attempt to convince audiences with an exaggerated appeal to patriotism. Good citizens support governments that use reason, not hype, to justify their actions.

Faulty Cause and Effect
If you are citing causes and effects, be sure that the cause does indeed produce the effect you claim. Have you considered all the variables that may lead to a particular result? Is it true that

> If you eat less, you will lose weight?
> If everyone in Canada spoke French and English, there would be equal opportunity for all?

Poor Analogies
Comparing your idea to something that the audience understands can be helpful. However, be sure the examples and analogies you use do not detract from the credibility of your argument. For instance, is it auspicious to compare planning a wedding ceremony to mapping out a military campaign? Is marriage really war?

Mayor Jean Drapeau of Montreal predicted that the Montreal Olympics could no more have a deficit than a man could have a baby. This analogy caught headlines (perhaps its purpose), but it was so far-fetched as to make the point laughable.

Be sure the analogy works.

Overly Emotional Appeals
Emotional appeals have a place in a speech, but not as the sole factor in a reasoned argument. A speech opposing nuclear arms that consists only of the spectres of nuclear winter, blasted landscapes, and the end of the human race will offend, repel, and

alarm your audience. However, they may not be convinced. Avoid, as well, a maudlin approach, a sickeningly sentimental play for support. No one will fall for the description of over-worked bankers, besieged by critics, as they work unstintingly for the good of their clients.

Using Isolated Abuses to Attack the Whole Policy

There are always individuals and groups who will abuse their rights. This is true of every aspect of life. However, the fact that something can be abused is no justification for its being pro-hibited to all. What's wrong with the following?

1. Eight people in one college filed false information on student loan applications. All they used the money for was a trip to Florida in study week. Student loans should be abolished.
2. Some women do not take proper birth-control measures. Then they seek abortions to get rid of unwanted pregnan-cies. Abortion clinics should be banned.
3. Last year federal authorities denied entry to 38 people who claimed to be, but weren't, political refugees. If we don't tighten up our laws, the country will be swamped with illegal immigrants posing as refugees.

EXERCISE: Logic

The following activities provide an opportunity to test your understanding of what is logical and what is not.

Logical Pursuits: How Many Errors Can You Find?

Do you remember that game on the children's page in the news-paper? An apparently normal picture is loaded with illogical

HOW MANY ERRORS CAN YOU FIND?

details: planes flying upside down, bicycles missing a wheel, children wearing only one shoe, batters swinging at footballs. The object is to find and identify as many mistakes as possible.

Tune into an interesting radio or television current events show and relax. While eating popcorn, tape an excerpt of a speech that contains some errors in logic. Political announcements or interviews are excellent sources. Play the excerpt in class, and present your list of logical bloopers, using the categories already outlined.

IMPERSONATION: The Great Pretender

Divide into teams of five or six people and plan brief speeches on the topic "Bald is Beautiful." Pack it with as many errors in logic as you can, at the same time *attempting* to sound reasonable. One person from each team delivers the speech while the other group tries to spot and identify as many thinning arguments as possible. (If, for obvious reasons, this assignment would be insensitive, alter the title to "Left-Handed People are Brilliant.")

Riding the Wave

Cast aside your practical down-filled jacket and duofold underwear. Beneath the sensible surface of every Canadian speaker is the derring-do of a surfing wizard. If you've followed the advice of the preceding chapters, you are ready for the thrill of catching the currents of audience reaction and riding the wave of oratorical brilliance. Even more, you should be ready to *enjoy it*.

The secret lies in your preparation: the plan and the practice. By the time you're ready for a major speech, you know how to organize. Your notes are clear, colour-coded, and precise, but there's more. *Advanced* note-card technique requires that you list your thesis, main proofs, and supporting ideas the usual way, *and* list alternative or additional material on the side, in case it's needed.

Imagine you have prepared a speech on eating disorders for an audience of teenagers. However, as you circulate in the foyer, you notice a fair sprinkling of parents and teachers. Have you any information about parent support groups, or anecdotes about families who were baffled for months by someone's odd eating habits? Get out your pen and jot down reminders of that information and ****asterisk****·them so you'll notice the addition. It's even better to predict·this at home, but perfection comes next year.

What happens when inspiration hits? As David Nichol, President of Loblaw International Merchants, says:

I like the security blanket of those little cards. But when you get off to a good start, when you're enthusiastic, you can forget about the

> *notes, and let the good times roll. When the spirit hits you, when you've spent a lot of time planning and you're totally prepared, then you don't need the notes.*

He's right. You don't need them—for a while.

Two examples illustrate the *brilliant* improvisation of students. A hospitality student was speaking on shy rights, the need to protect the dignity of the reticent and scared-to-death. As he walked to the lectern, a full-front, three-sided structure, he suddenly ducked behind and into the lectern, and started with the words, "I'd much rather make my speech this way than face you. Whenever I have to look at people to talk, I get so shy I can't say a word." He won his audience immediately.

Another student, in a book and magazine publishing course, made a speech on the legalization of prostitution. As she spoke on the financial reasons for some people turning to prostitution, she noticed that most of the class was with her, except for two obviously unconvinced men. Looking directly at them, she said, "Look around you. Can you be sure everyone here has enough money to pay the rent and buy food?"

Then, looking at each section of the audience individually, and speaking right to them, she said, "I'm not so sure what I may have to do in my lifetime to care for myself and my children, and I'm not going to knock anyone for what she or he may have to do to survive." She cared a great deal for her subject and her audience, and the rapport she established was moving. The feeling in the room caused the dissenters to listen carefully to her point of view; agreement was not necessary, but open-mindedness was.

How do you ride the wave without wiping out? Here are a few pointers. I can tell you from experience that you sometimes surprise yourself with how *good* you are. Afterwards, you may shake and wonder how you did it. That's the fun of public speaking: the skills you learn and the hours of practice make winging it possible.

Watch Your Audience Closely

The way your audience sits, nods, nudges each other, and talks to you with their eyes, gives you clues to their reaction to you. If you touch an unexpected nerve, there will be visible signs of agreement. Laughter is a sure indicator. Unconvinced audiences may respond to a plea for a fair hearing, and once you have them listening you can explain your honest intentions. Choose faces and eyes that will support you and give you a fair indication of how you are doing.

Prepare Extra Material

Speakers also list additional examples or proofs that may come in handy. Pretend you're a musician doing a set in a club. You know the musical taste of the usual clientele but still have a list of "extras" and "standbys" taped to your guitar.

When you practise at home, ask your friend or partner which anecdote works better, which example has more impact.

Have Faith in Yourself

You are good. Students in our universities and colleges make some of the finest speeches there are: they are accurate, moving, committed, convincing, *superb*. When you decide to tell a story that just came to you, or you remember yet another and better proof, go for it.

Use Your Plan

You knew it! First you're told to "go for it"; next is "use the plan." The plan is there to make sure that you come back to the topic, back to the thesis, back to the *reason you are speaking*. You may get carried away by your unexpected remarks and get confused. "What was I talking about?" The notes tell you. They also help you to—

Finish Strong and Finish on Time

Running five minutes overtime is normal; running 25 minutes overtime can be *boring*. Help the organizers keep their schedules by keeping to yours. That's the purpose of your notes. After you have spoken extemporaneously, check your cards to make sure you are still on track.

Good speakers leave the audience wanting more. End on a high note. You can build your conclusion with alliteration, a series of parallel questions, or repetition. Jesse Jackson, in the California primaries in 1988, promised different segments of his party to "compete without conflict and differ without division." Eddie Greenspan concluded his speech on the futility of the death penalty by referring to Donald Marshall, a New Brunswick Indian convicted of a crime he did not commit. Greenspan asked:

> Which of you, sitting here today, could have pulled the bag over his head? Which of you could have fastened the rope around his neck? Which of you could have sprung the trap door which sent Donald Marshall to his death?

Rose Anne Hart, in the speech that concludes this book, urges her audience to pause:

> When you meet someone who is different from you because of nationality, or colour, or religion, obesity, handicap, or sexual orientation, before executing that clever imitation, before making that witty remark, before issuing that curt dismissal—think.

When you practise your speech, listen to your final words. Do you sound clear and strong. Have you put your whole heart into the finish?

By now you know that the secret of winging it is to prepare for anything. That way, if you want to improvise, you have the knowledge that you can do it. Your confidence will impress your audience and your reason, wit, and logic will convince them.

Speech Assignment: The Persuasive

You must care about the topic you choose for this speech; your commitment will make it easier for you to persuade others.

Allow two to three weeks for this assignment so that you can prepare well.

1. Choose a topic (some suggestions are listed below).
2. After preliminary research, write down the purpose of your speech, the *thesis*, and main supporting points. Discuss these with your instructor.
3. Prepare a persuasive speech five to eight minutes long. Your presentation will show how much you have learned about designing and delivering an effective speech.

Possible Topics

- Music in the workplace
- Diet centres: rip-offs or help
- The causes of math anxiety
- Hair styles: fashion or social comment
- Travelling by yourself
- Ethics in the workplace
- Franchising is the way to go
- Advertising in the fashion industry
- Medical advancements based on human and animal experimentation
- Medical dilemmas: euthanasia, surrogate mothers, financial cutbacks, organs for sale on the black market
- Closer ties with communist countries
- Unsung Canadian heroes: Jack McClelland, Jane Rule, Norman Bethune, Rosemary Brown
- Sale of alcohol in local stores
- Marriage vs. living together
- Muscles for women
- Mandatory age for suspending drivers' licenses
- 35mm cameras vs. instamatics
- Swimming in the ocean
- The key to finding a job
- Costume jewellery vs. real jewellery
- Square meals vs. gourmet
- Streetproofing children
- Bob Marley's popularity is due as much to his

philosophy as to his music
- Price of long distance telephone calls discriminates against students (ordinary Canadians, kids, people in love, etc.)
- Minorities in the police and armed forces
- Stop biting your nails
- Become a block parent
- Car seats for babies
- Legalizing prostitition
- Strikes for teachers or doctors: necessity or crime?
- Danger in sports
- The relative safety of different products
- Changes to be made in an institution, or government agency or ministry
  Group brainstorm for more

DELIVERY TECHNIQUES TO REMEMBER

1. Use your voice to move your audience: pause, vary volume, excite, ask questions.
2. Make connection as you speak. Be aware of your audience and use their moods.
3. Polish your intro and conclusion. Give your all to a strong finish.
4. Build ethics into your delivery as well as your content. Move others but don't exploit their feelings.
5. Take time to feel the experience and enjoy it.

INTERVIEW

June Callwood

Journalist and Social Activist

April 13, 1988

June Callwood is a journalist, novelist, indefatigable speaker and fundraiser. More than any other Canadian, she has the ability to perceive the needs of a community, and form co-operative working groups to fulfil those needs. She founded

Nellie's, Jessie's, and Casey House in Toronto, and was an early advocate of palliative care. Her energy, her generosity, her joy make her a national hero, one who coined her own watchword: "Eventually you save the world. And if someone has to do it, it might as well be *you.*"

Q

In the convocation address you urged the audience to do something outrageous every day. Do you?

A

I think my whole life is outrageous. I'm suffering somewhat from the fallout from a series of columns I've just done on women who have lost custody of their children. I think I live outside what is considered normal behaviour.

Q

Why do you speak? You must spend almost all of your personal time speaking.

A

Well, I turn down fifteen to twenty speeches a week. I give them for two reasons: it's for a cause I support, like the opposition to the censorship bill, or for Nellie's, [a shelter for battered women] or Jessie's [a centre for single pregnant teenagers] or Casey's [a hospice for people with AIDS], or for palliative care, or better services for children, or the problems of poverty and homelessness. I frequently speak at fundraisers for battered women's shelters; soon I'm going to Ottawa and

Bracebridge to speak for interval houses there.

Public speaking is also my pension fund. As a freelancer, without a company pension plan, I have to plan for my own retirement, and I am paid for a number of my speeches. As an older woman, it will be a good income for me.

Q

You speak well to audiences made up of people of very diverse backgrounds. How do you approach your audiences?

A

I make a lot of assumptions. I see it as a very personal relationship, and that a belligerent or scolding tone, hectoring, or a critical approach is going to mean you're not going to be heard. People aren't going to listen to you.

I also assume that no matter how people look (and I don't mean their physical appearance but the stoniness of their faces, or the fact that they don't look like an interesting group), there's going to be a lot of surprises. I never underestimate an audience. I assume I'm speaking to highly intelligent, well-informed people. I also make the

assumption that they share my views, as long as I stick to the ethical component which is responsibility for one another. I urge them to open themselves to participating in their society more fully. It's a gentle message but it's very, very important.

Q

What public speakers do you admire?

A

Eddie Greenspan is probably the best in Canada. Alan Borovoy is dynamite; Julian Porter is a remarkably fine speaker. I once heard Ralph Nader, and understand why he is such an important consumer advocate. He's a great speaker. Rosalie Abbella is one of the best speakers anywhere.

Pierre Berton is compelling; you pay attention. It's his size, the big voice, and big thoughts. He has a big view of the country that he communicates.

Q

How well do people do at introducing you?

A

I've had some awkward ones, including the ones where they get your name wrong. One student at the University of Toronto, Scarborough College, introduced me as the founder of NATO. It was a bit much. I have also been thanked and introduced with wonderful elegance.

Q
How do you prepare for a speech?

A
I work only from notes. I'm getting five honorary degrees this spring, and four would like me to do the convocation address. They also want a print copy of the speech—but I don't have one. The second speech I gave was entirely written, and I nervously read every word. I found that I'd left the last page on the seat where I'd been sitting. I had to leave my seat and come down the stairs to get the page, and I've never had a written speech since. I prepare by giving a lot of hard thought to the audience, what experience they've got, and where they're at. I don't want to patronize people with information they already have.

You don't tell social workers about the feminization of poverty— they knew that ten years ago.

I think about what kind of expertise I'm

addressing and where it is that I've got anything that's useful or helpful. Most of the time, you're there because someone on the planning committee thought you have information that is useful for the group. They don't always know exactly what it is, but you take their ideas, and add your own judgment of where that group is at, and what would be useful to them from your experience, for you to talk about. I write in note form, sometimes full sentences, on folded pieces of white paper. Never any longer than five sides of notes. Just one word will sometimes remind me of a story. I take care with the opening and with the end.

Q
Can you see the audience when you're speaking to them?

A
Yes, I watch carefully; I watch faces. Usually, I find several faces that are sympathetic. I couldn't talk to a hostile face; I'd stop looking at that person. It would discomfort me too much. I look at fairly sympathetic faces and I watch them carefully to see what's happening. I

check them over and over again.

Q
Do you regret any of your speeches?

A
In Halifax in the late 'sixties, I spoke at a luncheon for couples attending a service-club conference. It was a time when everything was very open and I was still in full stride as a hippie. They seemed very stiff and uncomfortable so I said to them let's touch one another, let's care about one another. People cried and gave me a standing ovation, and I felt I had manipulated them. I was sick with shame. *Of course* everyone is lonely, and people need to touch. To have pulled a real evangelical trip on them was inexcusable. It's easy to make people cry when you touch their loneliness but it's unethical. You open them all up, and when it's over, you're on a plane. To my credit, I knew it was awful and never did it again.

Q
Do you still get nervous?

A
Some audiences. The convocations are nervewracking. I didn't

finish high school, and was intimidated being at a convocation at all. I'm nervous of extremely well-dressed people; it always has bugged me. When I was a kid we were awfully poor, and clothes were a way you could tell we were poor. Teenagers with better clothes always made me feel vulnerable, and I envied them, so a room of extremely well-dressed people still makes me feel vulnerable.

I really sweated over a speech to the Canadian Bar Association, Ontario. It was a very prestigious group, and I worked all day trying to figure out what would be of interest to them. I spoke on altruism.

Q
What speech do you remember?

A
Psychiatrist John Rich, a friend of mine, once said there are two kinds of people: the ones who remember only their mistakes, and those who remember only their victories. Lamentably, I only remember the duds.

If I've misjudged things, or been picketed and gotten distraught, been attacked in question periods, I can't forget. I don't rise to that kind of challenge, I sink. I have a resilient ego, and I don't take it personally, and I believe they're wrong, *but* I can't take the anger in their looks, the bitterness. It's how they behave when they attack: the lack of compassion, humanity, generosity, and civility. The bad manners depress me terribly. It's much more complex than what they're attacking; I feel the same way, when they attack someone else.

Q
What advice do you have for beginning speakers?

A
Be prepared! Know the content. The most nerve-wracking thing in the world is not being sure of what you're doing. It's awful to get up with notes half done, poorly phrased, not well thought out. It's terrible to get halfway through and have nothing more to say.

Get the material ready and be sure you know it. Whether you're using notes or a prepared speech, be absolutely comfortable with it. You're going to be uneasy anyhow the first few times, so concentrate on knowing your material.

You know your subject; you have a good reason to be there. Take heart from the fact that people asked you to speak because you do know your subject.

People don't want to see you fail; nobody enjoys a speaker's pain. The audience takes no pleasure at all when a speaker can't find a place, or the voice or paper shakes. The audience feels so uncomfortable. They don't want to watch you make a mess of it. They yearn for you to do well, they're totally on your side, and there's very positive energy going for you.

June Callwood

Speech: It Might As Well Be You

This is a convocation address given at a community college. June Callwood spoke from brief notes, and used humour to engage her audience and build rapport. You can hear the vigour and humour with which she touches her audience, and the incredible directness with which she leads them to action. Her style is at once homemade and eloquent.

I take my cue from our oldest child's graduation 21 years ago from McGill University. When I asked her about the convocation address (which I missed while taking our four-year-old to the washroom), she replied, ''It was superb. It was ten minutes long!'' So, that's what I'm aiming at—to give a superb address. You'll be comforted to know.

You'll notice I don't wear anything that indicates I graduated from anywhere; I didn't get enough education to qualify for this school, let alone graduate from it.

I hasten to assure all the graduates that not a moment you have laboured to reach this achievement has been wasted because the world is vastly more complex and alarming than when I began to work on a newspaper when I was 16 years old (and that was forty-six years ago.)

You've mastered technology, you're full of facts, and most important of all, you've learned how to learn. That's a process that begins with the awareness that there is something you need to know, then enough organizational skill to give that gap a heading so you know what it is you want to find out, some library skills to find a resource centre or a resource person, the nimbleness to assimilate and substitute....So you're all set. Also you must be terrified. I've

heard nothing but how few jobs there are—it's a most encouraging way to start a convocation. There is the yawning unknown that begins tomorrow, and that really is not so much a question of a job, but what kind of life you'll have. I can't speak of jobs and opportunites—I've been a freelancer for 41 years. I know a good many of you, maybe all, will succeed despite the odds. You may find another career path. But nothing is lost in the universe; whatever you've learned now—nothing is lost.

However, I can speak with some authority about how devastating it is to be a young person, to feel injustice as acutely as young people do, to have ideals, to believe that there is honour and consideration, and compassion, and that's what you want for yourselves. Adolescence is very painful; it's filled with the high tides of infatuation and hope, and the twists of self-disgust and depression. But your eyes are still open. It's not beyond your imagination to sense that most people experience depression, and that most people have hope destroyed, and most people suffer agonies of remorse.

What I ask is you don't lose that empathy. No one, *no one* is really a stranger to you. The commonality between men and women—and I'm a feminist; this is what a feminist looks like: this is the profile of a feminist, this is full-face, this is a feminist! —but there is commonality between men and women, between the races, and between religions, and between your parents and yourself, and between workers and management. What we all share is our vulnerability and our mortality. In that sense, there is nothing between you and anyone else you know, or have ever hated, or have ever admired. You're made of the same substance. You can be warm and caring but you've got to trust that people are like you, that inside people are alike. They have the same fears as you have. We humans are a tribe, we're herd animals. And we need one another, we need to trust one another, and we need one another's kindness.

One thing more. Hannah Arendt said this; it is the thing that has meant the most to me. When she was analyzing the evil of Eichmann during the holocaust, she looked to find the essence of evil. What is it? Six million people killed. What is the essence of that magnitude of evil? She came to the conclusion after a long time that the real evil is not so much what Eichmann was. The real evil was the apathy of people who did nothing, who were spectators.

That's what I want to leave with you. There is no innocence in the spectator. If you do not get involved in an accident, in a racist or sexist slur, or someone being even mildly humiliated, or someone in need. If you don't get involved, you are as much the cause of what is happening as the person who is actually doing it. If you're aware that something is unfair and plain wrong, you've got to act!

You have to be nonviolent, I think; you have to be calm, you have to be resourceful, but *don't just stand there*. Everyone longs to be the good person

that is inside, and there is a splendid person inside. That's the person we want to come out, but it takes a little practice. Gloria Steinem said, ''Do one outrageous thing every day.'' Say to the bank manager, ''How come the bank managers in here are always all men. There are these lovely little old ladies who've been here for 45 years, and 27 of you young men have been coming in and out as managers?'' Say that. Go to the president of Loblaws and say that you're very anxious to shop at a Loblaws that has a woman manager. Could he just tell you where the nearest one is.

It just takes practice. You start by helping a small child who is sobbing away about a broken crayon. Easy to do, eh? Then you politely tell someone it's not fair to cut in on a line-up for a movie. Then you protest in some visible way the pollution in the drinking water. And so on.

Eventually you save the world. And if someone has to do it, it might as well be *you*.

I salute you. I honour and I treasure you. May the wind ever be at your back and the sun on your face.

June 13, 1986
Centennial College
Scarborough

OUTLINE OF A PERSUASIVE SPEECH

Name: _____

Date of Speech: _____

Purpose Statement: _____

INTRODUCTION

    Grabber:

    Thesis:

    Overview:

BODY

    Supporting Argument #1

    Supporting Argument #2

    Supporting Argument #3

CONCLUSION

    Reference to purpose (thesis):

    Summary of main steps:

    Zinger:

SELF-EVALUATION FORM

This form is to help you evaluate your own speech. It can be kept private or shared with your instructor or peers.

Type of Speech: _____

Name: _____

Title: _____

Date: _____

DELIVERY
Physical Presence

Did I make eye contact with others?

Was my posture natural and appropriate?

Was I aware of my facial expressions and hand gestures?

Were there any distracting mannerisms that I was aware of?

Did I feel good?

Could I feel an energy exchange with my audience?

VOCAL DELIVERY

Was my voice under control?

Did I sound confident?

Was I aware of breathing calmly?

How was my enunciation?

Did I manage to avoid um's and ah's?

Did I sound interested/excited/committed?

How did my voice sound to me?

DESIGN AND CONTENT

How well did the introduction and conclusion work?

Did the framework unify my speech?

Was there a natural progression from point to point?

Did my notes keep me on track? Did I use them?

Did the audience seem to understand the organization of my speech?

Was the information clear?

What was the energy level of the conclusion?

What would I change the next time?

What worked very well?

OVERALL EFFECTIVENESS

Did I connect with this audience?

Did I achieve my purpose?

What do I remember most about making the speech?

What unexpected or unforeseen things happened?

What am I most pleased about?

OTHER COMMENTS

Grade:

PEER EVALUATION FORM

Peer evaluation should be done in a constructive and supportive fashion. The speaker may choose people to do assessments or they may be assigned alphabetically. Some groups maintain the same speaker/assessor teams for the entire course; others change for each speech. The instructor may wish to see this evaluation before it goes to the speaker.

Type of Speech: _____

Speaker: _____

Title: _____

Assessor: _____

Date: _____

DELIVERY
Physical Presence
Did the speaker maintain eye contact?

Did she or he establish a rapport with the audience?

Were gestures natural and effective?

VOCAL DELIVERY
Did the speaker sound convincing/spontaneous/excited?

Was his or her voice clear and loud enough?

How did you respond to the speaker's mood?

DESIGN AND CONTENT
Did the introduction interest you?

Did the overview give you an indication of the main proofs?

Did the speech flow easily and logically from one point to another?

Was the conclusion strong and memorable?

Did the conclusion reinforce the thesis and main points?

What was the thesis of the speech?

OVERALL EFFECTIVENESS
Did you learn something new or worthwhile from the speech?

Were you moved by it?

What was the most outstanding part of the speech?

What changes do you recommend?

What parts should the speaker definitely keep?

OTHER COMMENTS

Grade:

EVALUATION FORM

Type of Speech: _____

Name: _____

Title: _____

Length of Speech: _____

Date: _____

Legend:　　S = SUPERIOR　　E = EFFECTIVE　　NW = NEEDS WORK

DELIVERY
Physical Presence
Eye Contact

Rapport with Audience

Posture

Gestures

Use of Notes

Appropriate Use of Audio-Visual
Support Material

VOCAL DELIVERY
Naturalness/Spontaneity/Enthusiasm

Clarity

Variety (Tone, Pitch, Pace)

Volume

Absence of Verbal Tics (um, ah,
okay, like)

Sense of Control and Calm

DESIGN AND CONTENT
Use of Framework for Introduction
and Conclusion

Clear Thesis and Overview

Coherence/Use of Transitions

New/Interesting Information

Strong Finish

LANGUAGE
Word Choice

Impact on Audience

Grammar

OVERALL EFFECTIVENESS
Treatment of Topic

Intelligent Awareness of Audience

Achievement of Purpose

Impact on/Connection with Audience

OTHER COMMENTS

Grade:

Flying On Your Own: Last Words Of Advice

You reach out and you fly, there isn't anything that you can't do.

(RITA MacNEIL)

TIPS FOR SPEAKERS

1. Build speeches to be proud of: speak from the heart and connect with your listeners.
2. The checklists will help *if* you remember to use them.
3. Breathe deeply and—
4. GO FOR IT!

I t takes a teacher to write this chapter. After working your way through all the exercises, you're ready to strike out, to leave the learning environment and graduate to the real world of public speaking. Imagine you're sitting in my classroom; this is my last chance to impress upon you the lessons, secrets, tricks real speakers know and use.

This chapter is short: ten tips, a series of checklists, and a final example, a speech that had the greatest impact on a class that I've ever experienced.

Do you remember the parallel between good speakers and good skiers? They make it look so easy. Others comment, ''I wish I could do that—you weren't nervous at all.'' When you take the time to learn a sport or a skill well, the hours of training result in apparently effortless performances. What should you remember as you take off and fly down that hill?

1. Keep This Book

This book is a valuable resource for your professional, personal, and community activities. It has helped you learn to make good speeches, and it will be there, with outlines and reminders for future assignments.

Students in their first years of marketing, physiotherapy, environmental science, and so on, rarely have to make speeches outside the classroom. However, what happens during your co-op placement when you are required to speak to community groups? Speaking is required in almost every job: fire-crew bosses, lab technicians, graphic artists—they're all expected to make presentations.

This is a resource book that belongs on your shelf.

2. Use Your Nervousness Well

Have you ever had nightmares in which you are on a stage and can't remember your speech? I have. Several days before an important speech, I'll wake up in a panic from a nightmare in which I can't read my cards and can't think of anything to say. That's my good-luck sign; it terrifies me into checking my speech again. You can bribe your friends, your family, your cats, your canned goods, to sit there and look interested as you demonstrate how easy it is to make a cream liqueur.

Your anxiety is used well if it prompts you to review and revise your presentation. Go over it on the way to work, polish phrases in spare moments, redo your note cards. Practise until you're comfortable.

3. Build a Speech to be Proud of

As this chapter was being written I took part in a panel discussion regarding community safety and awareness. Another presenter fumbled through her notes, limped from one comment to another, and sat down when she'd finished the list of random ideas that she had, in her own words, "thrown together." She wasn't a careless person; she was nervous. Too nervous to discipline herself to analyze the audience, and to *plan*.

Build a speech that you can be proud of. Remember David Nichol's comment about Gordie Howe? Show enough respect for yourself and your audience to speak as well as you can.

4. Polish Your Intros and Conclusions

You may want to write your intros and conclusions out in dramatic fashion, with pauses and emphasis noted. The example on p. 84 shows how this is done. Now, remember, *you don't read the intro and conclusion*. Before you start, pause, make eye contact, glance at your intro, and address your audience with full eye contact. To conclude, pause in a dramatic fasion while you check the conclusion, and then *give it to them*. If you can grab your listeners with an interesting remark spoken in an intelligent and confident fashion, and leave them with a strong, memorable statement, they'll remember you *and* your speech.

5. Do Not *Read* to Your Audience

Several years ago, I went to a public forum to make a presentation to the provincial Minister of Natural Resources. As I represented an association, and had specific arguments to advance, I wrote out my speech. My own classroom warnings came true: *the more you have to read in front of you, the more you will read*. Like magic, my eyes were drawn to the page, and away from the audience. If I dared to look up, I immediately lost my place and had to fumble my way back. I looked like a bumbler, and worse: the presentation was *boring*. As a written statement it was fine, but it was a poor speech.

Don't tempt yourself. Prepare cards, use them wisely, and you'll be able to forge a bond with your listeners. Even better, they'll think that you did it without notes—and for some reason, that greatly impresses people.

6. Recycle Your Memory Work

At last, you've made it through traffic to the annual luncheon of the Canadian Blackfly Society. As you slide into your seat, anticipating a wonderful feast, the president slips you a note, "Please thank the speaker—I know I can count on you." It's at times like these that one or two passages of memory work can help you enjoy a meal. I'm not good at memorizing and can only remember four short quotations, but I have used them all many times, altering a word or two to suit the group. Here they are: the first one is often attributed to Bobby Kennedy, proof that he too had a good stockpile of versatile quotes.

> *You see things, and you say "Why?" But I dream things that never were, and I say, "Why not?"*
> *(GEORGE BERNARD SHAW)*

> *Every writer needs a built-in, foolproof crap detector.*
> *(ERNEST HEMINGWAY)*

> *Get to the point as directly as you can; never use a big word if a little one will do—[these are] about the same principles I used in painting.*
> *(EMILY CARR)*

> *There are strange things done in the midnight sun*
> *By the men who moil for gold.*
> *(ROBERT SERVICE)*

I would have used the quote from G.B.S. for the C.B.S.

If you wonder why I'm getting to such basic details, just remember—these are all real examples.

7. Be Prepared: Car Keys, Extension Cords, Spare Notes

Car keys

When I get keyed up before a speech, I'm so determined to be on time that I often race from the car to the cleaners, or the restaurant, leaving my keys in the ignition *and* locking the car. It's not too serious if you're already at your destination, but it's not good if the car is running, or your notes are inside, or you have to get home later. Carry an extra set of keys. Better still, take along a friend to do the driving and to offer moral support.

Extension Cords

Even if you are not using a projector, someone else may be, and the rule holds true: the nearest plug is *always* three feet farther than the cord will reach. Everyone's energy is focussed on moving the projector, or fussing about the delay. This may detract from the event, and from the build-up to your part of the program.

Spare Notes

On my way to the wedding of my best friend, my purse, containing the groom's ring and my speech, was stolen. Of course I had rough notes but they were at home, and I had not yet taught my cat to answer the phone. Take an extra set of notes with you.

FORGET YOUR NOTES?

8. Private Moments

This is really called "Adjust Your Clothes in Private" but I wanted to be tactful. Many beginners are so intent on their speech that they get swept away on a wave of greetings and seating arrangements. Then, in front of 50 or 500 people, they are seized by an urge to pat their hair, check to see if their buttons are fastened and their flies done up.

Schedule a private moment.

A professional media consultant who coaches corporate executives confesses that the most common advice required is, "Don't adjust your underwear in public." I once got on a hotel elevator all set to go to a meeting where I was the keynote speaker. As I stood there, I noticed that my dress felt especially silky underneath my coat. I checked. There was no dress; I was on my way clad only in my slip.

Make sure you have time to check your appearance before you start.

9. Coach Yourself: Breathing Exercises

What are you doing during the speech preceding yours? Listening to be sure, *but* you are also doing your deep breathing exercises, "In-2-3-4, Out-2-3-4, In-2-3-4, Out-2-3-4."

If you need further coaching on your way to the podium, try:

RELAX   BREATHE   PAUSE
EYE CONTACT   RELAX   BREATHE
PAUSE   EYE CONTACT   SMILE!!

Some people write their coaching on their notes:

PAUSE HERE/   LOOK AT MAP/   BREATHE/
WAIT FOR LAUGHTER

10. Go For It!

You can do it. People will give you their support and their good will. You have the technique and the experience to step into your speaker's skis and *fly!*

Rose Anne Hart
Speech: The Golden Rule

Rose Anne Hart is a graduate of a Traveller Counsellor programme, the mother of eight children, a community worker, and a person now pursuing her third "22-year plan." During her public speaking course, she discovered that real examples worked best for her; through anecdotes, she could get involved in her material. In her introduction, she heads off a "ho-hum" reaction, and goes on to outline a clear three-part plan. In the last part of her speech she anticipates being charged with over-simplification, and provides a rebuttal.

I want to speak to you today about a very old-fashioned idea, one you've heard a thousand times. In fact, you've probably heard it so often, that it's become meaningless to you. I want to talk about the golden rule, "Do unto others, as you would have others do

unto you." I'm going to tell you a story to illustrate some of the errors we make in dealing with people, the consequence of these errors, and I'm going to tell you how to avoid ever making these errors yourself.

I had a friend named James; he was in his forties, had his own business, and was a loving and caring member of his community. I met James when we were both volunteers for a care-giving organization here in Toronto. I was a counsellor and he was in fundraising. In his spare time, James crotcheted blankets for the people we helped; I remember one time he brought me a small red one and asked me to save it for a Chinese baby, because he had heard that to the Chinese red is a symbol of good fortune.

My friend was gay. He had many of the mannerisms we see parodied on TV, and in nightclub comedy routines. He had a longstanding relationship with another man; they owned a home in the community; and they attended church regularly where they helped out with all the functions. At one point James's friend became very ill. In fact, the doctors told him that they didn't expect him to live very long. James phoned the church and asked the clergyman to make a housecall. The clergyman agreed, but a little while later, he phoned back and told James that he had thought it over, and he felt it would be giving scandal to the community if he was seen entering their home.

James's friend recovered, but James never did.

He fell into a depression which caused the breakup of his relationship, and eventually caused him to take a bottle of sleeping pills. And as if that weren't enough, he wrapped a garbage bag around his head, and secured it at the neck with tape. He was determined to die and he was successful.

Now, we all know that not every slight is going to have such tragic results, and we know too that James's death was not caused by a single incident but rather by a lifetime of small hurts piled on top of another to form one unbearable burden. I don't expect my speech today will heroically save lives, but I would be delighted if it would save one of us from adding one more measure of pain to someone else's growing burden.

Being aware of the consequences of our actions is one sure way of guarding against ever having to use the saddest of all phrases, "I just didn't know." As the Roman philosopher Plutarch put it, "Boys throw stones at frogs in sport, but the frogs do not die in sport. They die in earnest."

I didn't tell you this story to make you feel sorry for James. I told you this story to make you think. When you meet someone who is different from you because of nationality, or colour, or religion, obesity, handicap, or sexual orientation, *before* executing that clever imitation, *before* making that witty remark, *before* issuing that curt dismissal—think. Think about how you would want to be treated if your roles were reversed. If we follow this one simple rule, "Do unto others as you would have others do unto you," we can *never* go wrong.

April, 1987
Scarborough

Using the Checklists

When you sign up with a canoe club to paddle the Nahanni River, they send you a package of trip information. Most valuable are the checklists. By referring to these lists, you can quickly determine if you have done sufficient preparation and have all the equipment necessary for each facet of the trip: personal belongings, repair and survival kits, nature books and charts, kitchen gear.

Use these checklists in the same way. Start with the *main menu* of checklists and then consult those appropriate to your situation. A quick glance will remind you of the main lessons of this book and essential items to take with you. The only trick is to remember the lists!

Checklists: Main Menu

Use these lists to remind you of various aspects of your preparation. Then consult the ones most appropriate to your situation.

1. Equipment to Take With You
2. What to Ask Your Contact Person
3. Questions to Ask About Your Audience
4. Matching the Format to the Audience and Occasion
5. Purpose of Your Speech
6. Is Your Speech in Shape?
7. What to Check for in a Rehearsal

1. Equipment to Take With You

1. speech notes
2. extra set of notes
3. pen and paper
4. mini flashlight (for reading notes during slide presentation)
5. tapes/slides/film
6. handouts: reports, outlines, booklets, manuals, forms
7. watch
8. extra glasses/lens cleaning solution
9. identification and health insurance numbers
10. medication
11. props
12. A-V equipment if necessary and spare parts
13. extension cord
14. clothes pegs or spring clips or masking tape to fasten notes to podium in breezy conditions
15. timetable
16. address of meeting and map
17. name and telephone number of hotel
18. name and number of contact person and *back-up contact*
19. business cards
20. press release
21. umbrella
22. tissues or handkerchief
23. comfortable shoes
24. change of clothes in case of accident (jacket, shirts, tie, blouse, stockings, etc.)
25. cash for personal expenses

2. What to Ask Your Contact Person

1. TIME   DATE   PLACE
2. Exact directions to the meeting place, even if you are being met
3. Name and phone number of local contact and back-up contact
4. Time limit
5. Names and topics of other speakers
6. The occasion
7. Dress guidelines
8. Will the proceedings be taped? Does it matter?
9. Questions about your audience: see Checklist 3
10. Have you *told* the contact person how to recognize you, your time of arrival, and any dietary needs you may have?
11. How will your expenses be covered? When will you be paid?
12. Where is the most convenient place to park?

3. Questions to Ask About Your Audience

1. Why are you being asked to speak?
2. What group or organization is inviting you to speak?
3. What is the occasion?
4. What does the audience know about the subject?
5. Are they interested/uncertain/hostile about the subject?
6. Has anybody ever talked to them about it before?
7. How much background should you provide for maximum understanding?
8. Do you expect them to ask questions?
9. What sort of local colour would be useful to you?
10. Do they know the level of experience or expertise you bring to the subject?
11. Will they expect a formal or informal presentation?
12. Is there a possibility of a negative response? Can *you* handle it?
13. Is there anything special about the date, place or group?
14. Basic information:

    age
    gender
    occupational background
    rural or urban experience
    race or nationality

traditional or alternative family groups
level of education
disposable income
interests and hobbies

4. Matching the Format to the Audience and Occasion

1. How much time have you been given?
2. Are you the only speaker?
3. How much does the audience already know about your subject?
4. What is their attention span?
5. What time of day and where in the programme are you speaking?
6. Would a speech followed by a question-and-answer period allow people with some experience to have input in the event?
7. Would a serious or information-packed presentation be made more lively by having a question-and-answer period afterwards?
8. Are you prepared to be put on the spot?
9. If you only have ten minutes to give an outline of a vast topic, is it better to try to cover it all or highlight a few significant aspects?
10. Would your speech be strengthened by A-V material?

5. Purpose of Your Speech

agitation?
demonstration?
education?
entertainment?
evaluation?
information?
inspiration?
interrogation?
persuasion?

1. Is it to advocate a position?
2. Is it to change your listeners' minds?
3. Is it to be liked?
4. Is it to reinforce a belief?
5. Is it to explain or demonstrate?
6. Is it to advance your own position? (pass the test, interview, etc.)

7. Is it to speak your mind on a matter you consider important?

6. Is Your Speech in Shape?

1. Is there a thesis and three main points?
2. Is the grabber effective?
3. Does the conclusion wrap it up well?
4. Do you stick to the topic?
5. In one sentence can you state exactly what you want to prove or express?
6. Do you need all of the speech?
7. Do you need to supply a title for the program. Is there a good line or example to appeal to the audience's curiosity?
8. Are there ethical, logical and emotional appeals?
9. Have you avoided errors in logic?
10. Are there smooth transitions from one point to another?
11. Is the speech suitable for
    • the audience?
    • the time allotted?
    • the occasion?
12. Have you chosen your words and examples carefully. Have you avoided sex, race, and class bias?
13. Is the language lively?
14. Have you practised with your note cards?
15. Are your cards numbered and in order?
16. Does your test audience like and understand your examples?
17. Have you timed your speech? Does it fit into the space allotted? (Never be guilty of using the phrase: "I know I'm running overtime, but I just have 6 more points.")
18. Does your speech sound like you?
19. Do you believe in what you are saying?

7. What to Check for in a Rehearsal

1. *How do you sound?* A speech is far different from reading aloud; reading over your notes is *not* the same as an actual rehearsal.
2. Are you getting better with practice? Start at least two days before the speech to develop assurance.
3. Practise with the notes you will use.
4. Listen to yourself:
    • Are you rambling?
    • Do you sound confident?

- Is your material interesting?
- Do you vary your tone and pace?

5. Make eye contact with your cat, a friend, the bedpost.
6. Make sure your words come out naturally.
7. Rehearse in front of a mirror to check out your body language.
8. Time yourself! Have you kept to the timeframe you were given? (If there are no limits, assess the audience: 20-30 minutes is plenty for an after-dinner address to adults and adolescents; an hour or more may be appropriate for specialists who want plenty of information and time for questions.)
9. Rehearse in front of a friend or partner. Which of your examples did he or she enjoy or remember?
10. Does your speech seem logical and complete to your test audience? Does it raise unanswered questions?
11. Can you handle props and visuals easily?
12. Get rid of clunkers—overly complicated examples, awkward or affected language, boring and unnecessary statistics.

8. On Arrival

1. Greet the organizer.
2. Put belongings in a secure place.
3. *Private time:* check notes, adjust clothes, attend to personal details. **Be sure to have this time before events speed up.**
4. Check the room with one of the coordinators:

   Is the seating and number of chairs appropriate?
   Is the lighting adequate?
   Is there a watch or clock to monitor time?
   Is there a lectern?
   Is there water handy?
   Is the microphone working? *Test it.* Can you find the off/on switch?
   Meet the A-V technician if necessary, explain your needs, and test the equipment ("May I see the first three slides to make sure they are in the correct order?")
   Are pen and paper handy if you expect questions from the floor?
   Are floor mikes or question boxes (or runners) ready for a question-and-answer period?
5. Mingle with other speakers or panelists, and compare content if necessary.
6. Talk to audience members for a feeling of the group.

7. Check in with the moderator and the person introducing you. Has she got your name right?
8. Make sure your notes are ready.
9. RELAX. BREATHE. ENJOY.

9. Are You Prepared?

What if...
1. the electricity goes off?
2. a fire bell rings while you are speaking?
3. the room is set up in a different way than you requested?
4. double the number of people show up?
5. you lose your notes?
6. the translator or signer is late?
7. you can't find the room?
8. the speaker ahead of you rambles on and on?
9. there's a snowstorm and you're an hour late starting?
10. you can't go at the last minute?
11. other panel members don't show up?
12. the microphone doesn't work?
13. your speech isn't geared to the audience?
14. someone heckles you?
15. you spill food on your clothing?
16. the media shows up unexpectedly to cover the event or do an interview?

10. When You Coordinate a Meeting Remember These Physical Arrangements

1. Speakers' needs determined *in advance*
2. Fair and realistic agenda
3. Materials translated, duplicated (and circulated if necessary) in advance
4. Noticeboards and directional arrows
5. Room: adequate size, air flow, light, fire exits
6. Comfortable chairs
7. Good sight lines and acoustics
8. Washrooms and directions to them
9. Secure coat storage
10. Meals scheduled to fit the agenda and participants' needs
11. Meals to fit a variety of dietary needs

12. Coffee/tea/juice and variety of snacks for arrival and breaks
13. Name tags: printed large enough to be read easily, names spelled correctly
14. A-V ready and tested *that day*
15. Technician on duty
16. Power supply tested for extra video cameras, etc.
17. No smoking signs posted and smoking areas indicated
18. Moderator and those doing introductions prepared and on hand
19. Extra runners/ushers/food coordinators/registrars/money handlers/salespeople
20. Credit-card machine and licence (if necessary)
21. Gift/cheque/expense sheets for speakers

11. When You Are Part of a Panel

Before You Leave

1. What is the purpose of the panel presentation?
2. Why have you been asked to participate?
3. What position have you been asked to represent:
   - supplier of background information?
   - proponent/opponent of a particular stand?
   - representative of an interest group?
   - community member?
4. Are different points of view allocated fair amounts of time?
5. Do they have equally good slots on the agenda?
6. What is the format:
   - individual presentations followed by questions?
   - one speaker followed by questions to or from a panel?
   - presentations only?
   - questions only?
7. How will questions be handled:
   - moderator assigns questions?
   - panelists volunteer responses?
8. Is the moderator unbiased? His or her attitude may be shown in the treatment of each speaker, the limiting of discussion, and the assigning of questions.

When You Arrive

1. Talk to the other panelists. Is there adequate variation in presentations?
2. Do *you* have enough information and experience to change your approach if there is too much overlap?
3. Listen carefully to the other speakers. You may be able

to make direct links with their remarks *or* find significant points of difference.
4. Give direct eye contact to each speaker: the audience
will notice if you read, look around, or appear bored.
5. Remember your body language is important during the
entire program. You are speaking, verbally or non-
verbally, all the time you are present.

12. Using Audio-Visual Support Material

Before You Leave
1. Does your A-V material support your speech?
2. Is it big enough?
3. Is it colourful enough?
4. Is it simple enough?
5. Does it speak to the mind or the emotions?
6. Did you choose graphs with a minimum of lines?
7. Do maps or charts show enough detail?
8. Have you rehearsed with the back-up material?
9. Does your test audience understand it immediately?
10. Have you edited your slides? Use only as many as you
need to make your point.
11. Are your slides in order and numbered?
12. Do you have the props, slides, film, overheads, etc. in
your hand when you leave home? If you are flying,
make sure they are in your carry-on luggage.
13. If you are supplying equipment, do you have the
proper machinery, spare bulbs and parts?
14. Pack that spare extension cord!

When You Arrive
1. Is there a technician?
2. Does she or he know exactly what you want?
3. Can you supply a script with cues?
4. Test the microphone and other equipment *with* the technician.
5. If you are doing your own work, find the electrical
outlets.
6. If you need a screen, is it in the right place?
7. Can you work the controls without fumbling?
8. If you have an assistant, have you outlined the cues
carefully in advance?
9. If lights have to be dimmed at certain points, does the
assistant have a good script with the cues highlighted?
10. Do the flipcharts flip?

11. Are there plenty of markers?
12. Is the overhead projector already focused? Are your overheads in order and easy to handle?

13. Using Tapes

1. Does the sound fill the room comfortably?
2. Do you have all the tapes with you?
3. Are the tapes and equipment compatible?
4. Is the tape set to go without any fiddling?
5. Do you or your assistant know how to work the controls?
6. Do you or your assistant know the cues?
7. If you have to fast forward, have you noted the exact numbers on the tape counter?
8. Have you rehearsed?
9. Is there back-up equipment on site?

14. Using Projection Equipment

1. Have you rehearsed with the visuals and equipment?
2. If you are using an illuminated pointer (an arrow) can you handle it well and evenly?
3. Make sure the equipment is set up well ahead of time.
4. Does it work smoothly?
5. Have you got the right film or slides? Are they in order?
6. If you are using an assistant, pick someone well ahead of time. Supply a written script with cues (script would be significant phrases and approximate time into speech). Note if lights have to be turned on and off.
7. Rehearse with the assistant if there is a lot of A-V.
8. Check the sight lines by sitting in the seats and looking at the screen and speaker's position.
9. If you are handling equipment, thread film before the event and test it!
10. Focus the projector and *set volume level* in advance.
11. Have a spare bulb and know how to change it.
12. Know how to remove a slide that sticks.
13. Be sure slides are in the correct way, not reversed.
14. Be sure the operator has easy access to the machinery.
15. Tape down extension cords so that people won't trip over them.
16. Turn off the projector at the end so that people aren't blinded by a dazzling white screen.
17. After using the equipment, leave it alone until the presentation is complete.

18. Locate the light switches in advance! Electrical panels may have banks of switches; find the ones you need and label them for your assistant.
19. Always be prepared to do your speech without the material. If a mechanical breakdown occurs, do not tinker with the machinery until your audience is frustrated. Apologize and go ahead without it.

15. Saving Face When You Make Mistakes

1. Admit the mistake.
   "You are right. I made a mistake; I'll check this point and get back to you."
2. Don't over-apologize.
   People can accept a mistake; they get impatient when you refer to it frequently.
3. Move on.
   "Aside from this error, the point is still valid," *or* "Now that I've acknowledged this error, how can we proceed?"

16. Speech Breakdowns
Questions You Can't Answer

1. Repeat the question into the mike so the audience can hear it. Use your discretion regarding which questions to repeat.
2. Admit you don't know the answer.
3. Promise to get back with the information.

Hecklers

1. If the comment is valid, pause, repeat it to the audience, and deal with it.
2. If the remark is rude or inappropriate, ignore it.
3. If the speaker is too disruptive to ignore, offer to speak to him or her later.
4. Remain cool. "Look, why not allow me to finish. I was *asked* to speak here."
5. If you anticipate hecklers, think up a few responses in advance.
6. Appear patient and more courteous than your attacker. If you are ruder than your questioner, or if you use heavy sarcasm, you'll seem frightened. You may even lose audience support.

Unexpected Media Coverage or Interview Requests

1. Keep to the checklist "On Arrival"
2. Do not be unnerved (or overly flattered) by an insistent reporter. Be courteous and firm.
3. Ask how long the interview will take.
4. Offer to do a brief interview, *if* you have time and can still keep to your timetable. Take care of business first.
5. Be sure to leave yourself five minutes between the interview and your speech.
6. Offer to do the interview after your speech; avoid being rushed.
7. Check out the interview and the timing of it with the moderator.
8. If the proceedings have attracted a lot of media coverage, don't be anxious. Concentrate on your speech and the *audience.*

Running Late

1. *You* won't run overtime because you will have practised your speech.
2. If problems arise because the speakers before you are running late, what can you do?
   a) Assess the situation: Are you presenting an opposing point of view and need all the time you were originally allotted? Are you presenting a complementary position? Can you allow a colleague to elaborate?
   b) Pass a note to the moderator outlining how long your speech is. Suggest that she or he make the decision to go overtime or give the present speaker a time signal.
3. If the moderator does not take action, and you need to give your full presentation, explain to the audience that the schedule is running late, but you trust they want to have the full story. Alternatively, you may suggest that the topic is of such significance, that you need their feedback to your ideas. Assume that you are dealing with reasonable people.

17. Evaluation

1. Did you say what you wanted to?
2. How did you feel at the end of your presentation?
3. Was there a good feeling in the room?
4. What was the feedback from others—audience members and organizers?

5. What did audience response or questions raised tell you?
6. What will you change the next time?
7. What will you keep the next time?

18. Inclusive Language: Avoiding Sex/Race/Class Bias

1. Do you avoid sexual and racial stereotyping?
2. Do your words value each person for his or her intrinsic potential and avoid suggesting that all members of a gender, race, ethnic group or class are the same?
3. Do you use non-sexist words for occupations, professions, and other general terms?

Avoid:	Use:
anchorman	anchor, anchorperson
businessman	businessperson, manager, executive
cameraman	cameraperson, technician
cleaning lady	cleaner, housecleaner
chairman	chairperson, chair, convenor, coordinator, facilitator
female doctor	doctor
fireman	firefighter
forefathers	ancestors
freshman	first-year student
girls (for adult females)	women, colleagues, manager, office staff
heroine	hero
mailman	letter carrier
manned observatory	staffed observatory
history of mankind	history, our heritage
policeman/policewoman	police officer
saleslady/salesman	sales person, sales representative
spokesman	spokesperson, speaker, representative
stewardess	flight attendant
waiter/waitress	server
weatherman	weather forecaster
workman	worker, employee, staff member
workmen's compensation	workers' compensation

4. Do you avoid statements which promote stereotyping? Rather than:
   "Ask a doctor about allergies. He has the facts."
   "Adequate manpower is essential for the project."
   "Men and their families suffer from increased taxation."
   use:
   "Ask a doctor about allergies. She or he has (or they have) the facts."
   "An adequate workforce is essential for the project."
   "People (or families) suffer from increased taxation."
5. Do you avoid using adjectives that, in certain contexts, have questionable racial or ethnic connotations or racist overtones? Such words as primitive, black, yellow, savage, fall in this category.
6. Do you avoid using the adjective white as a symbol for goodness?
7. Racism is often a result of omitting anyone who is not of the dominant race or culture. Does your speech mirror the experience of a cross-section of our society?
8. Do you honour a person's origin? Do you make an effort to pronounce names correctly and to be precise about geographic locations?

CREDITS

The following publishers have generously given permission to use extended quotations from copyrighted works: Excerpts from *The Cross-Country Skier's Bible* by Ervin A. Bauer, copyright 1977 by Ervin A. Bauer. Used by permission of Doubleday, a division of Bantam, Doubleday, Dell Publishing Group, Inc. From ''Professionalism and Responsibility in the Technological Society,'' by Conrad Brunk. Reprinted by permission of Conrad Grebel College. From *Rick Hansen: Man in Motion*, by Rick Hansen and Jim Taylor. Reprinted by permission of Douglas and McIntyre. From *Joining Together: Group Theory and Group Skills*, by David Johnson and Frank Johnson. Reprinted by permission of Prentice-Hall, Inc. From ''Flying On Your Own,'' by Rita MacNeil. Reprinted by permission of Rita MacNeil. From ''We Hold Up Half the Sky,'' by Arlene Mantle. Reprinted by permission of Arlene Mantle. From *Saint Joan*, by George Bernard Shaw. Reprinted by permission of the Society of Authors on behalf of the Bernard Shaw Estate. From *Metamorphosis*, by David Suzuki. Reprinted by permission of Stoddart Publishing Co. Ltd. From *Joe Wallace Poems*, by Joe Wallace. Reprinted by permission of Progress Books. ''Welded at the Hip,'' lyrics by Nancy White, music by Doug Wilde, published by Multinan Inc., 1986, is from the cassette *Nancy White: Unimpeachable* produced by Mouton Records, Box 128, Station E, Toronto, M6H 4F2.

PHOTO CREDITS

p. 1 Doris Anderson (*Toronto Star*), William Lyon Mackenzie (National Archives of Canada, 5434), Nellie McClung (National Archives of Canada, 30212), David Suzuki (Fred Phipps, Courtesy of CBC); **p. 8** The slouch versus the real listener (Bruce Gibson); **p. 15** David Suzuki (Fred Phipps, Courtesy of CBC); **p. 37** Rick Hansen in Australia (Courtesy of Man in Motion Tour); **p. 42** Weird Postures to Avoid (Bruce Gibson); **p. 48** Rick Hansen (Bill Cunningham, Man in Motion Tour); **p. 73** Cynthia Patterson (Liz Armstrong); **p. 92** Eddie Greenspan (Courtesy of Eddie Greenspan); **p. 140** Roberta Bondar (Courtesy of National Research Council Canada); **p. 156** Rick Hansen and Jeanne Sauvé (Drew Gragg, Courtesy *The Citizen*, Ottawa, Canada); **p. 167** Practise handling a microphone (Bruce Gibson); **p. 184** Jeanne Sauvé (Karsh, Courtesy of Jeanne Sauvé); **p. 230** David Nichol (Masao Abi); **p. 244** Rehearse your speech (Bruce Gibson); **p. 268** June Callwood (Randy Haunfelder); **p. 283** Rose Anne Hart (Bruce Gibson).